Mobilizing Interest Groups in America

*Jack Lamar Walker, Jr.*

Photograph by Bob Kalmbach.

# Mobilizing Interest Groups in America

## Patrons, Professions, and Social Movements

Jack L. Walker, Jr.

*Prepared for publication by*
Joel D. Aberbach, Frank R. Baumgartner,
Thomas L. Gais, David C. King,
Mark A. Peterson, and Kim Lane Scheppele

*Ann Arbor*
THE UNIVERSITY OF MICHIGAN PRESS

Library of Congress Cataloging-in-Publication Data

Walker, Jack L.
    Mobilizing interest groups in America : patrons, professions, and
social movements / Jack L. Walker, Jr.; prepared for publication by
Joel D. Aberbach . . . [et al.].
        p.       cm.
    Includes bibliographical references and index.
    ISBN 0-472-10276-1 (cloth : alk.).—ISBN 0-472-08164-0 (paper :
alk.)
    1. Pressure groups—United States.  2. Lobbying—United States.
I. Title.
JK1118.W35  1991
324'.4'0973—dc20                                        91-24922
                                                            CIP

A CIP catalogue record for this book is available from the British
Library.

*For*
*Max Lamar Walker*
*and*
*Samuel Robinson Walker*

# Foreword

Scholars, like everyone else, live with the expectation, or at least the hope, of a long and productive life. Although endurance into old age is more common than untimely death, tragedies sometimes befall even the most vital and spirited of us. On January 30, 1990, an hour into his fifty-fifth birthday, Jack L.. Walker lost his life, an innocent victim in one of the most pernicious signatures of modern civilization, an automobile accident. In addition to the enormous loss suffered by family, friends, and colleagues, Jack's death also took from our discipline one of its most lively, enthusiastic, and incisive practitioners.

At the time of his death, Jack was enjoying a year of sabbatical in California at the Center for Advanced Studies in the Behavioral Sciences (CASBS). In addition to perfecting an already accomplished tennis game, Jack was crafting the chapters of a book manuscript. The book was to be the culmination of a decade-long empirical investigation of interest groups and representation in America. We knew that in the manuscript pages that Jack had already written, and in the other work that Jack intended to use as the basis for subsequent chapters, there was a book that could, and must, be completed. We offer that book here, as Jack had planned it and, except for a few minor editorial adjustments, as he and his collaborators had executed it.

A fascination with interest groups grew naturally out of Jack's evolving perspective on American politics and governance. Perhaps that view can be best summarized by the response he would typically give his father when queried about what it was he did every day as a professor, a response that Jack shared with the fellows at CASBS in a lecture he presented just hours before his death: "I am interested in the processes through which emerging social problems are recognized and defined. I study the avenues outside of conventional political parties and elections through which individual citizens can be mobilized for political action. And I am trying to identify the major factors that stimulate policy change and social learning in the American political system." It did not occur to the Center fellows to give his father's ritual response: "And they pay you for that?"

Jack's fascination with the ways emerging social problems stimulate policy change in the United States was long-standing. It grew from his concern about the representation of disadvantaged people in the American political process.

At his intellectual core, Jack was a democratic theorist, with an interest in understanding governmental systems well enough so that the cause of full democracy could be furthered. His doctoral dissertation was the basis for early publications on black protests against injustice in Atlanta, Georgia, his home town (1963a, 1963b, 1963c, 1964). His now classic article with the provocative title "A Critique of the Elitist Theory of Democracy" (1966) set off a debate in the field that echoes to this day. Jack aimed to counter the emphasis on the virtues of political stability and the neglect of social movements that he saw in postwar writing on democracy. The work he did with Joel Aberbach on the disturbances in Detroit in 1967 resulted in a book entitled *Race in the City* as well as several well-known articles, including an examination of the meaning of slogans like *black power* to those affected by the profound social and political unrest that convulsed American cities in the 1960s (Aberbach and Walker 1970a, 1970b, 1970c, 1973).

The work reported in this volume on the origins and maintenance of interest groups was also strongly rooted in Jack's interest in the disadvantaged. A major concern was how and why some groups are mobilized and others are not. How, and under what conditions, do social movements spawn groups to represent their goals? How do those usually unable to mobilize on their own, such as the poor, elderly, or handicapped, find an organized expression of their interests? How do the rules, processes, and institutions of the American system affect who gets represented and in what ways? Jack wanted to know the answers to these questions, not only because they are important to political science, but because he believed deeply that "the American system could be changed if we wish it to be different" (chap. 1). None of the rules, processes, and institutions that shape our system, he said emphatically, "are products of natural forces beyond our leaders' control."

Jack was a doer in life, and he had real goals in mind when he studied and wrote. But as a successful doer, he was also realistic enough to recognize that one must see a situation in a hard-headed manner in order, eventually, to achieve anything of significance. Therefore, while this book, like his other work, is grounded in moral concerns, it follows his previous work in taking a systematic, empirical approach. The goal was to understand better the way the political process works so that a foundation might exist for making the process more equitable in the future.

Jack began his study of interest groups in the spring of 1977, when he hired his first two graduate students to start collecting data. His original interest centered on the role of public agencies in stimulating and directing political mobilization in behalf of policies in their areas. This interest largely grew out of his dissatisfaction with the current views in the discipline about the role of interest groups, protest movements, and other organized political activities in the administrative and policy-making process. In particular, Jack believed that the development and elaboration of interest groups in the United States were not a cause but a consequence of the growth of government and, especially, of the federal bureaucracy. He believed that intense, spontaneous political activities were the exception in our political system, and that highly organized and effective political activities required institutional and, particularly, governmental patrons except in extraordinary periods of social or political upheaval. Jack thus expected that most of the growth in political organization would come late in a policy area, after the major legislation had been enacted and new agencies had been established. It would occur during one of those infrequent periods of major policy innovation in American political history, such as the New Deal or the Great Society, as a result of exceptional political conditions.

But these specific expectations hardly exhausted the ideas, values, and ways of looking at things that Jack drew upon throughout the study, many of which he had developed in his earlier writings and empirical studies.

*The Primacy of Institutions in Structuring Politics.* Jack disagreed strongly with the tendency he saw among some political scientists to portray government as "a black box that carried out the dictates of representatives who themselves reflected social or economic forces" (1978). He saw the modern administrative state as imposing a considerable amount of structure on the nation's politics and society. This assumption of governmental or institutional primacy is found in many of Jack's earlier writings. One part of Jack's critique of the "elitist theory of democracy" argued that political scientists cannot assume the inevitability of observable patterns of political behavior—such as the widespread political apathy and incompetence among citizens during the 1950s and early 1960s. The apathy may, in fact, have been the consequence of the nation's political institutions and might thus be changed through the patient and deliberate building and amending of institutions by enlightened leaders.

*The Historical or Evolutionary View.* Jack not only believed that government institutions structured the nation's politics, he also believed that an understanding of those institutions—and how they could be changed—had to take into account their historical development. Jack always looked to the past to explain the particular characteristics of specific institutions. Of course, he also saw recurrent patterns of social learning and innovation—as his work on agenda-setting in the U.S. Senate (1977) and innovation among the states (1969) demonstrated. But he often used these patterns and models to account for the specific, historical, or contingent institutional outcomes, which to Jack's mind were often very important. The interest-group study did not emerge from a historical vacuum—Jack initially saw the study as an attempt to understand how the enormous political changes in the 1960s, and particularly the surge of legislation in the Great Society years, affected our political institutions and processes.

*The Concern for Socially or Economically Disadvantaged Citizens.* As noted previously, Jack was drawn to the study of interest groups because he was interested in the conditions under which socially and economically disadvantaged groups could be effectively represented in government. Jack's initial expectations were that the current political system allows certain kinds of disadvantaged citizens to be well represented—particularly if there are well-developed professional communities or government agencies that serve those citizens and can act as third-party advocates—but that many others are shut out. Jack wanted to call attention to these institutional conditions in order to demonstrate that the nation has a choice—that more citizens can be represented if only our institutions were further elaborated.

*An Appreciation of the Necessity of an Open Political System.* The interest-group study and Jack's approach to interpreting the data clearly showed his long-standing distaste for any claims that political participation in the United States was in need of stronger limits. The study began in the late 1970s, during the zenith of neo-conservative writings about "government overload" and the rise of the so-called special interest state. But Jack was very suspicious of calls for reduced or more orderly participation in politics, just as he was suspicious in the 1960s when reacting to "elitist" conceptions of democracy. Jack believed that the "messiness" and "crowdedness" of politics in the 1970s and 1980s reflected the growing functions of government and its institutional complexity. Since those functions are legitimate and unlikely to be rescinded, attempts to reduce participation levels or shield government from contending groups would simply suppress legitimate representation. Although Jack believed that government, and particularly the federal bureaucracy, contributed to the development of the interest-group system, he did not believe that mobilization was arbitrary or illegitimate. He generally saw government institutions as helping to organize groups that are deeply affected by new policies in situations where they face many barriers to getting organized by themselves. If that process produces a messy and crowded politics, that is as it should be. Any system that is less messy or crowded would lose legitimacy and its long-run stability by failing to recognize and channel legitimate claims.

*The Central Role of Policy Communities.* Finally, Jack was quite interested in exploring several ideas about the development and structure of "policy communities," or networks of interest groups active in a particular policy domain or representing a similar constituency (1989). Part of the project was, in fact, structured around these communities, and Jack wanted to examine some fairly subtle processes of innovation, learning, and specialization within them. This subject was extremely challenging empirically as well as theoretically, but Jack reached the point of understanding several critical and interrelated differences among these communities. Most of the ideas about policy communities and their internal processes had been developing for many years—in his work on cue-giving within policy communities among state officials, in his theoretical work on the dynamics of ideas within professional communities spanning the public and private sectors, and the patterns of leadership and learning he found in the U.S. Senate. Indeed, some of the most important concepts in the interest-group study were first developed in these earlier projects—he first used the idea of *patron* when discussing the supply of analysis within communities of policy professionals.

These five major themes or ideas had been developed first in Jack's earlier writings on pluralism, race relations, and policy innovation, but they led him easily to the study of interest groups. Jack saw the intimate connections between the interest-group system and our governing institutions, and thus undermined the claim that the growth of such groups was "cancerous" or alien to the proper functioning of government. Jack also collected systematic information and saw the gaps that needed to be filled in the interest-group system (rather than fretting about the possibility that there may be too many groups). And where some observers saw an amorphous mess of diverse organizations, Jack's earlier work helped him discern several layers of structure in the interest-group system—around broad sectors of the economy, within policy communities, in specialized strategies, in relations with the party system, and in connections with political patrons.

The results of his 1980 survey of interest groups gave Jack the opportunity to examine, in depth, the important themes about interest-group development and behavior that concerned him and that previously lacked the empirical foundation his project now made possible. He produced several articles and papers based on the 1980 data set that enlivened debate about interest-group politics, including: "The Origins and Maintenance of Interest Groups in America" (1983) published in the *American Political Science Review*, and winner of the 1988 award for an article of unusual significance in the field sponsored by the Section on Political Organizations and Parties of the American Political Science Association; "Three Modes of Political Mobilization" (1984), winner of the 1985 Franklin C. Burdette Pi Sigma Alpha Award from the American Political Science Association for the best paper presented at the previous annual meeting; "The Mobilization of Political Interests" (1983), a theme paper for the 1983 annual meeting of the APSA; collaborating with Thomas Gais and Mark Peterson, "Interest Groups, Iron Triangles, and Representative Institutions in American National Government" (1984), for the *British Journal of Political Science*; and, together with Thomas Gais, "Pathways to Influence in American Politics: Factors Affecting the Choice of Tactics by Interest Groups," for the 1983 annual meeting of the Midwest Political Science Association.

For all of its richness, the 1980 survey also revealed the limitations of a single, cross-sectional study and therefore the benefits to be derived from entering the field again at a later date. In his proposal to the National Science Foundation to support a second survey, Jack offered three basic justifications. First, "a second survey would allow me to create a more dynamic and realistic portrait of the interest-group system, and would also allow me to make estimates about its stability, permanence, and adaptability." Second, the later survey would "allow for much more reliable estimates of the causal significance and interrelationships of key dependent and independent variables identified in the initial phase of my analysis." Third, the efforts of the Reagan administration to reduce the scope of federal domestic programs, instigated since the 1980 study, constituted "a kind of natural experiment in the transformation of relationships between government and interest groups."

The 1985 survey, therefore, made possible a second, large-scale cross-section of the interest-group system and the creation of a panel data set of groups responding to both surveys, producing a unique opportunity to directly assess change in national voluntary associations during a particularly agitated period of interest-group politics. The results of the 1980 survey provided direction in improving the survey questions to acquire more information about group networks, revenue structures, institutional relationships, and ideological positions. Based on the panel data set joining the 1980 and 1985 surveys, Jack and Mark Peterson wrote "Interest Group Responses to Partisan Change: The Impact of the Reagan Administration upon the National Interest Group System" (1986) for a Congressional Quarterly Press volume; Jack collaborated with Kim Scheppele to write "Interest Groups and Litigation Strategies" (1986) for the annual meeting of the Midwest Political Science Association; and with David King he produced "The Provision of Benefits by American Interest Groups" (1989) for the annual meeting of MWPSA.

Besides the two major surveys of American interest groups, Jack also made efforts to study the group system in other ways. One was through mass surveys. Having queried group leaders about their memberships and activities, he wanted to survey the mass public about their affiliations with groups. As was typical of Jack, he was not content with how others had investigated this topic in the past. Therefore, he and Frank Baumgartner proposed a new series of questions for the National Election Studies, and eventually they were able to collect data on group affiliations in this way. The articles that they published on this topic ("Survey Research and Membership in Voluntary Associations" [1988] and "Response to Smith's 'Trends in Voluntary Groups Membership: Comments on Baumgartner and Walker': Measurement Validity and the Continuity of Results in Survey Research" [1990]) generated considerable interest among those who had previously studied the issue. Jack always wanted to collect the most accurate and complete information possible, and he bristled at the thought of accepting measures that were not as good as they could be. Jack's respect for the research process, and his desire to base his conclusions on the best available data, demanded that he often create new measures, or conduct his own surveys.

In another project with Frank Baumgartner, Jack was concerned with establishing a comparative perspective for understanding the relations between the state and groups in a policy community. This led to their article "Educational Policy Making and the Interest Group Structure in France and the United States" (1989) in *Comparative Politics*. They showed that state support for interest groups was very similar in both France and the United States. The governments in the two countries apparently used very similar decision rules in granting subsidies to outside groups, but the degree of conflict among groups in the two countries led to dramatically different relations with the state and even to different public policy outcomes.

In all of this work, Jack's interest in the nature of representational government and the group process was combined with an insatiable appetite for finding evidence on which to base his conclusions. Even two national surveys of interest groups in America did not satisfy Jack; his curiosity led him to collect data that allowed him to gain a perspective on interest groups from a variety of angles.

As the interest-group project continued during the 1980s, Jack pursued active agendas in other domains as well. He served the University of Michigan as a tenacious and forward-looking administrator, first as an associate dean of the College of Literature, Science, and the Arts, and second as the chair of the Department of Political Science. (He had previously been the director of the Institute of Public Policy Studies from 1974 to 1979.) In each of these positions, he was relentlessly enthusiastic, coming up with what some have described as "a grand plan an hour." His leadership seemed effortless, and his curiosity and vision were contagious. On Jack's watch, for example, the number of students applying for graduate work in political science more than doubled, and the amount of money available to graduate students more than tripled. At the same time, Jack tried laying out a multidiscipline vision for the department's future faculty hiring and drafted the conceptual foundations for new institutes and programs at the university.

Though Jack relished wheeling and dealing as an administrator, his first love was intellectual give-and-take. Make that intellectual combat. Administrative duties ate away hour after hour of his days, but he always found ways to keep the interest-group project alive. One year, while department chair, Jack gave David King an office down the hall where Jack could hide from the phone and his secretary. As far as the main office knew, Jack was "gone," but in his hideaway he escaped into his interest-group project—poring over ideas and printouts with abandon. When results fell into place, Jack would pump one fist in the air, screaming "gotcha baby!"

In those afternoons in his hideaway Jack found lots of "gotcha babies," and what remained was putting them together in manuscript form. Though he had started a few detailed outlines of an interest-group book before the 1985 survey, as of early 1989 Jack had not yet settled on just what the book would look like. On one hand, he wanted to write a data-rich book that would be admired by the most methodologically sophisticated readers. On the other hand, he wanted a large audience that would include undergraduates and the general public. While at the Center for Advanced Study in the Behavioral Sciences in California, he outlined a "readable monograph" to reach the largest possible audience, and he decided that his more technical treatments would be reserved for journal articles. Based on that plan, he launched into writing the chapters for the book.

Although most of us had departed from the University of Michigan by the time of Jack's death, all had written with Jack before and none of us was very distant from his project. Thomas Gais, now with the state of Wisconsin's Department of Transportation, began the project with Jack in 1977, contributed to the formulation and implementation of its research design with the 1980 survey, and remained deeply involved until leaving Ann Arbor in 1984. Mark Peterson, currently at Harvard University, joined the early information collection stages of the project in 1978 and carried through managing the second group survey before leaving in 1985, taught with Jack, and continued as a collaborator until Jack's death. Frank Baumgartner, now of Texas A&M University, had worked with Jack since 1979 and joined the project in 1983, assisted in completing the data collection and participated in expanding the scope of the project until his departure in 1986, after which he also remained a collaborator with Jack. David King of the University of Michigan joined the ranks in 1987, continuing the research enterprise and assisting with the data analysis for the book at the time of Jack's death. Kim Scheppele, a colleague of Jack's in the Department of Political Science and the Institute of Public Studies (IPPS) at Michigan, collaborated with him on the nexus between public law and interest-group behavior. Joel Aberbach, now at UCLA, was a friend and colleague of Jack's for more than two decades, a coauthor, and was also until recently a fellow faculty member in Michigan's political science department and IPPS.

Because of our close association with the interest-group project and Jack's extant work, each of us was paying close attention to his progress on the book, a volume that we anticipated. It was only natural, therefore, that immediately after Jack's death we each independently came to the conclusion that we should carry forward the last strokes required to finish the project. At first the reality of such an undertaking instilled a bit of trepidation in the group, as we contemplated the task of producing a manuscript that suitably fulfilled Jack's plans and hopes for the book. Not long after working with the available written material, however, we realized how much of the work was already done. Jack had completed drafts of the introductory chapters to the book. His extensive outline told us much about what he planned to do in later chapters. We were able to take papers he had done with collaborators (all such chapters are jointly signed) and, with some editing and reorganization of material, produce this volume. We decided that chapter 10 would serve well as a concluding chapter and that we should add only an epilogue on Jack's unfinished research agenda. In the chapters that are jointly signed, the collaborator played the primary role in making the last revisions. Frank Baumgartner was responsible for chapters 1 through 3, and Tom Gais for chapter 10. Joel Aberbach helped us all by reviewing and suggesting revisions to all parts of the manuscript. In sum, this was a collective enterprise. While each of us took primary responsibility for particular chapters, we also read and commented on the others. We followed a simple rule in making these last revisions: when in doubt, make no changes. What follows in the chapters ahead, therefore, is the unmistakable crispness of Jack's voice, marshaling the ideas and empirical support that are the hallmark of his assessment of the group system and its role in defining the opportunities for representation in the American political system.

Work on this project was aided by numerous friends and colleagues during Jack's lifetime, and many helped or gave an extra measure of assistance after his death. We hope that our list is inclusive, but if we have inadvertently left someone out, our sincere apologies.

First and foremost, each of us would like to express our appreciation to the Walker family for their support and encouragement during this process. Linda Walker provided more than only encouragement, since she also helped us gain access to Jack's materials and made numerous helpful suggestions throughout the revisions. We especially want to thank her for her constant support. We were privileged to meet Jack's father, Jack L. Walker, Sr., his brother, Anthony W. Walker, and his sister, Marianna W. Malone. Of course we already knew Jack's two sons, Max and Sam; we can only hope that our completion of this book will mean as much to them as it has to us.

Helene C. McCarren, assistant director for Administration and Budget at the University of Michigan's Institute of Public Policy Studies, made contributions to the project at every stage. The editors particularly acknowledge her efforts in facilitating work on the preparation of the final manuscript during an intensive two weeks in Ann Arbor in June, 1990. Helene worked with Jack during his years as IPPS director and became a close friend of the entire Walker family.

Jack and his coauthors were indebted to many scholars who commented on their work. We are pleased to acknowledge their help. Sincere thanks go to the following: Thomas Anton, Jeffrey Berry, Henry Brady, John Campbell, John Chamberlin, Jeffrey Cohen, Stephen Elkin, Morris Fiorina, Elizabeth Gerber, Edie Goldenberg, Edward Gramlich, Bernard Grofman, Richard Hall, Bruce Heady, Hugh Heclo, John Jackson, Charles Jones, William Keech, John Kessel, John Kingdon, Garrison Nelson, Susan Olson, Norman Ornstein, Roy Pierce, Nelson Polsby, Michael Reagan, Steven Reed, Michael Reich, Randall Ripley, Bert Rockman, Stephen Rosenstone, Olaf Ruin, Robert Salisbury, Kay Schlozman, Clarence Stone, Norman Thomas, Margaret Weir, Janet Weiss, Ernest Wilson, Graham Wilson, James Q. Wilson, Mayer Zald, and William Zimmerman.

Fourth, several people made contributions to Jack's work not only by their comments on manuscripts but through long-term intellectual support. These include: Robert Axelrod, Arthur Bromage, Michael Cohen, Paul Courant, Lane Davis, Joel Grossman, Donald Johnson, Donald Kinder, Michael Lacey, Theodore Lowi, Vincent McCarren, Andrew McFarland, Lawrence Mohr, William Newman, and Robert Putnam.

Philip Converse is a part of this last group also. We single him out to further acknowledge the fact that, in his role as director of the Center for Advanced Study in the Behavioral Sciences, he and his able staff did all that was possible to help Joel Aberbach and David King sort through the mountain of project material that was in Jack's office at the Center and ship it to Ann Arbor.

The editors would also like to thank Catherine Rudder, executive director of the American Political Science Association, and Tom Mann, director of the Governmental Studies Program at the Brookings Institution, for their help and encouragement in organizing the panel at the 1990 APSA convention at which we presented this work. Further, we would like especially to thank Theodore Lowi and Andy McFarland for their comments as discussants at that presentation.

Jack worked with numerous students, other than those already mentioned, on the interest-group project. On his behalf, we thank the following for their assistance: Gordon Adams, Brian Christjohn, David Ericksen, Fran Featherston, Gina Hoeffer, Carol Kowecki, Barbara Lahr, Mark Messura, Cynthia Robinson, and Catherine Shaw.

Jackie Brendle, Judy Brown, and Judy Jackson of the IPPS staff typed the original papers and provided excellent production assistance.

No project like this can be done without financial assistance, and Jack was a master at securing it. In his papers and articles he thanked many generous institutions for their support, including the University of Michigan's Institute of Public Policy Studies, the Center for Advanced Study in the

Behavioral Sciences, the Earhart Foundation, the Guggenheim Foundation, the National Science Foundation, and the Woodrow Wilson International Center for Scholars.

In the hope that scholars will continue to make use of the unique data sets that Jack collected, and in accordance with Jack's wishes, we have assembled the data sets, given them proper documentation, and turned them over to the Inter-university Consortium for Political and Social Research (ICPSR) at the University of Michigan for the most widespread dissemination in the scholarly community. Those who might be interested by some of the findings reported here are encouraged to contact the ICPSR for the data. We hope that many others will find them as rich as did Jack, and perhaps that someone may improve upon them in a future study of the topics covered in the following pages.

As a last acknowledgement, the other editors would like to thank Frank Baumgartner for his work in coordinating the preparation of drafts of the book manuscript at Texas A&M, and acknowledge the work of Marcia Bastian, who was skillful, thoughtful, and quick-witted while helping to prepare the final manuscript and figures. Frank also served as liaison to the University of Michigan Press. On the other hand, this was the least Frank could do after all the times Jack allowed him to win their tennis matches.

Finally, a few words about our own experience in putting the finishing touches on this book. When we met in Ann Arbor, we were all pleased to do what we could to bring the book to completion, but we also dreaded what we were about to do. Jack was a very special friend and colleague, and this symbolized the end. But once we got down to work, everything lightened up. We had great fun, actually, because Jack's special qualities shone through the pages of the manuscript. We think it is a vital, exciting piece of work that represents the man as we knew and loved him. We interacted again with Jack through this task, remembering his enthusiasm, his expressions, his style. We are proud to be associated with the book as we were to be associated with the man.

Joel D. Aberbach
Frank R. Baumgartner
Thomas L. Gais
David C. King
Mark A. Peterson
Kim Lane Scheppele

## Acknowledgments

Chapter 2 is a revised version of "Interests, Political Parties, and Policy Formation in American Democracy," which appeared in *Federal Social Policy: The Historical Dimension,* edited by Donald I. Critchow and Ellis W. Hawley (Pennsylvania State University Press, 1988).

Portions of chapter 5 appeared in "The Origins and Maintenance of Interest Groups in America," *American Political Science Review* 77 (June 1983).

Chapter 7 is a revised version of "Interest Groups, Iron Triangles and Representative Institutions in American National Government," *British Journal of Political Science* (April 1984). Copyright © Cambridge University Press. Reprinted with permission of Cambridge University Press.

Chapter 8 is a revised version of "Interest Group Responses to Partisan Change: The Impact of the Reagan Administration upon the National Interest Group System," which appeared in *Interest Group Politics,* 2d ed., edited by Allan J. Cigler and Burdett A. Loomis (Congressional Quarterly Press, 1986).

# Contents

CHAPTER 1

# Introduction

Interest groups have been fixtures in the nation's capital from the founding of the Republic, but during the past three decades the interest-group system in Washington has undergone a dramatic transformation. Although there has never been an accurate census, the number of political organizations seeking to wield influence over the policy-making process in Washington has at least *tripled* during the past 30 years. Real estate values in the city have soared as more and more trade associations and professional societies have staged a determined March on Washington, moving their headquarters into the nation's capital and away from New York, Chicago, or other regional capitals.

All these groups feel the need to get closer to the daily political life of the federal government in Washington. Most of their efforts are directed at helping their members obtain favorable tax rulings, amendments to administrative regulations, grants for the development of new products, or contracts to supply goods to federal agencies. Beyond these daily efforts to make the huge federal establishment work to the advantage of their members, however, some groups go further by endeavoring to make fundamental changes in the country's public policy. With the advice and counsel of experienced lobbyists, public relations specialists, and law firms in the city, many interest groups are able, at times, to compete quite effectively with the president and the congressional leadership for the attention of the mass media and for the loyalty of elected representatives facing tough decisions about tax policy, environmental concerns, abortion rights, or federal aid to education. Although these ubiquitous advocates and representatives do not always get their way, almost no important decision is made in Washington without the active, continuous involvement of some parts of the interest-group system.

Political leaders and commentators have not greeted the recent explosion of organized advocacy with much enthusiasm. In fact, from the founding of the Republic to the present day, America's political leaders have feared that the free-for-all of democracy would lead to the frustration of the common interest and eventually to such unrestrained conflict that it would tear the country to pieces, as it almost did during the Civil War. George Washington, in his farewell address in 1796, warned of the "baneful effect of the spirit of party" that through "selfish misrepresentations" tends "to render alien to each other those who ought to be bound together by fraternal affection" (Commager 1973, 169).

Almost two centuries later, President Jimmy Carter, in his farewell address, expressed almost the same concerns when he said:

> Today, as people have become ever more doubtful of the ability of the Government to deal with our problems, we are increasingly drawn to single-issue groups and special interest organizations to ensure that whatever else happens, our own personal views and our private interests are protected. This is a disturbing factor in American political life. It tends to distort our purposes, because the national interest is not always the sum of all our single or special interests. We are all Americans together, and we must not forget that the common good is our common interest and our individual responsibility. (Carter 1981, 156)

When most commentators speak of *special interests* they usually are referring to groups that represent business, such as the Automobile Manufacturers of America, the American Petroleum Institute, the American Bankers Association, or the Iron and Steel Institute; or to trade unions like the United Auto Workers or the Teamsters. Large associations also exist in Washington, however, that represent interests in the nonprofit realm, such as the nation's teaching hospitals, municipal transportation authorities, or the land grant universities, and there are many familiar organizations in the city that are dedicated to the furtherance of causes, such as the American Civil Liberties Union, the Sierra Club, or the National Organization for Women.

It is not surprising to find that large manufacturing companies feel the need for representation in Washington, or that they were able to find the resources to create and maintain organizations that serve them. It also might be expected that some extremely popular causes or large social movements might somehow lead to the creation of interest groups in the nation's capital. But would we have anticipated the creation of the Railroad Passengers Association? It seeks to represent a group of individuals that certainly have shared interests, but the level of fares or the quality of service is not the kind of concern that normally would attract the time and energy of the busy people hurrying anonymously through crowded train stations on their way to work. There are many more passengers riding on buses than railroad trains, yet there is no association in Washington that seeks to represent them. We might also be surprised that groups like the International Committee on Sports for the Deaf, or Partners for a Livable Planet, or Peace Links: Women Against War ever managed to come into being. It is not that the causes these groups are furthering are unworthy, but such organizations face towering financial and administrative obstacles. How did they overcome all these problems and successfully get under way? How have they managed to rent office space, hire staff, and issue publications?

The existence of these somewhat unlikely associations is especially puzzling because of the many obvious gaps in the universe of interest groups. College and university students are represented in Washington by small, struggling organizations that can barely afford to mount programs, while in some European countries there exist many large, active organizations that purport to represent students. There are several large groups in Washington seeking to represent the interests of children and the mentally ill, elements of the society that are exceedingly hard to organize for collective action since the constituents of the movements are themselves unable to join interest groups. On the other hand, there is no group in the city that has as its central focus the interests of the nation's unemployed, certainly a body of vulnerable and distressed people much in need of an advocate for their interests.

In this book I attempt to explain the uneven coverage of interests in the universe of national advocates and to answer a fundamental question about the interest-group system: whom does it represent and, just as important, whom does it leave out? One of my primary goals is to identify the forces behind the recent expansion in the number of interest groups at the national level of government. I want to explain how these organizations came into being, and how they are able to maintain themselves year after year. How are they organized, and in what kinds of issues are they interested? What tactics do they employ in their efforts to wield influence over the policy-making process, and what factors affect their choice of tactics? How do interest groups relate to each other? Are there discernible patterns of cooperation that create long-standing alliances among groups, or is the interest-group world simply a war of all against all, devoid of structure or form? What are the relationships between interest groups and the nation's political parties, and are these two different kinds of political organizations inevitably in conflict with each other, or is their evolution guided by the same underlying forces? What can be learned about the future of the system of interest groups in America, and how does the evolution of this element of the political system affect the general health and well-being of American democratic institutions?

## The Subject of the Study

This is a broadly focused study that attempts to address a series of important questions about the national system of interest groups, but as soon as the investigation began, it was evident that if the study was ever to be brought to a conclusion within my lifetime, many equally important questions would have to be ignored, or at least left aside for research at some other time. The problem I was facing is the same one that bedevils anyone who tries to investigate any aspect of the governmental process. Everything seems to be connected to everything else! It would have been easy to transform this study of interest groups into a study of congressional lobbies, campaign finance, the permeability of the executive agencies, political participation by individual citizens, or even the way in which news is gathered in Washington. At the outset, it was necessary to create clear boundaries around the subject matter under investigation. I had to decide which questions to ask, which types of organizations to study, and, most important, what to leave out.

In his classic study of interest groups, David Truman used the term *interest group* to refer to "any group that, on the basis of one or more shared attitudes, makes certain claims upon other groups in the society for the establishment, maintenance, or enhancement of forms of behavior that are implied by the shared attitudes" (Truman 1951, 33). This broad definition covers categoric groups within the population, such as women or the elderly, that both have shared attitudes and are generally agreed on the actions that should be taken to advance their interests. Truman argued that any kind of group could be regarded as political once it made any effort to influence the government to achieve its goals. Truman's definition covers almost any grouping within the society, ranging from what he called *potential groups*, people who share attitudes but are not formally organized into functioning associations, to the more conventional organizations that maintain staffs and make easily observable efforts to take part in politics.

I have not attempted to cover the entire universe of human interactions, as Truman did. Several generalizations are made in this book about the broad system of interest groups and institutionalized advocates at the national level of government, but my principal focus is limited to functioning associations in the United States that are open to membership and are concerned with some aspects of public policy at the national level. Most of the organizations that are included in the study have headquarters in Washington, D.C., but not all of them do. Some have a handful of members, while others have tens of thousands. Some have tiny staffs made up of part-time employees, while others have hundreds of staff members and annual revenues amounting to millions of dollars. The process by which my sample of national interest groups was constructed may have left uncovered a number of tiny interest groups made up of a handful of individual citizens. I am confident, however, that the data presented in this book constitute a reasonably accurate picture of the entire spectrum of interest groups operating in the nation's capital. It represents all organizations that can reasonably be described as voluntary associations, and that are seeking in one way or another to petition the government on behalf of some organized interest or cause.

Let me note some important groups that are not included in the study. Trade unions are not generally included, partly because membership in them is not usually voluntary. Unions were included in the original sample for this study, but the organizational directors to whom the questionnaire was sent apparently felt that many questions were not appropriate for them. More than for any other type of group, questionnaires returned from unions often had entire sections left blank; worse, many did not return the mailing at all. Because of this low response rate for unions, data reported in this book generally exclude the union respondents. There are a few occasions where it was possible to have confidence in the responses from unions, for example, the questions dealing with collective bargaining, allocation of member benefits, and the use of the courts, areas where striking differences occurred between union responses and those of other types of groups. Therefore, when questions were particularly appropriate for the union respondents, their answers are reported. Typically, however, this study does not include unions.

Besides trade unions, lots of other very important organizations are not included in this study. By focusing on groups that admit members, I excluded the public affairs divisions of private corporations such as the Ford Motor Company, Sears, Roebuck and Co., General Electric, or Xerox. There are hundreds of such offices in the city, and many of them maintain large, active staffs of lobbyists. My study also excluded hundreds of nonprofit corporations and "think tanks," such as the Brookings Institution, the Heritage Foundation, Resources for the Future, or the Police Foundation, all of which play some role in the formulation of public policy. There was no coverage of either conventional or public interest law firms, some of Washington's most distinctive institutions, that contain some of the most influential lobbyists in the city. I also did not collect data on university-based research centers, independently financed study commissions, private foundations, public relations firms, specialized policy newsletters (of which there are several hundred), or the increasingly active national lobbying efforts of state governments, large cities, large university systems, hospitals and other health-care providers, many of which maintain full-time representatives in the national capital. Similarly, foreign governments are not included, although their embassy staffs are often to be found bargaining with American agency officials over trade questions. All these entities are integral parts of the increasingly complex representative system that has emerged in Washington during the past three decades, and a truly comprehensive study would have to include them all. My study obviously would have been stronger if data were available on the entire system of interest aggregation, agenda setting, and influence, but the information we do have will provide many important insights into the origins and maintenance of the broader universe of organized interests.

By limiting my data collection to associations that are open to members, however, I have not entirely lost touch with business firms, universities, city governments, or the other large organizations that maintain their own staffs of lobbyists in Washington. These organizations remain in my study as important members of many of the voluntary associations that fall within my sample. A company like General Motors, for example, operates a large office of public affairs in the city that handles most of the firm's direct relations with government agencies, members of Congress, and the press. The company also retains several Washington law firms that sometimes engage in lobbying on its behalf, and controls several political action committees that make campaign contributions at both the state and national levels. Beyond these independent activities, however, General Motors holds memberships in dozens of specialized trade associations like the Automobile Manufacturers Association, the Transportation Institute, and the Truck Body Equipment Association, and it also is a prominent member of a number of peak business organizations like the Chamber of Commerce and the National Association of Manufacturers. The company's influence is also promoted by its employees, who often play central roles in the professional associations in their respective occupational areas, such as the Institute of Transportation Engineers (often all dues and travel expenses connected with membership in these associations are paid for by the company). Multiple memberships are the rule, so even by addressing only those groups that are in the sample, we came in contact with the vast majority of those seeking representation in Washington.

It is important at the outset to understand that the interest groups we are studying are not composed exclusively of autonomous individuals seeking some benefit or public policy goal of their own. Even though most recent theories about the logic of joining interest groups overlook these differences among members, many group members have joined explicitly in order to represent the interests of their employers, not only themselves. In fact, national interest groups are pretty evenly divided among those whose membership is composed primarily of individual citizens (like the League of Women Voters or the Wilderness Society) and groups that are composed almost entirely of the representatives of large institutions, business firms, or state and local governments (such as the International Hospital Federation, or the United States Cane Sugar Refiners Association). As Salisbury (1984) has pointed out, it is important to keep in mind the important role played by institutions in the affairs of political interest groups when interpreting their behavior.

Early in the planning for this study another important decision was made that further limited its scope: This study does not attempt to measure the degree of power or influence actually wielded by the interest-group system. This is an extremely important question, but one that would require a research design quite different than the one that was eventually adopted. Many scholars have struggled with the problem of how to measure political power, but there is certainly no consensus among students of the field about how to accomplish this difficult task (see Hunter 1953, Mills 1956, Dahl 1961, Bachrach and Baratz 1962, Polsby 1963, Crenson 1971). Rather than join in this effort, I decided to operate on the assumption that interest groups wield significant influence in the policy-making process, but to make no effort in this study to measure systematically the extent of their power. The study concerns, instead, the crucial questions of how interest groups originate, how they maintain themselves, how they relate to other groups, the government, and the political parties, and why groups have been successfully organized in certain areas but have not emerged in others. The ultimate aim of the study is to specify the principal financial, political, and organizational factors that determine the origins, maintenance, and behavior of interest groups operating at the national level in the American political system.

**Research Strategy**

Once the principal questions to be answered in this study were specified, it was necessary to decide how these questions might be addressed. What kind of evidence would be the most useful in dealing with each of the central questions being posed? Most scholars who have studied interest groups have concentrated in great depth upon one group, such as McFarland's excellent study of Common Cause (McFarland 1984), or have conducted comparative studies of groups in one policy area, such as Berry's study of public interest groups (1977), Gelb and Palley's survey of feminist groups (1982),. or Browne's analysis of agricultural interest groups (1988). Others have studied the role played by interest groups in the resolution of an important policy issue, such as Robyn's study of trucking deregulation (1987), or Bosso's investigation of the regulation of pesticides (1987). All of these studies are enormously useful because they provide the texture and detail required to sharpen our insights into the impact of interest groups on the policy-making process, but since there are many different kinds of groups operating in Washington, and each policy area has a number of unique characteristics, it has been difficult for scholars to construct reliable generalizations based upon the existing case studies that would apply to the entire system of interest groups.

The lack of intellectual coherence in this field arises in part from the fact that each case-study writer has employed a slightly different scheme of classi-fication and has emphasized different aspects of group operations. Having multiple focuses is not peculiar to studies of interest-group influence but is common in the field of public policy in general. Efforts to build comprehen-sive theories are often frustrated by the range of activities to be explained (see Greenberg et al. 1977). But in the end, the difficulties scholars have had in building generalizations are due not so much to the quality of the available case studies as to our lack of understanding of the broader outlines of the interest-group system. Without this crucial element of perspective, it is difficult to be sure what each case study is a case of.

One of the most important goals of this book is to provide an intellectual road map that will guide us in our efforts to build general explanations based upon the rich heritage of description left us by earlier scholars. Rather than collecting hundreds of pieces of data concerning a limited number of groups, I decided to collect a small number of pieces of data about hundreds of groups. My aim is to create a more accurate ecology of the entire American interest-group system, as well as a better understanding of the principal social and political forces that seem to be driving the development of this system. I chose to study several hundred associations—ranging from large citizen groups with hundreds of thousands of members that exist largely through direct mail solicitation to tiny trade associations with a handful of business firms as members and only a single Washington attorney acting part-time as their executive secretary. This broad survey of the entire spectrum of voluntary associations operating in Washington should enable us to identify theoretically crucial differences among different kinds of interest groups so that the many case studies of individual associations in the literature can be placed into proper perspective.

## The Data

The argument presented in this book is substantiated mainly from the results of two surveys of the entire system of national interest groups, but it is not confined to those data. One important source of information derives from several dozen personal interviews with staff members of interest groups and congressional committees, elected representatives, and other observers of the Washington policy-making process. These interviews were open-ended, and all the respondents were promised anonymity. They ranged in length from about 30 minutes to almost 2 hours in one case. They were designed mainly to prevent me from losing touch with the everyday reality of interest-group management, and they allowed me to experiment with arguments and interpretations with people immersed in the details of administration, fund-raising, and lobbying. Many of these interviews were conducted before the first mail survey was attempted, beginning in 1979, and several more took place after those data were collected in an attempt to better understand the results I had obtained. Besides these personal interviews there are references throughout the book to scholarly studies of the history of interest groups and to many case studies and other monographs that provide vivid descriptions of the process of policy-making in Washington.

The heart of the study, however, is the statistical analysis of the results of two general surveys of national interest groups conducted by mail during the 1980s at the Institute of Public Policy Studies of the University of Michigan. Detailed descriptions of the samples and response rates are reported in appendix A. The respondents were the executive secretaries or other officers who bore principal responsibility for managing the associations, and efforts were made to contact every association open to membership and concerned with national policy issues in Washington, D.C. The 1980 survey had 734 usable responses (55.4 percent response rate); the 1985 survey, 892 cases (54.5 percent response rate). The panel data set includes 448 groups that responded to both the 1980 and 1985 surveys. Generally, this book reports the 1985 data whenever possible. Each table or figure reporting data indicates the data set used to create it.

## The Structure of My Argument

My explanation of the operation of the interest-group system will unfold over the course of the chapters of this book, justified and reinforced in as many places as possible with empirical evidence. Rather than presenting my analysis piecemeal, however, thus running the risk that objections to one portion will color the reader's reactions to other parts of the story, I have decided to lay out the central findings of the study in capsule form at the outset, thus running the risk that readers will never even finish the introductory chapter. The propositions I am about to present will be elaborated and filled out in the chapters to come, but, in essence, my conclusions are simple and can be summarized in a few paragraphs.

Early in the history of most interest groups, leaders settle upon an organizational and financial strategy that includes methods to maintain the loyalty of the membership and to attract the sympathy and support of important patrons. Some groups adopt an "inside" strategy based primarily upon close consultation with political and administrative leaders, relying mainly upon their financial resources, substantive expertise, and concentration within certain congressional constituencies as a basis for influence. Other groups become dedicated mainly to "outside" strategies based upon appeals to the public through the mass media and efforts at the broad-scale mobilization of citizens at the "grass roots." These fundamental strategic choices are determined by the group's niche in the constituency and policy communities of which it is a part and by four crucial environmental factors: (1) whether their membership is based on certain occupational or institutional roles or open to individual citizens regardless of their institutional affiliations, (2) the array of patronage sources available, (3) the nature of the resources available to the group, and (4) the degree of conflict the group experiences with organized political opponents of various kinds. These variables determine the type and mix of benefits groups of all kinds provide to their members and the fundamental tactical stance they adopt.

The larger interest-group system has a relatively stable structure within which associations maintain identifiable roles and ideological positions. The system is organized around coalitions of groups striving to represent a set of constituents, such as the handicapped or Hispanic-Americans, and also by an overlapping set of policy networks or communities concerned with policy areas like national defense, elementary and secondary education, or consumer protection. These constituency and policy communities anchor the system and orient it toward the two major political parties, but their relations with the parties are complex. Some groups are closely connected with a party, but others have independent organizational lives. These groups are not much affected by the change in partisan control over the Congress or the presidency. Their relations with the permanent government of agencies and congressional committees are more important to them than who is serving in the White House.

A growing number of interest groups report, however, that their access to governmental decision makers and the amount of financial support they receive from government agencies are directly affected by the outcome of elections, especially those for the presidency. In order to protect or enhance their own influence and financial well-being, interest groups that maintain fairly clear liberal or conservative ideological positions and are experiencing conflict with other groups or political leaders are likely to make efforts to influence the outcome of national elections and may also become attached to loosely coupled coalitions with links to one of the two major political parties. The partisan electoral system and the interest-group system are slowly becoming more closely intertwined.

About 80 percent of American interest groups have emerged from preexisting occupational or professional communities. From the beginning of the development of the interest-group system, there has been a sharp cleavage between representatives of the profit and nonprofit sides of the economy—a cleavage that carries great political significance. Professionals working on a fee-for-service basis have organized separate groups from professionals who work for salaries in universities, nonprofit hospitals, or other types of public bureaucracies, and they often find themselves on opposite sides of political debates, providing representation for different elements of the society.

In the profit-making side of the economy, companies compete with each other in the marketplace but realize that they share a common interest in important public policies. Companies that manufacture aircraft engines, for example, have a common interest in such questions as the size of the nation's Air Force, measures meant to reduce air pollution, or the amount of subsidies supplied to cities and towns that wish to build airports. These shared interests lead firms to create an association designed to represent their interests, often under the prompting of the largest companies in the industry and sometimes even with the encouragement of the principal government agencies in the field. Large firms often act as "member patrons," paying a disproportionate share of the costs of this process of mobilization, a phenomenon described by Olson as "the exploitation of the strong by the weak" (1965). Business interests will not avoid political conflict if it becomes necessary but normally choose to pursue "inside" strategies of influence that capitalize upon their wealth and prestige rather than becoming involved in open controversies that would be featured in the mass media.

Trade unions arise from the shared interests of workers in collective bargaining with powerful employers, but many efforts to create industrial unions were unsuccessful until the right to organize was officially recognized by the government in the 1930s and a legal framework was provided within which peaceful organizing drives could be conducted. Today's trade unions are the most flexible organizations in the system when it comes to the selection of tactics to pursue their goals. Their ties with a mass membership and their traditions of social protest make them more likely than trade associations and professional societies in the profit-making realm to pursue a mixture of "outside" and "inside" strategies.

Where public welfare or other governmental or nonprofit services are concerned, officials in local agencies offering services to the public realize that they have an interest not only in the well-being of their programs but also in exchanging information and comparing administrative techniques with other professionals operating similar programs in other cities or states. Often such public sector professionals are initially brought together by officials in federal agencies that have their own policy agendas. These federal officials wish to improve coordination of local, state, and national efforts through the creation of associations and also hope that the resulting organizations of professionals or state and local agencies eventually will mobilize support in Congress for the agency's programs. Groups of this kind are most effective in policy areas characterized by low levels of conflict because they rely heavily on public bureaucracies for patronage, and these agencies are careful to avoid becoming the object of attack by powerful political leaders. The social service professionals also wish to protect their reputations for neutral competence and expertise and are fearful of intervention in their internal affairs by partisan politicians should they become too openly involved in the advocacy of what may be regarded as controversial causes.

The remaining 20 percent of the nation's interest groups are not based upon preexisting occupational or professional communities. They usually arise in the wake of broad social movements concerned with such problems as the level of environmental pollution, threats to civil rights, or changes in the status of women. The groups formed to act as representatives of these social movements often are created by political entrepreneurs operating with the support of wealthy individuals, private foundations, or elected political leaders who act as their protectors, financial supporters, and patrons. These patrons provide the crucial seed money needed to mount the expensive campaigns required to convince thousands of people to affiliate with these fledgling organizations. Groups seeking to further a cause thrive on controversy and must gain the attention of the mass media in order to convince their patrons of the organization's potency, and also to communicate effectively with their far-flung constituents. The structure and operation of these citizen groups is determined by the requirements of an "outside" strategy of influence.

As a result of the legal, financial, and organizational factors that determine the origins and maintenance of interest groups, three principal modes of mobilization become available to political entrepreneurs in the American political system. The first, and most prevalent, is the straightforward mobilization of relatively small groups of people with shared economic or professional interests who wish to petition the government either to gain some form of privilege or to protect themselves against regulation or taxation. This form of mobilization from the bottom up, with elements of the society organizing in their own immediate interests to influence the government, is the most familiar and best understood type of political action by citizens in a democracy. Often, such groups actually get their start with subsidies provided by the largest firms or organizations operating in the area, so that the image of spontaneous mobilization from below is an illusion. This is especially true where peak organizations representing generic activities (such as retailing, manufacturing, scientific research, or health care) are concerned. In these cases, all the familiar dilemmas of collective action arise, and successful organizing efforts often require crucial assistance from the area's largest organizations or from government agencies or political leaders, especially in launching associations and seeing them through their formative years.

The second mode of political mobilization emerges from social movements that sweep through society from time to time, normally arising from the educated middle class. Movements to abolish slavery, prevent the production and sale of alcoholic beverages, shut off immigration, ensure civil rights for minority groups, or protect the natural environment have long been a central feature of American political life. Spontaneous movements for reform represent a form of mobilization from below that governmental leaders are almost compelled to recognize if they expect to maintain their legitimacy. The forces leading to the emergence of social movements are not well understood, but even less is known about the way in which tangible associations arise that purport to represent these movements. Successful efforts to organize such groups require a widespread perception among the potential membership that fundamental rights or crucial public goods are being threatened, and they also require that large amounts of patronage be secured, usually from business firms, trade unions, private foundations, wealthy individuals, or sometimes from the government itself, to pay the costs of attracting members who eventually will pay dues or make contributions that will sustain an expensive program of advocacy and public education.

The third mode of political mobilization, and the least well understood, involves people usually unable to mobilize on their own because they are poor, elderly, physically or mentally handicapped, or without the capacity to represent themselves, as in the case of children. Successful organization where such vulnerable constituents are involved usually is initiated from above with social service professionals in the lead, gaining crucial assistance, in the early stages, from government agencies, private foundations, and elected officials. Mobilization for political action begins among those who wish to provide some new form of social welfare services, and eventually, if no organized opponents appear and conflict is held to a minimum, and if public sympathy can be gained for the proposed recipients of the programs, groups may also be organized in which the clients themselves or their immediate guardians are the featured membership. Such broadly based organizations, however, normally appear only after major pieces of legislation have been passed that bring large government agencies into being, because such bureaucratic organizations are required to supply the crucial patronage needed to maintain groups made up of such vulnerable members of society.

Not all elements of the population or all types of interests are able to find a successful formula for organization employing one of these three principal modes of mobilization. The interest-group system lends itself to the organizing efforts of some groups much more readily than to others, which means that, at any one time, the associations actually operating in the city of Washington are not a perfect reflection of the shape of public opinion in the country. There are many more types of people represented in Washington by organized advocates in the 1990s than there were in the 1950s or the 1920s, but the interest-group system is still prevented by administrative, political, and financial obstacles from responding to the intensely felt needs of many elements of the population.

Despite its shortcomings as a sensitive register of the passions and desires of the American public, however, the interest-group system does allow for the expression of concern about emerging new problems, such as the growing menace of air pollution or the rising aspirations of black Americans for political equality. The issues around which interest groups form do not always fit perfectly with the fault lines within the polity created by the party system. Both the opponents and proponents of abortion rights, for example, come from social groups traditionally allied with both the Republican and Democratic parties. Such an issue cuts sharply across the traditional coalitions that support the two parties. Aspiring politicians usually strive to avoid issues that divide their followers, so party leaders cannot be relied upon to deal with some important problems that capture the attention of large numbers of people. The interest-group system provides a mechanism in an increasingly complex society through which emerging issues and ideas can be offered up as possible new items on the national political agenda. When interest groups begin to attract resources and attention to their causes, the parties are forced to alter their programs and reformulate their supporting coalitions to accommodate to shifts in the public's principal concerns. Seen in this light, the two forms of political organization are complementary and together constitute a much more responsive and adaptive system than either would be if they somehow operated on their own.

## A Preview of Coming Chapters

The book begins with two chapters designed to provide the historical and theoretical context within which the results drawn from my survey data can be interpreted. Chapter 2 is concerned with the evolution of the modern American system of interest groups and political parties that began to take shape in the latter half of the nineteenth century. The history of this system has been shaped by the rapid growth of a highly complex urban-industrial society, and by pressures from wave after wave of newly emerging elements of that society—immigrants pouring into the country from Europe, Latin America, and Asia; new professions, occupations, and industries; religious groups fighting to establish themselves in a sometimes unwelcoming culture; women making demands for political, economic, and social equality; and racial minorities struggling to overcome the legacy of slavery and discrimination—all clamoring for political recognition and a legitimate role in the political system. America has been experiencing a continuous crisis of participation for over 100 years, and during this period many innovative political organizations have been created to provide for the peaceful accommodation of a broader and broader spectrum of political demands.

The growth of so many new forms of political organization and advocacy led scholars to search for fresh understandings of the American political system. By the early years of the twentieth century, many new theories were being offered that were designed to explain the process through which public policy is formulated, interests are accommodated, and conflicts resolved in the American political system. Chapter 3 describes and offers a critique of this theoretical tradition. It also describes the theoretical stance I will take, thus setting the stage for the analysis of systematic data on the contemporary state of the national system of interest groups gathered in my surveys.

The analysis of systematic data on national interest groups begins in chapter 4, where the outlines of the system are presented, and several possible schemes of classification based upon the nature of the membership of groups, their policy goals, and their place in an elaborate mosaic of policy communities are evaluated and compared. A picture of an interest-group structure with a discernible, relatively stable ecology emerges from this chapter. The system is engaged in a continuous process of change and adaptation, so the purpose of the chapter is not to provide a perfectly detailed description of the complex system of interest groups in Washington. Its purpose, rather, is to sketch the larger outlines of the system and, in fact, to justify the use of the term *system* in describing the array of interest groups operating in the nation's capital.

In chapter 5 the focus changes from the macro- to the micro-perspective, and an explanation of the origins and maintenance of individual interest groups is offered. Special attention is given to the crucial role of outside patrons in the creation and daily management of interest groups. In order to be successful, group leaders must somehow assemble a mixture of resources that come in different proportions from outside patrons and their own members. Presumably, both their patrons and their membership will respond to some mixture of incentives or benefits, and these combinations vary according to several crucial variables, including the degree of conflict groups experience, the amount and type of patronage they receive, and the nature of their membership. Many different combinations of patronage and benefits are conceivable, but once an organizational recipe is chosen by group leaders, many other aspects of the association's organization and functioning are also determined.

Once an interest group is established and manages to secure the resources it needs to operate, it finds that it has narrowed the number of pathways to influence that are open to it. The political environment it faces, especially the kind of organized opponents it faces, will influence the choice of tactics it may exercise in any given situation. In chapter 6, we find that a group's early financial and organizational decisions, along with the nature of the interest it represents, usually determine whether it adopts a predominantly "inside" or "outside" strategy. Groups must make a series of strategic choices, such as whether to engage in electioneering or steer away from partisan conflicts and whether to engage in protests or other kinds of activities that will generate publicity for their proposals. Beyond establishing the group's fundamental tactical stance, group leaders must also choose whether to approach Congress, the bureaucracy, the presidency, the court system, or some combination of these avenues in order to reach their policy goals.

The discussion of the forces affecting the origins, maintenance, and tactical choices made by interest groups leads me back to a consideration, in the next three chapters, of the larger role played by interest groups within the national political system. Groups vary in the degree of access they enjoy to the principal centers of decision making in Washington, and these differences are partly a result of the types of interests they represent, the tactics they employ, and the efforts groups make to influence the outcome of partisan elections. The access and cooperation that most interest groups experience with the permanent government in Washington are hardly affected by the outcomes of national elections, but during the 1980s it was increasingly difficult for group leaders to insulate themselves from the tides of national partisan politics. This could be a temporary effect caused by the aggressive effort of the Reagan administration to alter so many settled public policies in the domestic realm, but there seem to be forces at work in the political system that are breaking up the infamous "iron triangles" through which so many groups in past years mediated their relations with the government. Chapter 7 focuses on the development and breakdown of "iron triangles" and "subgovernments" up through the 1970s, chapter 8 assesses the efforts of the Reagan administration to alter the group structure in the 1980s, and chapter 9 focuses on the use of the court system by America's interest groups.

Interest groups engage in many different types of activities, but their efforts are ultimately directed toward the political mobilization of the individuals and institutions that they represent. As the system of interest groups grows in size and the number of interests being represented grows, more and more people are brought into closer contact with the governmental process. In chapter 10 the findings of this study are integrated in a discussion of the three principal modes of political mobilization available to political entrepreneurs in the American political system: (1) the organization of small homogeneous groups of people or institutions that share a distinct economic or professional interest, (2) the creation of organizations meant to represent the aspirations of many people involved in a broad social movement, and (3) the mobilization of individuals willing to act as representatives for other, less fortunate or less competent members of the society. Many of these efforts at third-party representation are backed by the government itself, or by other patrons of political action in the nonprofit realm.

Some features of the interest-group system encourage innovation and facilitate peaceful change. Yet it is clear that some elements of the population who are experiencing great distress remain without representation unless they can find a sponsor or patron able to foster their mobilization. Some interests are granted advantages by the American system, while others find it almost impossible to make their voices heard. No governmental process could ever provide equal access or influence to every conceivable interest, and it might be wise, in some cases, to sacrifice accessibility in order to improve the system's capacity to reach closure and manage conflict. Whenever such choices are made, however, some interests must be favored over others, and such choices have distinct moral implications. Every political system is organized around a distinct constellation of interests that is the product of its rules, processes, and institutions, none of which are products of natural forces beyond our leaders' control. The American system could be changed if we wish it to be different.

# CHAPTER 2

# The Mobilization of Political Interests in America

Most people, most of the time, are able to find better things to do than participate in politics. Even if some method could be devised to allow all citizens to be consulted on every governmental decision, few people would have the time or inclination to participate. Study and informed debate are required to decide whether the tax code should be amended to allow machines used in manufacturing glass containers to be depreciated on an accelerated schedule, or whether a program is required to subsidize students taking graduate degrees in mining engineering. Yet those are the kind of narrow, technical questions that elected legislators must deal with every day. They manage to address these questions through an elaborate system of specialized committees and with the assistance of thousands of staff members. Most citizens would not be able to comprehend the information generated by the congressional staff, and even if they could, there is little reason to think it would interest them. People have better things to do. Legislating in a modern democracy has become a highly specialized, full-time job.

Most people do not know how their representative votes on most issues that come before Congress. The little they hear in the mass media about new legislation is usually obscured by confusing talk of conference committees, parliamentary maneuvers, floor votes, presidential vetos, or administrative rulings. Some people may have personal dealings with their representatives when they ask for assistance in negotiations with the Social Security Administration or receive information about a governmental program that might assist them in their business or profession. Members of Congress refer to this kind of activity as *case work,* and it is an excellent way for incumbents to increase their popularity. However, even the most active members of Congress manage to render personal assistance to only a tiny proportion of the voters in their districts (see Fiorina 1989). Newsletters can be sent by mail, government publications can be sent to those who might need them, but the majority of citizens never have any direct contact with their representatives and know almost nothing about them.

The linkages between citizens and their representatives, however, are not as tenuous as this sketch would imply. Legislators may not communicate often with each individual voter, but they are in contact, almost every day, with professional advocates who claim to speak for the elderly, manufacturers of plastic pipe, teachers in the public schools, or some other specialized segment of the public. When members of Congress visit their districts, they consult with a small circle of confidants who have an impression of how the public might react to certain issues; representatives also gain impressions of public sentiment during visits to local Chambers of Commerce, civic clubs, churches, and other community institutions (see Fenno 1978).

When elections take place, these same organizations make efforts to communicate with their members and provide helpful cues about the records and platforms of the candidates, although political parties usually are the most active linking mechanisms between citizens and the government during elections. Even though most individuals have little information about the activities of their representatives, they can still cast votes for the candidates most likely to advance their interests by supporting those with the most appropriate partisan labels. Party workers contact millions of citizens during election campaigns, urging them either to register, contribute money to the campaign, or to go to the polls and vote. All of these institutions—voluntary associations, trade unions, interest groups, and political parties—serve to link the public with their elected representatives. They provide channels of communication through which important political messages may flow.

## Political Parties versus Interest Groups as
## Agents of Mobilization

There is little doubt in the minds of most political scientists about whether political parties or interest groups are preferable as mechanisms for political mobilization in a democracy. The parties win, hands down. During the early years of the 1980s, a review of all scholarly articles published in political science journals found more than ten times the number of articles on political parties than on interest groups (see Walker 1972; Janda 1983; Cigler 1989). Any observer of American politics who had not been trained as a political scientist but whose reading included publications like the *Washington Post* or the *National Journal* would surely regard this as a curiously lopsided investment of intellectual resources, far out of line with the significance of each type of organization in the daily struggle over public policy in Washington. Why would the scholarly discipline of political science lavish so much attention on organizations that are widely believed to be of declining significance in the American political process? Why are comparatively little time and energy spent on the world of interest groups, corporate public affairs officers, law firms, think tanks, and even government bureaucracies—the featured players in journalistic descriptions of political life in Washington?

Political scientists devote so much of their resources to the study of political parties mainly because of their historic commitment to the task of convincing anyone who will listen that democracy cannot be successful without the existence of vigorous, competitive political parties. Interest groups also have been an important object of concern since the discipline was founded, but, from the beginning, many scholars have been noticeably uncomfortable with the phenomena they were studying (Garson 1978). Walter Lippman complained as early as 1914 about the inability of the sprawling American political system to establish coherent goals or carry out comprehensive plans in his aptly titled *Drift and Mastery* ([1914], 1961). Many writers have warned that, if the interest-group system is allowed to overwhelm all efforts to enact comprehensive legislative programs, there is a grave danger that our highly decentralized system will be unable to adapt to new economic and social developments. By seeking to appease every concern and objection by hundreds of selfish, conservative, special interests, the American system runs the risk of contracting a chronic case of perpetual political deadlock.

Not all interest groups, however, are narrow-minded defenders of the status quo. Many new citizen groups have emerged in recent years advocating extensive reforms and pushing controversial causes, sometimes attracting hundreds of thousands of members. These broadly based associations also attract the complaints of disapproving commentators who refer to them as "single-interest groups" that threaten to "overload" the government with unreasonable demands, polarize debate, and render compromise impossible, eventually leading to a dangerous breakdown in consensus (Huntington 1973 and 1981; King 1975; Rose and Peters 1978).

Besides the tendency of the interest-group system to fragment the system and undermine any semblance of party discipline, charges often are made that interest groups are not representative. The insistent advocates for business or labor represent narrow, selfish, and, for the most part, upper-class interests. Even the new citizen groups are supported mainly by well-educated members of the upper middle class (McFarland 1984). "The flaw in the pluralist heaven," Schattschneider argued in a much cited passage, "is that the heavenly chorus sings with a strong upper-class accent" (1960, 35).

Political parties are often portrayed as the solutions to these looming problems of fragmentation, drift, and class bias, since only they are capable of providing broad policy direction, and reliably representing the many unorganized and vulnerable elements of the society. They are the only institutions capable of aggregating demands from conflicting interests, coordinating the constitutionally divided branches of the federal government, concentrating authority, and allowing for the exercise of leadership in the American form of government. Political scientists have long argued that strong political parties were beneficial, whereas powerful interest groups posed a threat to the representative process.

The party system and the interest-group system are often regarded as being fundamentally at odds. When groups increase in power or influence, the fragmentation they create causes parties to decline in influence. When parties are able to gain control of the agenda of debate, the influence of interest groups surely will recede (see Schattschneider 1942, 1948, 1960; see also Dahl 1982, 190–91). There is such a strong consensus among political scientists about the importance of strong political parties in the American system of government that warnings are frequently issued from leading scholars about the demise of parties, and measures are proposed that would lead to their renewal (see Committee on Political Parties 1950; Ladd 1977; Kirkpatrick 1978; Pomper 1980).

The real live American political parties, however, are not so consistently dedicated to mobilizing the public or coordinating the government as the advocates of party government might wish, nor is the interest group system, taken as a whole, as selfish and narrow as it is portrayed in these accounts. The two systems are not fundamentally antithetical. The party system is most active during elections and when the government is being organized, while the interest-group system predominates during the period between elections, when public policy is being formulated and implemented. Most interest groups are careful to avoid becoming involved in partisan politics. Only 33 percent of the groups in my surveys report that they engage in any form of electioneering. Furthermore, most politically active people who take part in party politics are affiliated with several interest groups at the same time (Baumgartner and Walker 1988 and 1990). Since the late 1970s, parties have begun to offer more consistent, ideologically distinct programs to the public, but during this period the interest-group system has been steadily expanding rather than declining, and even continued its growth in the face of the Reagan administration's consistent hostility toward all liberal organizing efforts during the 1980s (see chapter 8; see also Peterson and Walker 1986). Far from fading away, many elements of the interest-group system expanded and became more active at the same time the party system's role as a coordinating and mobilizing force, especially within the government, also began to strengthen.

The American public is much more thoroughly mobilized for political action in the 1990s than it was 35 years ago, and both political parties and interest groups have contributed to this development. Any harassed member of Congress, under pressure from powerful party leaders while being overwhelmed with thousands of pieces of mail per month and flooded with contacts and overtures from Washington lobbyists, will readily attest to this development. The somewhat contradictory dangers of polarization, political fragmentation, class bias, and legislative deadlock have plagued American democracy from the beginning. They remain serious problems in the 1990s—perhaps even more so because of the rapid mobilization of the middle class for political action while voting turnout continues to be low, especially among members of the lower and working classes. These problems call out for solution, but they cannot be intelligently addressed until we grasp the roles being played in the political process by all types of political organizations, both political parties and interest groups.

The best way to understand the directions being taken by contemporary political parties and interest groups is to review their recent history. What form did parties take 100 years ago? How did their development affect the development of the interest-group system? And what is the likely future of both the party and the interest-group systems? Are we seeing a dangerous trend toward political fragmentation with dire consequences for our democracy, or are we in the midst of a steady, evolutionary change in the rules of the American political game that will lead to a stronger and more resilient national political community?

## The Party System: A Capsule History

After assuming their modern form in the 1830s and 1840s, the parties entered a golden age soon after the Civil War as the chief organizing devices of American politics. (For reviews of the American party system, see, in particular, Chambers and Burnham 1972; Klepper 1981.) For more than three decades, until the Republican party achieved hegemony after the political realignments of 1896, the outcomes of most national elections were in doubt, precinct-level organizers were hard at work for both sides, large numbers of recent immigrants were mobilized into the political system, turnout at elections soared, and the policy agendas in Washington and many state capitals emerged almost entirely from the clash of the two major parties. (For the most approving description of this period of party hegemony, see McGerr 1986.)

These powerful nineteenth-century parties were decentralized organizations composed of largely autonomous state and local units. They were built upon ethnic, religious, and regional loyalties, but the key to their success was the vast supply of material resources at the disposal of party leaders in the form of patronage jobs, government contracts, exclusive franchises for local services and utilities, and privileged access to judges and other public officials. Party leaders were able to reward those who cooperated and punish their opponents with tangible rewards and sanctions. They used this power to maintain their organizations, control party nominations, and shape the policy agenda, but their methods were not always within the law. The boss, the machine, the gerrymander, the graveyard vote, and many other unsavory metaphors became part of common parlance in America during this golden age of party government, and politicians acquired a sinister reputation that lingers today.

As the twentieth century began, a cultural transformation was underway in almost all realms of American life. Large, centrally managed, bureaucratic hierarchies were emerging in the business world with names such as International Harvester or United States Steel, and national professional communities were being formed in fields such as education, accounting, engineering, and the law, based largely upon technical or scientific values (Hays 1957 and 1969). Pressures soon arose for the creation of government agencies in which these new professional specialties could be pursued without the corrupting interference of partisan politicians. The slogan of the advocates of reform in urban government was: "There is no Democratic or Republican method for paving a street!" Educational leaders wanted to get the public schools "out of politics," just as military planners, public health officers, policemen, forest rangers, and other managers of the new public services wanted to free themselves from kickbacks, graft, partiality, and all the other tainted aspects of partisanship (Skowronek 1982).

As these debates over the delivery of public services intensified in the first decades of the twentieth century, political parties were usually depicted as the chief enemies of good government. Party leaders were under attack for corruption, but the conflict actually ran much deeper. Reformers did not believe that such parochial, decentralized, geographically limited organizations could serve as the centerpieces of representative democracy in an industrial society. Local and state political machines often opposed the expansion of government into new services such as public health or city planning, especially if it meant the incorporation of more professionals into the public service who would refuse to submit to party discipline (McDonald and Ward 1984). In the eyes of those who wished to meet the social problems of an industrial society or exploit the nation's potential as a world power, the political parties developed in the nineteenth century were among the chief obstacles to the modernization of business, government, and the professions in America.

The clash between party leaders and reformers that began in the late nineteenth century did not end in one climactic battle. It dragged on in isolated struggles in cities and states all over the country during the next 50 years. As sources of patronage were eliminated and social services were expanded and professionalized at the state and local levels, the material resources required by party leaders to maintain their organizations began to disappear. Political machines collapsed one by one, party organizations fell into disrepair, and their capacity to mobilize potential voters or control their own nominating procedures steadily declined. Besides these serious organizational setbacks, the party system that emerged from the New Deal realignment of the 1930s also began, by the 1950s, to lose its capacity to shape the agenda of American politics. The unlikely alliance of trade union leaders, big city bosses, Northern liberals, and Southern conservatives that made up the Democratic New Deal coalition was able to shepherd the formulation of a program of social reform during the 1950s, but the programs themselves could not be enacted into law until the Kennedy-Johnson years and the overwhelming Democratic victory in 1964 (Sundquist 1968).

During the Truman administration and throughout the 1950s and early 1960s, stubborn resistance from an alliance of Southern Democrats and Northern Republicans successfully prevented most efforts at domestic reform, creating what James MacGregor Burns called a "deadlock of democracy" that frustrated liberals and, above all, prevented resolution within the legislative arena of one of the country's most serious and potentially explosive domestic problems—racial segregation in the South (Burns 1963). Factions within the Democratic party urgently wanted to address this problem and majorities in favor of national civil rights legislation clearly existed after World War II, but the ruling party was unable to produce legislation on this subject out of fear that its supporting coalition would be blown to pieces by the conflict created by such a debate. Far from being a force for further mobilization of the unorganized and disadvantaged, the party system became a major obstacle to change. Proponents of civil rights were forced to look to the presidency, the courts, and eventually the streets as the only forums where the dilemma of racial segregation might be resolved.

At the state and local level, party organizations were also unable to adjust to the rapid shifts in population and the growth of suburbia after World War II. Representatives of the burgeoning suburban middle class were demanding expensive new government programs in education, health care, transportation, recreation, natural resource conservation, pollution control, and land use planning. Once again, sufficient public support existed to enact these new programs, but established party leaders resisted and delayed, refusing to begin the tremendous expansion of state and local government that such new programs would require. Pressures mounted to reapportion state legislatures according to population so that suburbanites and city dwellers would have a greater voice. In many states during the 1950s, large popular vote majorities failed to produce a majority of legislative seats. Party leaders who profited from these arrangements defended declining rural interests against the rising urban and suburban middle class. When the Supreme Court decided, in *Baker v. Carr* (1962), *Reynolds v. Sims* (1964) and subsequent rulings, that state and local legislative bodies must be apportioned according to equal population size, it also opened the policy agenda in these jurisdictions to new issues that leaders of the majority parties had either ignored or bitterly resisted.

The immediate impact of reapportionment was rapid turnover in all representative bodies. Prior to reapportionment in the 1959 general election in

New Jersey, 20 percent of those elected to the state Senate were new members. In 1967, soon after reapportionment, 75 percent of those elected were serving for the first time. Many Southern states were engaged in protracted disputes over the issue that required many court orders and several reapportionments. No sooner was the issue settled than the 1970 census figures became available, requiring yet another round of redistricting. The Tennessee legislature, for example, was redistricted six times in the nine years from 1962 to 1973. This constant shifting of district lines fractured local political organizations, sent many politicians into early retirement, and led to the unsettling of state party systems for more than a decade (O'Rourke 1980). These decisions had their greatest impact on Southern states such as Georgia and Mississippi that had long been controlled by the dominant Democratic party, or Northern states such as New Jersey and Michigan, where carefully constructed coalitions based in heavily Republican rural areas and small towns had blocked proportional representation for predominantly Democratic urban areas. The decade-long turmoil emerging from the process of reapportionment fractured local political organizations in all these states, leaving their party systems in shambles.

The wrenching experience with legislative reapportionment was another of a long series of organizational body blows sustained by the party system in the twentieth century. With the disappearance of the kind of material inducements organizers had always used, and the decline in intensity of the ethnic and religious loyalties upon which the party system had been founded, some other bases were needed upon which party workers might be recruited. It soon became apparent that "Amateur Democrats" who wanted to achieve programmatic policy goals through political action would also expect to have a voice in party affairs and could not be counted upon for loyal support of all decisions by party leaders (Wilson 1962). In the midst of the turmoil caused by reapportionment during the 1960s, Democratic party organizations at the local level in several cities also became the target of protests over the Vietnam War. Volunteer workers concerned with advancing liberal reforms had centered much of their political activity within the party during the 1950s and early 1960s, but with the advent of an unpopular war conducted by a Democratic president, they turned against the party leadership, fracturing local organizations even further and creating a legacy of bitterness that lasted for years afterward (Ware 1985).

During the 1970s, a search for a new formula for organizational viability began in both parties. As the traditional county- and city-based party organizations continued to wither, a system of candidate-centered electoral politics arose, with campaigns staffed increasingly by professional consultants joined by volunteers whose loyalty was to the individual candidate much more than to the party organization (Ware 1985; McGerr 1986). In response to these developments, Republicans began highly successful experiments with direct mail solicitation for funds, the use of telephone banks, polling, special publications, and other techniques of mass persuasion (Crotty and Jacobson 1980; Harmel and Janda 1982; and Gibson et al. 1983). Through a series of reforms of their nominating procedures, Democrats opened their party to an unprecedented level of participation by volunteer workers and citizens who took part in caucuses, conventions, and direct primaries (Peterson and Walker 1990).

Although appeals to religious, ethnic, regional, and especially racial loyalties still played a prominent role in American electoral politics during this era of candidate-centered campaigning, such powerful symbolic and emotional issues were most often referred to indirectly and with extreme care. Blatant appeals to religious or racial prejudice were almost always counterproductive and had to be avoided. Party leaders found that they must pay more attention to the substance of public policy in presenting their case to the public. A new model of party organization began to evolve in the 1970s, aimed at the growing middle class, built around the latest techniques of mass communication, with centralized staffs of professional fund-raisers and campaign consultants who relied more than ever before upon broadly ideological appeals.

**The Interest-Group System: A Capsule History**

Interest groups have been a part of American life from the country's origins, but the modern system began to take shape only in the late nineteenth century, during the golden age of party government. The rapidly developing industrial economy, besides luring the millions of immigrants to whom the parties were making their appeals, was also spawning a great many new commercial and scientific specialties that served as the foundations for a number of trade and professional societies. These new associations were meant to exercise control over unruly competition within newly developing markets, provide forums for the exchange of information and the development of professional reputations, create knowledge about the latest methods or techniques in the field, and represent the occupational interests of their members before legislative committees or government bureaus (Mosher 1968; Johnson 1972). There is evidence that the membership of these groups waxed and waned with the economy and that there were spurts of development, especially around the national mobilization during World War I, when dozens of these groups were formed each year (Berry 1977; Schmitter and Brand 1982). A new set of linkages between government and the citizenry was emerging, based squarely upon the rapidly growing occupational structure of the industrial society.

## Occupational Interests: The Profit versus the Nonprofit Realms

The new, occupationally based interest-group system grew in response to several different forces. From the beginning, occupations carried on mainly in the public sector or in nonprofit institutions organized separately from those in the profit sector. Interest groups usually contained members who were mostly from one sector or the other, and conflict between the two sectors often stimulated the growth of even more interest groups (Walker 1983b).

Beginning in the 1940s, for example, a coalition of occupationally based organizations in the nonprofit sector, led by the American Cancer Society and the American Heart Association, began a concerted campaign to reduce cigarette smoking because of its links to cancer and heart disease. This campaign gained wide publicity and was joined by officials in the U.S. Public Health Service, including the surgeon general. The six large firms that dominated the tobacco industry—together accounting for 98 percent of domestic cigarette sales—immediately realized that there was a grave threat of government intervention in their affairs. To combat this threat, they joined forces in a defensive coalition and jointly funded both the Tobacco Research Council, a corporation designed to conduct research under industry auspices, and the Tobacco Institute, a trade association that would coordinate their lobbying efforts in Washington. A struggle began between these two coalitions—public sector professionals, nonprofit institutions, and government agencies on one side, and large corporate and commercial interests on the other—that has continued for more than 30 years, causing many additional organizations to spring up with elaborate coalitions being built on both sides (Miles 1982; Fritschler 1983).

This four-decade-long controversy bears little relation to the cleavages around which the political parties are organized, because it unites all regional interests, Republican and Democratic, where the tobacco industry is dominant. It also invites logrolling tactics in Congress with other bipartisan, regional-industrial blocs (such as the dairy industry, the timber industry, or the oil industry) that wish to protect generous subsidies or obtain favorable government regulations.

Most studies of the formation of business interest groups or trade associations have concluded that they tend to form not so much in response to conflict with organized labor, but rather as responses to threats of unwanted government intervention, as in the case of the tobacco industry, or when factions of an industry seek government aid or protection from their competitors. Antitrust laws prevent some openly collusive joint political efforts, but trade associations tend to form within relatively homogeneous industrial domains where most of the firms perceive the threats emanating from their political environment in much the same way. Associations are also more likely to be established within industries where a few large firms predominate, presumably due to their willingness to bear a disproportionate share of the costs of organizing because they expect to gain a disproportionate share of any benefits that result (Gable 1953; Pfeffer and Salancik 1978; Schmitter and Brand 1982).

The expanding scope and size of government not only stimulated the organization of business interests; even more directly they encouraged the rapid increase of new organizations in the nonprofit and public sectors. The growth, during the twentieth century, of public schools, parks and forest preserves, agricultural research stations, public hospitals, and social welfare agencies of all kinds stimulated the creation of numerous professional associations made up of the providers of these new public services. These groups often were created at the suggestion of public officials who realized the political value of organized constituents working to promote their programs from outside of government.

## Government Sponsorship

The growth of representation for the elderly provides a good example of mobilization from the top down with government encouragement and leadership. In the case of the elderly, the creation of the first pensions for federal civil servants during the 1920s soon led to the creation of the National Association of Retired Federal Employees that could lobby for increases in the program. A system of neighborhood centers for the elderly begun in New York State during the 1930s led to the organization of the social workers who managed these centers. This new professional society not only encouraged the exchange of information about managerial procedures and professional techniques but also pressed for greater financial support for neighborhood centers from all levels of government. A piecemeal process of mobilization of interests representing the elderly began, with the service providers taking the lead in the effort. The process was spurred on by ambitious civil servants in the Federal Security Agency, and eventually through a series of White House conferences in 1951, 1961, 1971, and 1981. With the federal government's assistance, organizations were created to plan and conduct these national meetings. In each case they remained in existence as independent interest groups, although they were often heavily dependent upon grants and contracts from government agencies or private foundations for their continued maintenance.

It was almost three decades after the mobilization of the elderly began before groups designed to enlist the elderly citizens themselves came into being. One of these groups, the National Council of Senior Citizens, was formed with the aid of trade unions and the 1960 presidential campaign for John F. Kennedy, while the American Association of Retired Persons, the largest and most powerful group representing the elderly in the 1990s, began in 1958 as a marketing device for a private insurance company.

By the 1970s, a large, potent array of interest groups representing both the providers and recipients of government services to the elderly had grown up in Washington; a system heavily subsidized by private foundations, churches, business firms, trade unions, and the federal government itself through the Department of Labor and the Agency on Aging. Most of these groups were founded *after* the great legislative breakthroughs of Social Security, Medicare, and the Older Americans Act of 1965. In this case, there was no steady buildup of a gathering force of lobbyists and citizens' associations that finally achieved their goals after decades of pressure upon the government. Much of the initiative for legislation in this field came from *within* the government itself. The associations representing the elderly—especially those that represent the clients of these programs rather than the professionals who deliver the services—were more the consequence of legislation than the cause of its passage (Pratt 1976).

The prominent role of government officials, activist legislators, and presidents in creating the interest groups associated with the mobilization of the elderly was not an aberration. The mobilization of the handicapped, the mentally ill, children, and many other disadvantaged or vulnerable elements of the population followed a similar pattern during the past half-century. The leading role of officials within the public sector in patronizing these movements matches the role of large national and multinational corporations in stimulating the organization of trade associations in the business and commercial sector. But governmental leadership in the mobilization of interests has not been confined to creating groups that advocate an expansion of the welfare state. Business firms have mainly been successful in organizing themselves around narrowly defined market sectors where homogeneous interests exist. Leadership from the government, however, has been necessary in almost all cases where broadly based associations have been created to represent the collective interests of all businesses in the management of the economy or the maintenance of the capitalist market system.

Secretaries of commerce have complained throughout the twentieth century about the weak and indifferent participation of business leaders in discussions at the highest governmental levels. In order to strengthen this voice, and presumably increase their own influence within their administrations, entrepreneurial commerce secretaries have assumed a prominent role in creating many business associations, including the U.S. Chamber of Commerce during the Taft administration; a number of trade associations during the Coolidge and Harding administrations; the Business Council and the Committee for Economic Development during the Roosevelt administration; the Labor-Management Group under the Kennedy administration; the National Alliance of Businessmen during the Johnson administration; and the Business Roundtable during the Nixon and Ford administrations (McConnell 1966; Silk and Silk 1980; Arnold 1982; McQuaid 1982; Vogel 1989).

Governmental leadership has also been crucial in the creation of many other broadly based organizations meant to represent the collective interests of distinctive sectors of American life. For example, the American Farm Bureau Federation began as a network of official advisory committees to county agents organized by the Department of Agriculture, the National Rifle Association was launched in close consultation with the Department of the Army during the nineteenth century to encourage familiarity with firearms among citizens who might be called upon to fight in future wars, and the American Legion was begun during World War I with government support to encourage patriotism and popular support for the war effort. One of the most important results of the New Deal was the relatively peaceful organization of large industrial unions under the supervision of the newly created National Labor Relations Board, following years of bitterly violent resistance to unionization by employers.

Even modern feminist organizations, representatives of a powerful social movement with access to many committed volunteers, received millions of dollars of support in their early years from a series of White House conferences during the Kennedy administration, from federal legislation sponsored by President Kennedy assisting in the creation of Commissions on the Status of Women in every state, from large grants to the International Women's Year of the United Nations, and both statewide and national conferences on women's issues paid for with public funds during the 1970s and 1980s. Once organized, many feminist organizations received much needed funds from grants and contracts with federal agencies for research, data gathering, and the conduct of demonstration projects. The National Organization for Women (NOW) itself was created in 1966, shortly after one of the annual national conventions of State Commissioners on the Status of Women, by a group of commissioners frustrated by the limits on political action placed upon them by their official status (Freeman 1973; Carden 1974; and Gelb and Palley 1982).

Although NOW moved on to create a mass membership base, it was typical of the feminist movement in that most of the interest groups it spawned "began as leadership or cadre organizations lacking a mass base" (Gelb and Palley 1982, 25). The women's movement would undoubtedly have made an important mark upon American life without leadership and financial support from the government in its early years, but the organizations representing it almost certainly would have been more narrowly focused, smaller, and more parochial. In addition, they would have found it much more difficult to attract the attention of the communications media or the political leadership.

The government has many means at its disposal for encouraging the growth of particular interest groups. Nonprofit associations, in particular, benefit from generous provisions in the tax laws without which the very existence of many of them would be imperiled. Gifts, even membership dues to many citizen groups, are fully tax deductible, so groups are better able to solicit contributions from a broad range of individuals. Not only for citizen groups does the tax system provide benefits, however. Professionals can usually deduct the costs of membership in professional societies, and costs of attending conferences as professional expenses. Large businesses typically pay the dues of their employees when membership in a group is for professional reasons, then the businesses deduct these expenses as costs. So the tax system has important implications for the financial health of almost all interest groups in America. Far from hurting the groups, generous provisions are typically given to promote membership and, thereby, to sustain the activities of associations of all types. In fact, the vast majority of membership organizations in the United States appear to avoid taxes altogether, representing quite a remarkable subsidy to their operations. As we will discuss in greater detail in chapter 5, over 90 percent of the groups responding to our 1985 survey reported having tax-exempt status.

Government agencies may provide large grants to various groups in order to carry out specific projects. Even if these are essentially fees for services provided, these large budget items often allow the groups to cover staff expenses, rent office space, and meet overhead expenses that help maintain the groups' financial health. In particular, if the contracts can be expected to be renewed over several years, they provide a long-term cushion against the constant worries of attracting a greater and greater membership base. Especially when groups can provide expertise on matters of public policy, they are particularly likely to garner large contracts from federal agencies. If the Justice Department wants to know something about the state of the profession in the area of law, to whom would it turn for information but the American Bar Association? If there were questions about the state of higher education, a group like the Association of American Universities would be well placed to win a federal grant to conduct a study. Now obviously such grants would not sustain an entire organization, but for many groups they can provide a relatively important and stable source of income.

Long-term financial support provides a base of financial security that many groups need. Foundation support is particularly important for many groups, in addition to government contracts. For example, the annual report of the Environmental Defense Fund (EDF) for 1990–91 gives the following analysis of the group's budget: membership climbed to an all-time high of

200,000; annual revenues reached a total of $16.9 million, of which 22 percent came from foundation grants, and 63 percent from membership and contributions. In the category of contributions, however, many foundations made longer-term commitments, not counted in the annual budget. "An additional $3.5 million of support has been recorded in the category of contributions designated for use in future years. This amount, which is not reported in current income, reflects the growing number of foundations that have committed themselves to long-term support of EDF programs by awarding multi-year grants" (EDF 1990, 18). Groups seek to avoid complete dependence on annual contributions from members by developing such long-term funding sources.

Anyone who has received dozens of mail solicitations for funds from a variety of interest groups can recognize another form of government assistance to the group system: postal rate subsidies. Nonprofit organizations, citizen groups, and others benefit enormously from this form of subsidy (though they are not the only ones to receive it). Without it, they would face millions of dollars in extra costs, or would have to curtail their solicitation drives, thereby further reducing their budgets.

To summarize, the American national government is an important sponsor of many interest groups. Of course, wealthy individuals, corporations, and foundations have greater freedom of choice in their decisions to underwrite the activities of groups that they support, and, for many groups, a single private sponsor may be their primary source of support. The federal government is unlikely to be the sole sponsor of a group; however, its overall impact on the group system, through tax incentives, contracts, and grants, is enormous (see Berry 1977, 44 ff and 1984, 90–91; Schlozman and Tierney 1986, 92–93; Shaiko 1991). Governments in most democracies play a similar role in encouraging the group system. For example, the French government provides thousands of civil servants to work full-time in a variety of citizens' organizations, such as educational associations, cultural groups, and labor unions (see Baumgartner 1989a; Baumgartner and Walker 1989). Government support is an important source of patronage for groups in the United States, as elsewhere.

## The Rise of Citizen Movements

Most of the groups seeking to represent women in Washington have emerged from social movements and are open to all citizens, regardless of their occupations or status. Other groups of this kind, such as the Anti-Saloon League, Marcus Garvey's Negro Improvement Association, the Townsend Movement, the Committee of One Million, the Society Against Nuclear Energy, or the Students for a Democratic Society made a dramatic impact upon the political life of their times. These groups often motivated thousands of people to put forth great effort in intense political activities, but soon they collapsed and disappeared, often with few discernible results. Not all "cause" or citizen groups experienced such rapid cycles of hyperactivity and collapse, but those that did manage to persist were often relatively small or were the exclusive preserve of a circle of dedicated activists sponsored by a few wealthy individuals or institutional patrons.

Citizen groups built around a compelling moral cause or single issue have always been greatly outnumbered in the modern interest-group system by associations founded upon occupational communities. They still are, but, in the 1990s, citizen groups constitute a larger proportion of national lobbying organizations than ever before. Evidence for such a shift in the composition of the group system is difficult to find because there has never been a comprehensive census of interest groups operating in the American political system. Still, comparing the creation dates of groups in my survey shows that over half of the citizen groups were created in the past 25 years, in a dramatic surge of growth that has changed the nature of interest-group politics in America. Profit sector organizations have not shown such a surge in growth, as will be shown in greater detail in chapter 4.

It is clear that groups such as Common Cause, the Sierra Club, NOW, the Moral Majority, and the Wilderness Society are important participants in the national debate over public policy and also appear to have achieved a degree of administrative stability that is unprecedented. With the growth of a large, well-educated middle class since World War II, and with the development of many new techniques of carefully targeted mass communication, such as computerized mailing systems, closed-circuit video conferences, and toll-free telephone lines, it has become possible to organize large, highly dispersed formations of citizens united only by their dedication to a cause or common beliefs about the appropriate direction of public policy.

When the public is surveyed concerning their memberships and contributions to voluntary associations, the vast extent of involvement becomes clear. Almost nine Americans in ten contribute to, or are members of, some kind of voluntary association. These not only are professional associations but include many associations concerned with social issues (see Baumgartner and Walker 1988 and 1990; for philanthropic organizations, also see Pifer 1987, 120–21). Millions of Americans are extremely active, making routine contributions to groups advancing such causes as consumer protection, environmental conservation, and civil rights, and there is evidence of a similar, perhaps even larger body of supporters willing to make contributions to groups advancing conservative social issues. Common Cause has managed to stay in existence for a decade relying almost solely upon direct mail solicitation. There have been ups and downs, but the group had almost 270,000 members in 1989 (McFarland 1984; Common Cause 1989). The Committee for a Sane Nuclear Policy (SANE), originally founded in the 1950s, was still in operation in 1984 with an expanding list of over 80,000 members (*New York Times*, 16 April 1984). The leaders of both political parties and interest groups are discovering that ideological commitment, under some circumstances, can serve as a sound basis for long-term organizational membership.

The early development of interest groups in the United States was based on occupational and professional groupings, with profit sector and nonprofit sector groups often organizing separately. Indeed, the organization for political action of one group often led to the countermobilization of others, as the interest-group system in America grew in the first half of the twentieth century. Government actions often played an important role in organizing constituents for action, as in the case of elderly Americans. The nonprofit sector saw encouragement from government and foundations, while profit sector organizations were often subsidized by large corporations. The nature of the American interest-group system has been transformed in the past 35 years, however, by a tremendous flowering of new citizen groups based on ideology more than on professional interests. The 1960s brought about dramatic changes in the nature of American politics, especially in how interests are organized for political action at the national level.

## Increased Mobilization in the 1960s

The system of political parties and interest groups underwent a transformation during the past 35 years in which new groups and civic organizations formed at an unprecedented rate, bringing many formerly quiescent elements of the population into closer contact with the nation's political leaders. The seeds of this organizational activity were evident in 1955, with the Montgomery bus boycott, and burst into flower with the sit-ins, freedom rides, and protest marches of the civil rights movement in the 1960s. Armed with the symbolic authority of affirmative decisions from the Supreme Court, and backed by a broad coalition of liberal religious groups, labor unions, and civic leaders from the white community, the civil rights movement called into question the moral foundations upon which political leadership had been based in the postwar years. Its demand for the immediate implementation of the American democratic creed led many other groups in the population (who also believed they were victims of discrimination) to make similar appeals.

White college students who were veterans of the early years of protest came home from the Mississippi Freedom Summer in 1964 and immediately attempted to convince their fellow students that they were somehow members of an oppressed class in need of liberation. Plans to give students an equal voice in curriculum development, academic tenure decisions, campus planning, and budget making were advanced—first at Berkeley in 1964 and later at other schools all over the country—and many universities were soon racked by civil disorder. Confrontations with college administrators and local police had all the rhetorical and tactical earmarks of the civil rights protests in Atlanta and Birmingham because the student leaders had often been initiated into civic life through participation in those protests. Regardless of whether they had been directly involved, they were using the heroic style of the Southern black students as their guide to political action.

The National Organization for Women has been described as the "NAACP of the women's movement," (Carden 1974) and consciously modeled itself after the civil rights organizations of the 1960s (Gelb and Palley 1982). The Mexican-American Legal Defense and Education Fund (MALDEF), one of the most active of the Hispanic groups in the 1980s, was incorporated by a former staff member of the NAACP (Broder, 1980). Hundreds of other groups were formed during the 1960s and 1970s representing Hispanics, women, the handicapped, homosexuals, and other disadvantaged elements of society in attempts to make the same kind of gains for their constituents that they believed blacks were achieving through the civil rights movement. These groups used class-action lawsuits, acts of civil disobedience, initiatives and referenda, as well as conventional electoral politics—the same mixture of tactics that had been pioneered by the civil rights movement. Established institutions were placed under great pressure as one group after another attacked customary procedures for hiring employees or measuring achievement. Most of the society's fundamental assumptions about human relations and the bases for authority were subjected to searching criticism.

Once this process of political mobilization of the disadvantaged sectors of the society was well underway, other kinds of social movements began to arise. At the beginning, these came mainly from the educated middle class, and they were dedicated to forwarding the rights of consumers against the power of large business firms, placing restraints on the ability of businesses and individuals to exploit the environment, or granting the government extensive powers to ensure higher standards of industrial health and safety. Many of the groups in fields such as civil rights or environmental protection had been in existence for decades and there had been a steady buildup throughout this century in broad public support for the values underlying these movements. The political atmosphere of the 1960s, however, provided the catalyst needed to create organizations dedicated to advancing these values.

## The Political Consequences of Increased Mobilization

The elaborate networks of associations and advocacy groups that grew up during the decades after World War II provided hundreds of new channels through which public preferences and opinions could be both molded and transmitted to the political leadership. The degree to which they transformed the political system was graphically illustrated by the striking differences in the reactions of the American public to the wars in Korea and Vietnam. When public opinion polls measuring support for the war in Korea in the 1950s are compared with the results of similar polls measuring support for the war in Vietnam more than a decade later, the patterns are remarkably similar. As casualties mounted and frustration grew over the limited goals of American forces in both conflicts, the numbers of citizens expressing disapproval of the war effort began to rise at about the same rate (Mueller 1973). Public approval of Presidents Truman and Johnson, as measured by the Gallup Poll, dropped rapidly as each war dragged on (Gallup 1980). Voters in both the national elections of 1952 and 1968 shifted toward those candidates who promised to end the fighting, but in the 1960s the more highly mobilized public, accustomed to unconventional forms of political expression, erupted in an angry series of public demonstrations. Members of Congress immediately began to receive questioning letters from their constituents, heard outspokenly negative testimony in congressional hearings, and were visited by delegations of concerned citizens. Political leaders found that they were no longer as well insulated as they had been only a little more than ten years before from the shifting tides of public opinion.

Most of the groups formed in the 1950s and 1960s were dedicated to liberal causes, but they were matched almost immediately by conservative countermovements that grew even stronger in the 1970s and 1980s. Planned Parenthood was soon confronted by the National Right to Life Committee; the Fellowship of Reconciliation encountered the Committee on the Present Danger; the National Council of Churches was matched by the Moral Majority. These new conservative groups, often employing organizing techniques introduced by the liberals, such as computer-assisted direct mail solicitation for funds, began campaigns of opposition to most of the central policies of the Kennedy-Johnson years. The New Christian Right, a complex of voluntary associations and nonprofit corporations centered around the Moral Majority, was similar in some ways to the civil rights movement. It grew up around an established network of fundamentalist churches, television evangelists, and bible colleges, each with its own sources of income and strong community ties. These established institutions provided the administrative and financial foundations upon which a national movement could be built (Leibman and Wuthnow 1983). While many of the particular organizations of the conservative movements of the 1980s have proved short-lived, others have taken their places, often based on similar appeals, with virtually the same mailing lists, contacts, and purposes.

Several new policy initiatives were launched by this rapidly growing conservative network and some, such as the tax limitation movement, began to have a major impact on the course of political debate in the country. These conservative movements, like the liberal ones that preceded them, drew many elements of the population—housewives concerned over abortion, business executives concerned with government regulation, and Protestant evangelicals worried about moral questions—into active participation in political life for the first time. With the help of sympathetic business firms and foundations, an imposing network was created consisting of think tanks, public interest law firms, and political magazines dedicated to conservative causes (Blumenthal 1986). This conservative movement, rising in opposition to the liberal movement that preceded it, was an extension of the process of political mobilization begun by the civil rights movement in the 1950s and 1960s. The civil rights movement had a profound impact on the American political system that has reverberated throughout the society for decades, steadily expanding the boundaries of the active political community, as Americans organized for action through a burgeoning network of voluntary associations. The nature of American democracy has changed, as massive numbers of citizens have begun to be represented through a variety of professional and issue-based groups.

## The Transformation of American Political Parties

Political parties have not been collapsing under the impact of the great upsurge of political mobilization during the past several decades; rather, they have been transforming themselves. Realizing that it is unlikely that parties will ever receive large public subsidies, or that restrictive legislation will be passed that would restore the virtual monopoly on representation enjoyed by political parties in the late nineteenth century, both the Republicans and Democrats launched efforts during the past decade to rebuild their organizations by employing many of the same techniques used by many successful interest groups.

Rather than trying to recreate the precinct organizations of a century ago, parties have tried to recruit millions of people willing to make small contributions. This money is used to develop large, sophisticated staffs that seek to coordinate national election campaigns, provide consultation for local and state parties, and provide advice for Political Action Committees (PACs) and other sympathetic contributors who want to back promising new candidates. This new approach to organizational viability must be founded on ideological appeals, or at least upon more consistent approaches to public policy than American parties have used in the past. The continued loyalty of small contributors, who are receiving mainly moral or ideological reinforcement in exchange for their support, can be assured in no other way. Parties, by adopting this approach, are beginning to compete with the ideologically based citizen interest groups for the loyalty of the affluent new middle class, the active core of the citizenry.

No matter how successful the parties are in adapting to the demands of campaigning in the age of mass communications and programmatic politics, however, it is hard to imagine a set of issues or ideological appeals that could divide the highly mobilized, contemporary electorate neatly into only two political camps. The social issues of abortion and public support for religious institutions cut across the constituency that supports national health insurance, and environmental issues divide this group in yet another way. None of these issues is likely to go away and all are promoted by well-financed policy communities made up of dozens of interest groups and other political organizations. These overlapping and conflicting policy communities create a constantly shifting, somewhat bewildering political agenda in Washington, but they also make the American system more adaptive and responsive by allowing citizens loyal to different political parties an opportunity to voice passionately felt concerns while remaining generally loyal to one political party. They supplement, rather than weaken, the political parties by insuring that debate about issues not consistent with society's basic partisan divisions takes place in democratic legislative forums, rather than in the streets.

Furthermore, if party politics does center more around fundamental public policy questions, and if national elections increasingly appear to pose significant choices between different ideological paths, there is good reason to expect an *increase*, not a reduction, in interest-group activity. Political parties might be reinvigorated in their new role as coordinators of large coalitions of interest groups, PACs, political consultants, and other political organizations, but if institutional patrons are freely left to sponsor political action, and the futures of many government programs enacted during the recent expansion of the welfare state are put in jeopardy at each election, those that support these programs can be expected to respond with vigorous efforts to organize new interest groups that will defend the gains they have made.

## Summary and Conclusion

The increase in the level of political mobilization in the American system during the past 35 years resulted from fundamental social changes, such as the growth of a large, new, educated middle class from the emergence of many new institutions prepared to subsidize political organizations, and from the steady expansion of the power and responsibility of the federal government. Increases in the number of specialized membership and nonmembership organizations involved in policy formulation and advocacy have led to a dramatic increase in the range of interests being represented and the number of issues being debated in Washington. In the past, most citizen groups that emerged from social movements simply faded away once the intense enthusiasm of their followers began to cool, or when a string of policy defeats caused marginal supporters to lose interest. In the 1990s, however, many of the citizen groups born during the past 35 years are still in business, with help from their patrons, even though public interest in their causes has declined. These groups promote concern for their favorite issues and stand ready to exercise leadership whenever there is a new burst of public enthusiasm for their causes. As a result of the expansion of the interest-group system and the change in its composition, the processes of passing legislation and evaluating public policies have become much more complicated, and policy formulation has become much more conflictual than ever before (chap. 7; Nordlinger 1981; Gais, Peterson, and Walker 1984).

This is a period of historic transformation in the relationships between interest groups and political parties in America. Many elements of the public that were largely inactive or completely quiescent 35 years ago, from blacks and ethnic minorities to Protestant evangelicals and the CEOs of large manufacturing corporations, have recently plunged into public affairs in greater numbers, causing a persistent crisis of participation that has lasted for a generation. The growth in the politically active core of the citizenry has stimulated the expansion in the size and power of the public sector, and this expansion has, in turn, stimulated more people to become involved in public affairs. In order to cope with the growing pressures for participation, many organizational and procedural innovations have been introduced into the political system, making the past three decades one of the most creative periods in the country's history. Public interest law firms, political action committees, campaign consultants, and think tanks have become familiar parts of the American political scene during this period, causing important changes in the opportunities and incentives available to both citizens and their elected representatives.

Access to government has been provided for many social groups that in the past had been either ignored or, as with blacks, brutally excluded from political life by force. There is little prospect that the interest groups in the nonprofit sector based upon the country's increasingly elaborate occupational structure will disappear—especially those that have emerged as a direct result of the expansion of the welfare state. The many newly founded citizen groups also have shown remarkable resiliency. Political parties have begun to accommodate this new, highly engaged, conflictual political environment and have begun to reorganize to adjust to the newly intrusive role of the mass media that it involves. America continues its risky experiment with democracy in the modern world. We have moved to a higher plateau of political engagement during the past three decades, from which there is no turning back.

CHAPTER 3

# Explaining the Mobilization of Interests

There is an interesting contradiction between the political science literature and the social reality of interest groups during the past three decades. Political scientists in the 1950s viewed the founding and maintenance of groups as the natural result of the mobilization of individuals sharing common interests, and yet this was a period of relative quiet among mass-based groups. Later, the 1960s saw tremendous growth in the number and size of groups, especially in the wake of the civil rights, environmental, and antiwar movements (all seeking collective or ideological goods), precisely as scholars focused on the difficulties of mobilizing citizens for action. This chapter reviews some of the major contributions to interest-group theories during the past 30 years and notes how explanations focusing solely on the individual psychological decision to join or to contribute to a group cannot account for the flowering of groups in America. Individual motivations are fundamental to our understanding of group activities, as many scholars have argued, but institutional factors must also be considered. A renewed focus on these institutional factors helps explain how so many groups could be formed even though they must overcome tremendous obstacles that are based on individual motives for behavior.

## Pluralism, Mobilization, and the
## Collective Action Dilemma

Given the explosive growth in the number and variety of interest groups in America during the past three decades, it is ironic that scholarly analysts during this same period spent much of their time explaining why it is nearly impossible to create voluntary associations representing broad collective interests. During one set of meetings held at Washington's Mayflower Hotel, scholars assessed the difficulties of mobilizing citizens for collective action. Scholars discoursed about the nature of collective goods and how it was virtually impossible for certain kinds of groups to mobilize effectively. As the participants left the elegant and socially isolated enclosure of the hotel, they walked right into massive demonstrations by tens of thousands of Americans who had not heard about the collective action dilemma, but who had apparently overcome its restrictions. Thousands of Americans were descending on

41

Washington at that time to press claims of all sorts on the government, just as scholars were elaborating theories about why they should never be expected to mobilize.

This curious disjuncture between the central themes of scholarly commentary and the burgeoning world of interest groups was the result of a revolt by group theorists in the 1960s against the operating assumptions upon which traditional group theory was based. Most group theorists prior to the 1960s assumed that once individual citizens began to experience some social or economic problem and became aware that they shared their difficulties with others, it would be perfectly natural for them to create a formal organization that would represent their joint interests before government decision makers. David Truman recognized that individuals might be too poor or isolated from one another to act upon their shared beliefs, or they might not be sufficiently aroused to take the necessary pains. If, however, they cared deeply enough and events produced a sufficient amount of interaction with other affected individuals, eventually "formal organization or a significant interest group will emerge and greater influence will ensue" (Truman 1951, 36). The process was believed to be more or less spontaneous, propelled by social disturbances arising from the growing complexity of the urban-industrial economy. Societies that did not forcibly repress this process or impose unreasonable legal constraints upon citizens' natural desires to form associations could be expected to spawn interest groups in waves of mobilization and countermobilization until a form of equilibrium was achieved, only to be disturbed by further social or economic developments, setting off another round of mobilization.

Truman was not alone in believing that individuals would organize for action when they realized that they had shared interests. Most writers who attempt to analyze the roots of political behavior employ several types of variables in their explanation, but, even so, most contemporary theories of political mobilization are founded upon a set of assumptions and hypotheses about the behavior of individual citizens. Robert Dahl, for example, begins his analysis of political mobilization in *Who Governs?* by dividing the population into two ideal types: Homo civicus and Homo politicus. The civic man is in search of direct gratifications, and, typically, politics appears to be a much less attractive source of pleasure

> than a host of other activities; and, as a strategy to achieve his gratifications indirectly, political action will seem considerably less efficient than working at his job, earning more money, taking out insurance, joining a club, planning a vacation, moving to another neighborhood or city, or coping with an uncertain future in manifold other ways. (Dahl 1961, 224)

The vast majority of the citizenry can be classified as members of the genus Homo civicus. They sometimes become involved in politics, but only if the actions or inactions of governments threaten their primary goals. Since there are few such instances, most people usually pay almost no attention to public affairs. If an immediate and tangible threat arises, such as an increase in taxes, the construction of a highway through the neighborhood, or a proposal for drafting young people into the armed forces, Homo civicus may become involved in public affairs, sometimes intensely, but members of this class can be counted on to lapse into inactivity as soon as the stimulus disappears, and to resume their search for gratification through more direct, nonpolitical means. In Dahl's words: "Homo civicus is not, by nature, a political animal" (Dahl 1961, 225).

Homo politicus is the mirror image of the civic man. A tiny minority of the population derives both direct and indirect gratification from political activity and the exercise of influence over others. Dahl provides no reason for this fundamental difference among citizens. He simply begins his argument with the assertion that, although most people avoid politics because it is too costly and boring, there remain a few who plunge into public affairs as if it were a calling. These differences are matters of taste and personal preference, but they also are the keys to the successful operation of a democratic political order. All political systems operate largely by habit and inertia and are vulnerable to changes in their economic or social environment. The energy needed to overcome inertia and engineer the changes in policy that are required to meet the challenges facing the system are supplied by gifted leaders from the political class. As in Schumpeter's classic analysis of the capitalist economy, Homo politicus acts as an entrepreneur, working constantly to gain influence over other citizens in order to assemble the political resources necessary to renew the system. In Dahl's words:

> Political man can use his resources to gain influence, and he can then use his influence to gain more resources. Political resources can be pyramided in much the same way that a man who starts out in business sometimes pyramids a small investment into a large corporate empire. To the political entrepreneur who has skill and drive, the political system offers unusual opportunities for pyramiding a small amount of initial resources into a sizable political holding. (Dahl 1961, 227)

An obvious danger arises in such a fluid system that some member of the political class will pyramid enough political resources to become a threat to the democratic order. Dahl has become increasingly concerned over the past decade with the power of great private corporations that control vast amounts of political influence and "loom like mountain principalities ruled by princes whose decisions lie beyond reach of the democratic process" (Dahl 1982, 194). These huge entities could potentially gain control of the civic agenda, resist the efforts of government agencies to control them, and even shape the preferences and ideologies of the citizenry through clever exploitation of the mass media.

Dahl recognizes these dangers to democracy and speculates that they may soon rise to the top of the political agenda. He not only forecasts these issues becoming controversial (1982, 184–85) but also recently made an effort to further the debate by offering a bold argument in favor of governing private corporations through democratic means (1985). He also believes that the democratic order has many built-in safeguards against tyranny. One important constraint on potential tyrants is the system of "dispersed inequalities." In any open system, there are many different kinds of resources available to different citizens, and these resources are almost always unequally distributed. People with social standing, for example, usually do not control large numbers of votes, cannot dominate all important organizations in the community, or cannot control all of its wealth. Dahl does not rely entirely upon fundamental cultural differences between citizens to explain why some people participate more actively in public affairs than others. Differences in education, occupation, levels of income, access to certain organizations, and other economic or social factors play a role in determining the extent to which any individual will seek to gain influence in the political system. In Dahl's opinion, however, almost everyone in the society, with rare exceptions, has access to some kind of political resources. The increasingly aggressive political actions of the business community are a threat, but a political order that maintains many competing political entrepreneurs within a system of "dispersed inequalities" will be able to offer strong resistance to centers of concentrated power.

The success of entrepreneurs from the political class in countering undemocratic tactics from their competitors depends, in the end, upon more than their skill in marshaling political resources and employing them decisively. The most important defense against tyranny in Dahl's theory is the consensus among all citizens on the essential importance of maintaining democratic procedures in the conduct of public affairs. If the system is to be protected and constitutional protections against tyranny are to be enforced, the citizenry must be willing to answer the call from members of the political class for action against potential tyrants. Even Homo civicus, according to Dahl, can be counted on to become active in the defense of the fundamental principles of democracy, and since potential offenders are aware of the possibility of such uprisings, they are not likely to challenge these procedural norms. If they are foolish enough to do so, however, other members of the political class can usually be counted upon to react to the danger by rallying the citizens against the offender.

Dahl's theory relies upon a broad consensus on the underlying values of democracy as the last line of defense against tyranny. He not only argues that such a consensus exists but also asserts that when average citizens become convinced that these values are being challenged, they will be willing to take action to defend them. The members of the genus Homo civicus, who normally pay almost no attention to the conduct of public affairs, nevertheless exercise a powerful indirect influence over the political leadership because they control the latent power to destroy the political career of any leader who violates the fundamental political consensus. Leaders are constrained by the fear of awakening this sleeping giant, and, thus, the seemingly passive citizens of a democracy are much more powerful than they look.

Both Truman and Dahl base their pluralist theories of the nature of American democracy on the actions of individuals. A large body of literature developed in the 1960s and 1970s that explicitly challenged these assumptions. Edelman, for example, showed how easy it was for political leaders to dissipate the energy and commitment of broadly based social movements by using symbolic gestures of reassurance (see Edelman 1964, 1971, 1988). When regulatory legislation is passed in a policy area and new agencies created with the responsibility to deal with problems arising from issues like monopoly control over markets, water pollution, or child abuse, the public's interest in the area quickly dissipates, even if the agencies are soon frustrated in their efforts to institute change. This process has been referred to by others as the "issue attention cycle" (Downs 1972). Once the public's concern abates, well-organized interest groups working steadily through the legislative process without fanfare or publicity eventually are able to modify and dilute the reforms intended in the enabling legislation (see also Salisbury 1984). Edelman's demonstration of the ease with which public attitudes could be manipulated through threatening or reassuring gestures underlined the inherent advantages of intense minorities over majorities in democratic systems, but it was Mancur Olson (1965) who mounted a full-scale attack on the conventional theories of political mobilization using a simple, deductive argument that had the most devastating impact.

Olson directly attacked the commonsense assumptions at the heart of group theory about the natural inclination of citizens to take joint action in their collective interest. He showed that rationally self-interested individuals, in fact, would *not* take part in securing a collective good for a large group, even if they were aware that they would be better off if the collective good were secured. Olson argued that, since the costs of collective action to any individual are usually larger than the personal benefits derived from participation, most people would not join in collective action unless they face at least one of two principal inducements. First, they might be coerced into joining an association, either by legal requirements, such as rules barring them from employment unless they join a trade union, or through strong social pressures arising within relatively small, homogeneous groups of people who saw each other frequently and could sanction those who did not contribute. Second, especially in larger groups, individuals might join associations engaged in collective action in order to receive selective material rewards (such as an invitation to an important meeting, an insurance policy, or merchandise discounts) that they could not receive if they remained outside the group as a free rider. Group leaders might provide these selective benefits in order to gain members, and, then, as a by-product of the successful inducement strategy, they might pursue the broader collective goals of the community they purported to represent.

As a description of some groups, Olson's theory seems to work well. Some groups attract members by providing tangible benefits such as insurance policies, special access to important information, or glossy magazines. The American Association of Retired Persons (AARP) has grown into the largest voluntary association in the country with more than 28 million members, and this growth has been fed by using a great variety of selective material benefits (Bureh, Koek, and Novallo 1989, 1234). Other groups, however, such as Common Cause, seem able to thrive while providing almost no material benefits to their members. These groups rely heavily upon appeals to conscience or calls to protect the public interest (McFarland 1976 and 1984). How can these different patterns of benefit provision be explained? What are the most important factors that determine which kinds of benefits groups will offer to prospective members?

Political scientists reacted to Olson's arguments, and many tried to show that group membership is not the illogical act that Olson implies. Others noticed that Olson's thesis is not so much about how groups might form in the first place, but how they are maintained once established. "The provision of selective incentives cannot be the general solution to the collective action problem. To assume that there is a central authority offering incentives often requires another collective action problem to have been solved already. Before a union can force or induce workers to join, it must have overcome a free-rider problem in the first place" (Elster 1989, 40; also see Frohlich and Oppenheimer 1970). At a minimum, then, an explanation of why we have the groups we have should detail both the origins of interest groups and the strategies these groups use to survive.

The most familiar "solutions" to the collective goods dilemma work within the framework Olson outlined but contend that individuals also respond to "solidary" and "purposive"—not just material—incentives (Clark and Wilson 1961; Salisbury 1969; Wilson 1973; Moe 1980 and 1981). Solidary benefits come from satisfactions gained through friendship and fraternity among individuals involved in a joint enterprise. Purposive benefits are more difficult to define, though they "are associated with pursuit of ideological or issue-oriented goals that offer no tangible rewards to members" (Berry 1989a, 47).

Yet there is something wholly unsatisfying about resorting to purposive benefits to make group memberships appear rational. Like the "sense of citizen duty" motive used by some to explain why people vote, the purposive category is a catchall that verges on a tautology. If we work within Olson's structure, the purposive argument goes like this: Why do individuals join a group to advance a collective good? Because they have a purposive desire to see that collective good advanced. Such a circular argument does not take us very far. As David Knoke writes (1990), Americans' decisions to join or to contribute to groups are based partly on hard-headed economic calculations, and partly on other factors, such as group norms and affective ties. Neither of these additional motivations is nonrational, but subsuming these approaches within the Olson model cannot be done, according to Knoke, "except by a tortuous logic that renders the latter concept universal and, therefore, useless" (43). Instead of attempting to include nonmaterial incentives in a model seeking to explain collective action, one should ask under what conditions individuals will join groups in order to advance purposive—which is to say collective—goals.

Cooperation to achieve collective goals is more likely if a threat arises that existing public goods will be destroyed. Tens of thousands of members recently were attracted to interest groups on the pro-choice side of the abortion debate, once a serious threat arose that existing legal guarantees of abortion rights would be withdrawn. Hansen (1985) argues that people are more likely to support interest groups if the object of collective action is the prevention of a collective bad rather than the creation of a new collective good. This makes a lot of sense, and it may be one reason for the march to Washington by businesses since the 1960s, as groups form to protect their members in the wake of increased federal regulations (Salisbury 1984; Vogel 1989).

Writers such as Hardin (1982), Axelrod (1984), and Johnson (1987) contend that free riding is much less likely when individuals are engaged in a game that is conducted over and over, rather than only once. When individuals face the consequences of their actions again and again, they may come to see, without inducements or sidepayments, that it is in their interest to cooperate by joining in various forms of collective action. The steady evolution of equity norms also encourages individuals to ignore opportunities to act as free riders (Marwell and Ames 1979; Elster 1989). Rothenberg (1988) has shown that as members learn more about the activities and demands of an organization, they become more likely to remain members. The impact of collective goals appears to be much higher than Olson predicts, at least according to the members of Common Cause, the group studied by Rothenberg.

Olson's theory of public good and individual incentives highlights the great obstacles facing those who wish to organize deprived elements within American society. A balanced representation of group interests cannot be achieved from entirely voluntary political action by individuals, since the marginal costs of participation differ so greatly among social groups and since individual incentives are generally so weak. Some of these obstacles are lifted during periods of great political stress, and some can be overcome through the efforts of organizational entrepreneurs (Moe 1980; Salisbury 1969), but there are limits to the impact individual leaders can have, no matter how energetic or clever they may be. Groups with large memberships that do not provide selective material benefits or employ coercion to hold their members attract mainly those with good educations and ample incomes. For their members, presumably, the annual dues represent a painless way of amplifying their ideological views and gaining a sense of involvement in the national political process. Such groups flourish in the American system. Associations representing socially disadvantaged elements of the society, however, those that depend entirely on support from their members in response to mainly purposive incentives, typically have been short-lived.

These leading theories of group formation and maintenance underscore the many obstacles standing in the way of those who wish to create mediating institutions to represent certain broad sectors of American life, particularly the poor or socially disadvantaged. So many powerful forces have been identified that prevail against the mobilization of large social groupings that it is surprising that any such groups exist. Despite the theories, however, many such groups do exist, and, furthermore, their numbers are steadily increasing.

## Institutional Patronage and Political Mobilization

If there are so many obstacles in the way of those trying to organize broadly based citizen groups, what accounts for the rapid increase in the number of such groups in recent years? By concentrating so closely upon the internal workings of voluntary associations, theorists following the line of discourse established by Olson have diverted our attention from the relationships between groups and the many established governmental, economic, and civic institutions in society. Corporations, foundations, government agencies, hospitals, universities, private charities, local governments, the presidency, national religious organizations, trade unions, and wealthy families often provide financial and organizational support that is the key to the maintenance and effectiveness of interest groups.

Working in the rational choice tradition, Olson took rational, autonomous individuals as his unit of analysis, and most subsequent works have followed this form. However, as Salisbury (1975 and 1984) and I (1983b) have argued, interest groups are very often composed of institutions, not autonomous individuals. Many people are members of organizations as part of their occupational duties. Corporate vice presidents for public affairs may have their names on many mailing lists and be members of many organizations, but they are acting for the institutions that they represent, not for themselves. Distinguishing between individuals acting for themselves (called *autonomous individuals* in this book) and those acting as representatives of larger organizations (called *organizational representatives*) is important in developing a complete understanding of group membership and organizational maintenance. Little is known about the differences in how these two types of potential group members react to and solve collective goods dilemmas, a subject I examine below.

The process of political mobilization cannot be fully understood until we realize that mobilizing efforts often come from the top down, rather than the bottom up (for a similar point, see Cameron 1974). Many groups are begun at the instigation of the leaders of large corporations or government agencies who often even recruit the entrepreneurs and sponsor their efforts in order to achieve policy goals that are meant to enhance their institutions' well-being. Political participation should not be conceived only as the spontaneous result of the psychological and social characteristics of individuals, but also as the result of the incentives, constraints, and opportunities created by the society's legal system and the intervention in political life of its largest economic, social, and governmental institutions, which often play a crucial role as the patrons of political action.

One of the most important reasons for the rapid increase in the total number of groups and the increasing prominence of citizen groups during the 1960s and 1970s was the emergence of many new patrons of political action who were willing to support efforts at social reform. Numerous private foundations were just being founded when the civil rights movement began, and their staffs saw in this and subsequent movements a significant opportunity for their institutions to play an important role in public affairs (Marris and Rein 1973; see also Karl and Katz 1987; McCarthy 1987; Pifer 1987; Sutton 1987). These new patrons, along with wealthy individuals, churches, trade unions, government agencies, and business firms, made an effort to direct the frustration being expressed by participants in the political insurgencies of the time into established channels. They began to support experiments in social activism and political mobilization that would have been impossible to finance even a few years earlier. Once this process of mobilization began, it had a contagious effect upon political activists representing other disadvantaged groups, leading to the creation of more organizations making appeals to additional patrons whose support added further to the process of mobilization.

Much of the antipoverty legislation of the 1960s, along with the bills protecting consumers or ensuring occupational health and safety, was passed without any large organized campaign in its favor; rather, it was the result of the efforts of activist legislators in search of national recognition (see Wagner 1966; Nadel 1971; Walker 1977). Once legislation was passed in response to the civil rights movement, and the government began to extend the welfare state and expand its regulatory powers in the 1960s, the balance of advocacy was upset, and a massive march to Washington was begun by groups who wanted either to emulate the success of others in gaining new benefits or to protect themselves against further governmental encroachments on their autonomy (see Vogel 1989). As the process accelerated, inhibitions against involvement in political controversy were reduced and many professionals, organized religious groups, long-established private charities, institutions for the performing arts, chief executive officers of major corporations, social scientists, and even writers and poets began to press the government for support, setting off the dire warnings about "government overload" and political bankruptcy (see Huntington 1973; King 1975; Rose and Peters 1978). Just as David Truman might have predicted, the decades of the 1960s and 1970s were marked by waves of mobilization and countermobilization as members of the system searched for some new form of political equilibrium.

The patrons who helped to create these new interest groups did not confine their advocacy to the support of voluntary associations. The same institutions that patronized interest groups also greatly increased their purchases of the services of lawyer-lobbyists, public relations specialists, and the other political guns-for-hire that are available in both the national and state capitals (Vogel 1989). Several large corporations and trade unions launched major advertising campaigns designed to combat what they believed to be prejudices against them among those in the mass media who write and interpret the news. Many new political magazines and newsletters, study centers, and think tanks were created, representing both liberal and conservative views, all financed mainly by wealthy individuals, private foundations, and business firms. The same institutions, in other words, that subsidize the formation and maintenance of membership associations have contributed, as well, to the recent flowering of many other types of nonmembership political organizations (Blumenthal 1986). These groups must also be included in any comprehensive inventory of the devices through which interests are formulated and communicated to the government.

Institutional patrons try to advance their interests through many different channels, and, in recent years, some institutions have supplemented these efforts by entering directly into the political arena to represent themselves.

Large cities not only join associations like the National League of Cities or the U.S. Conference of Mayors, but they also send members of their own staffs to the national capital to lobby for their interests. Agencies of the federal government not only play important roles in coordinating lobbying campaigns but also use their own personnel to contact legislators or their staffs. Most of the larger corporations mount important lobbying operations with extensive staffs operating out of their own offices of public affairs, and sometimes they even conduct grass roots lobbying campaigns—something unheard of in the 1960s—in which their employees, suppliers, and customers are encouraged to contact legislators to urge the passage of legislation affecting them. Record amounts of mail have been received in recent lobbying campaigns run by the banking industry, AT&T, and the Chrysler Corporation, rivaling any grass roots campaign ever mounted by organized labor or any citizen-style interest group (Vogel 1989; Wittenberg and Wittenberg 1989). With the new authority granted private corporations by the courts to spend funds to advance public policy positions deemed to be in the interest of the firms and to operate political action committees, business firms themselves are becoming important devices, in some ways like parties and interest groups, that serve as direct links between individual citizens and their government. The most significant recent expansion of the discretion of managers to involve their firms directly in politics is in the Supreme Court decision in *First National Bank of Boston v. Bellotti* (1978). Data will be presented in chapter 5 to show the prevalence of large subsidies for organizational maintenance from single or few large institutional members of particular groups, especially in the profit sector. Trade associations are especially prone to organizational structures in which a single member pays a considerable portion of the total annual revenues of the group, in effect subsidizing the dues of the smaller members.

## Social Movements and Political Mobilization

Even social movements—the most spontaneous form of collective political activity—cannot be fully understood unless one accounts for the role of private and public institutions in stimulating their emergence, affecting their choice of tactics, and determining their success (Zald and McCarthy 1979, 1980 and 1986). Social movements are often depicted by political scientists as spontaneous upwellings from below; little attention is paid to the broader political environment in determining their behavior. Samuel Huntington elaborates a cyclical theory of outbursts of "creedal passion" in American politics, for example. Huntington conceives of these movements as a kind of fever that breaks out within the population at regular 60-year intervals. Often, these are instigated by marginal figures venting their frustrations through anomic, disruptive acts of political deviance (Huntington 1981). Such theories leave the distinct impression that, during periods when no organized protest movements exist and in the absence of outright repression by governmental authorities, the country is relatively united. There have been, of course, some cases of widespread mobilization at times other than those identified by Huntington's cyclical analysis, but the idea of cycles implies generally broad support for the social and economic order most of the time, and that the public is mostly satisfied with its leadership save during the exceptional periods of mass mobilization.

The rise and fall of political insurgencies and their ultimate success in obtaining their goals, however, depend not so much on the character, attitudes, or motives of those who lead or participate in them; rather, they are a function of the amount of assistance they obtain from sympathetic third parties and the reaction of authorities to their challenges. In their study of efforts to organize farm workers, Jenkins and Perrow found that movements during World War II and those led by Cesar Chavez in the 1960s were remarkably similar in every detail, yet the earlier movement made little progress and attracted few followers, while Chavez was ultimately successful. The differences in result did not stem from greater determination among the protest leaders, more distress among workers, more money, better organization, or different tactics. The crucial differences seem to have been, first, the mounting of an effective boycott of nonunion lettuce and grapes by a huge, national, liberal constituency mobilized during the 1960s through the efforts of many groups working on many diverse issues; and, second, divisions during the 1960s among the leaders of government and business that led them to deal in tentative and uncertain ways with the challenges being offered by the farm workers (Jenkins and Perrow 1977; Jenkins 1985).

We must conclude that political insurgencies are not exclusively the result of social changes that create distress, eventually leading individuals to engage in protest. Farm workers had been distressed for years and, if anything, were better off in the 1960s than they had been in the 1940s. The same could be said of the Southern blacks or Appalachian whites who also mounted protests in the 1960s. Distress and anger over perceived injustice are a persistent fact of life among disadvantaged elements of any society and are only one of a number of factors that must exist before a social movement begins. A comprehensive explanation of unconventional political movements must reach beyond the motives and inclinations of individuals who lead or join the movement to include a description of changes in the larger political environment and the intervention of sympathetic patrons who provide fresh resources and crucial assistance for entrepreneurial leaders at critical times. Movements that receive aid from outside sources and are able to achieve a few initial breakthroughs begin to attract followers because the presence of potent allies provides enough hope for success to prompt their sympathizers to risk engaging in potentially dangerous political actions (Oberschall 1973; Gamson 1975; McCarthy and Zald 1978; Zald and McCarthy 1979; Gaventa 1980; McAdam 1982).

## Toward a New Explanation of Political Mobilization

A comprehensive explanation of political mobilization in America cannot be confined to generalizations about the attitudes and behavior of individual citizens and their relations with the leaders of interest groups. If patrons play an important role in the representational system, a complete explanation must specify the circumstances under which patrons of different types become engaged in political action. My research indicates, for example, that wealthy individuals are the most venturesome of all patrons, much more likely than business firms or government agencies to fund experiments in political action and to become involved in controversial policy areas (Walker 1983b). The necessary research has not been done, but it would seem plausible that individual patrons would be extraordinarily sensitive to changes in the tax code and might also be reluctant to commit themselves to political groups over a long term. They should, however, be more willing to grant support in return for purposive benefits, since the kind of material benefits that can be offered by most groups would be worthless to them. Substantial assistance can be rendered to a struggling interest group with financial gifts that constitute trivial expenditures for a wealthy person. Giving becomes even less painful if portions of the gift are tax deductible.

As I shall show in later chapters, most patronage for political action comes from large, complex institutions, not wealthy individuals. The professional managers who control these organizations engage in political activities in order to advance their institutions' interests. Although little research on this subject has been done, it seems likely that institutional patrons in the profit sector have more discretion to support political action than do government agencies or organizations in the nonprofit realm, such as private foundations, religious groups, or charitable organizations. Institutions can afford to wait longer than most individuals for the political results they seek. Such stability and autonomy have led institutions to be more consistent supporters of interest groups and to expect more in terms of advocacy and political action than would most individuals. As Salisbury has pointed out, the political activities of institutions are likely to follow different patterns than those of individuals.

> Institutions are *far* more likely to be part of relatively small, similarly situated groups—Olson's privileged groups—and thus be able to organize more readily and to anticipate being more effective politically than most individual citizens can expect. Second, although a given individual

may hold a large number of distinct values or interests and even embrace a considerable set of political causes, available resources for participation are quickly exhausted, and multiple modes of individual participation are comparatively uncommon. Institutions possess more resources which, combined with a greater sense of efficacy in political action, lead to a considerably increased probability of participation at any given level of intensity of interest or concern. (Salisbury 1984, 69)

In a revised theory of mobilization, the steady expansion of the power and responsibility of the federal government figures as one of the major causes of the recent growth of new organizational devices for linking citizens and their government. Elaborate networks of policy professionals have grown up around policy areas like agriculture, housing, or national security, or around constituencies like the elderly or disabled veterans. These policy networks or communities bring together public officials and policy specialists from Congress, bureaucracy, the presidency, university research centers, private consulting firms, think tanks, interest groups, law firms, and state and local governments (Heclo 1978; Walker 1981). An informal division of labor grows up within these communities. Some groups specialize in collecting data, while others specialize in conducting midcareer training for professionals in the field, engage in campaigns of public education or propaganda, or serve as technical advisors or consultants for public bureaucracies. Typically, this leaves only a small number of groups to take the lead in the more conventional tasks of legislative lobbying. As the representational system in each policy area matures, policy entrepreneurs and their patrons are able to devise many different formulas for organizational maintenance, creating highly specialized membership and nonmembership groups that are only viable because they fill a niche in a larger community of groups (Ross 1970; Browne 1977 and 1990; Hannan and Freeman 1978; Knoke and Laumann 1982).

## Conclusion

Political scientists interested in the growth and expansion of the group system developed theories to explain why groups would not grow at the very time that the American group system has shown its most impressive capability to generate more and more growth. More than ever, Americans send money, contribute their time, and devote their resources toward mobilizing for political action. Individuals do not contribute to groups in a vacuum, however. Government officials, the leaders of major foundations, the largest businesses, and many other important institutions in American society are powerful forces in encouraging or discouraging the development of new groups in response to major social developments. Patrons of political action, from both the private and public sectors of the economy, alter the public's opportunities for mobilization and for representation through the interest-group system.

The ecology of interest groups active in Washington varies tremendously by sector. Different types of groups have developed surrounding different areas of the economy because the various government and private sponsors of political action have followed different strategies of mobilization. Some groups exist within homogeneous professional communities where their main reasons for creation and existence were the development of professional standards, furthering the careers of professionals in the area, offering training seminars, or other nonpolitical activities. Other profit sector groups have been organized in response to perceived threats by government action or citizens' activity, in a mobilization-countermobilization cycle more directly related to political activity. In other areas, professional communities of social workers, health professionals, and other service providers have organized to provide representation for their clients or to protect the government programs on which they depend. Finally, patrons have often sought to provide support for the mobilization of large numbers of individuals. The next chapter describes the different types of groups active in the American system.

CHAPTER 4

# An Ecology of Interest Groups in America

*David C. King and Jack L. Walker, Jr.*

It is not surprising that huge, concentrated industrial groupings such as the automobile manufacturers or the major aerospace contractors have successfully organized to advance their interests in Washington, but it is not obvious that the American political system would inevitably have spawned groups like the American Alliance for Health, Physical Education, Recreation and Dance; the National Council of Puerto Rican Volunteers; the International Center for Social Gerontology; or the Friends of the Earth. Yet all these groups exist, along with hundreds more that crowd the office buildings and congressional hearing rooms of Washington. In this chapter, we describe what types of groups exist in America, and in the next chapter we will try to explain why and how these groups are maintained. Most previous investigations of interest groups have been designed to measure a group's influence but have taken their existence for granted. In this and the next chapter, the process will be reversed. We begin by taking for granted that, under certain circumstances, interest groups exert influence over legislators, bureaucrats, and the public. We concentrate our attention, instead, on the ways in which these groups are created and the means by which they remain in existence.

## The Universe of Groups

The histories of four distinct group types—profit sector, mixed sector, nonprofit sector, and citizen—were introduced in chapter 2. We argued that groups often pursue different pathways to influence and provide different mixes of benefits and inducements to join. Pathways to influence often use predominantly either "insider" strategies, like lobbying federal bureaus directly, or "outsider" strategies, such as staging public rallies. The profit, mixed, and nonprofit sectors have grown out of occupational patterns related to the marketplace (for profit groups) and government legitimization of service occupations (in the nonprofit sector). Citizen groups have open membership, and their membership appeals are unrelated to a profession and usually focus on broad ideals or issues.

57

Does our typology of groups, introduced in chapter 2, hold up to empirical investigation? Findings from both the 1980 and 1985 surveys reveal a fundamental cleavage within the interest-group system between the profit and nonprofit sectors of the economy. Respondents reported very little mixing of members from these two broad realms within their organizations, and separate sets of interest groups have emerged from these two sectors of society that often oppose each other and seldom engage in consultation or coordination.

All existing interest-group classification schemes present difficult problems of measurement, and when most scholars have tried to write comprehensive descriptions of the group system, they have usually ignored the more complex typologies. (Typologies abound in this field. For examples, see the work already cited by Wilson and Edelman, along with Lowi [1964] and Hayes [1981].) Most textbook authors simply subdivide groups into the policy areas in which they operate or the constituencies they claim to represent, with chapters on such categories as business groups, civil rights groups, environmentalists, and groups representing the handicapped (Zeigler and Peak 1972; Wilson 1973; Ornstein and Elder 1978; Schlozman and Tierney 1986). These popular divisions survive mostly by journalistic inertia and a lack of obvious alternatives, not for compelling theoretical reasons. The interest-group typology that we use throughout this book reflects the fundamental social structure of interest groups; it is based on a theoretical, explanatory foundation.

Several writers have argued that the central cleavage in the American political system is the clash between social elements organized around the business community and those organized around government and nonprofit institutions in the public sector. As E. E. Schattschneider (1960, 118) argued: "the relations of government and business largely determine the character of the regime . . . the struggle for power is largely a confrontation of two major power systems, government and business." (Also see Lindblom 1977 and Greenstone 1982; and for a thoughtful critique, see Elkin 1982.) These writers imply that there are two distinct realms within the world of groups: one incorporates the commercial interests in society that are defending themselves against intrusions by government or searching for government assistance to protect their specific interests; the other is composed of both the providers and the recipients of public services who are seeking to increase public investment in activities ranging from education for the physically handicapped to the performance of grand opera, which they believe will languish if left to depend upon the market economy.

In order to create an analytically useful typology grounded in a general theory of groups, we began by dividing associations into those groups that require members to possess certain professional or occupational credentials and those that are open to all citizens regardless of their qualifications. Groups that are open to all, such as large citizen interest organizations like Common

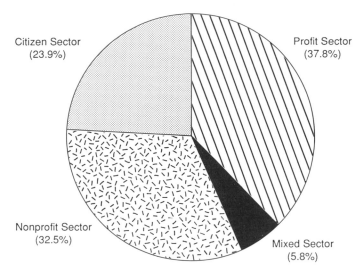

**Fig. 4-1. Classification of interest groups. (Data from 1985 Survey. *N* = 863.)**

Cause and the Sierra Club, have received much scholarly attention. Most groups, however, are not open to anyone who may want to join. The basis for mutual interest around which most groups are formed is an occupational specialty, not some broad social cause or abstract idea about the public interest.

Figure 4-1 reflects data from the 1985 survey, and the cleavages shown mirror those from the 1980 survey, which were reported in Walker 1983. Most national voluntary membership associations—76.1 percent of our sample in figure 4-1—emerge from pre-existing occupational or commercial communities. They include trade associations (such as the American Boiler Manufacturers) and associations of professionals (like the American Women's Society of Certified Public Accountants). Among these occupationally based groups, members in any given association are usually quite homogeneous.[1] Groups with homogeneous members share similar professional backgrounds

---

1. We asked for responses along a five-point scale ranging from "poor description" to "good description" in relation to this statement: "Members of this association tend to have similar occupational or organizational affiliations." A majority of responses tended toward this as a good description, with 421 (or 48.6 percent) selecting the most homogeneous response and 174 (or 20.1 percent) selecting the next most homogeneous response. Citizen groups were by far the least homogeneous. Percentages responding that the statement was a poor description were 35.4 percent for citizen groups, 8.2 percent for profit sector groups, and 5.5 percent for nonprofit sector groups.

and interests, and, significantly, they usually work exclusively either within the profit or the nonprofit sectors of the economy.

Roughly 38 percent of our 1985 group census arises from the profit sector, such as groups of professionals operating on a fee-for-service basis. Profit sector groups include the Mortgage Bankers Association of America, the Aerospace Industries Association, and the Airline Pilots Association. Another 32.5 percent of the groups are made up of representatives of nonprofit institutions such as colleges, hospitals, transportation authorities, or groups of professionals who operate as salaried employees in nonprofit or governmental agencies. Nonprofit sector groups include the National Association of Independent Colleges and Universities and the American Public Welfare Association.

Most groups that grow out of occupational roles fit clearly into either the profit or nonprofit sectors, but there were 50 groups in the 1985 survey whose members' backgrounds were so evenly distributed between the profit and nonprofit sectors that they did not belong to either category. This mixed sector (5.8 percent of the sample) includes professional societies, such as the Society of American Foresters, and some trade associations, such as the American Hospital Association or the National Association of Broadcasters. We therefore classify these as mixed sector groups because their memberships included employees from both the profit and nonprofit realms. The National Association of Broadcasters, for example, includes those working for public television and radio stations as well as private networks and stations. For the most part, however, individuals or organizations from the profit and nonprofit realms seldom find themselves in the same interest group. Of groups associated with occupations (76.1 percent of our 1985 census), more than 92.0 percent were either wholly comprised of members from the profit sector or wholly comprised of members from nonprofit occupations. Our 1985 census also included responses from 29 unions; because of this response rate, we will use the union data sparingly throughout this book (see appendix A).

The nonprofit segment of the group system includes what might be called public sector trade associations—groups representing a certain type of government agency or nonprofit organization, such as the Association of American Medical Colleges, the National Association of Counties, or the American Association of Homes for the Aged. It also includes professional societies made up mainly of individuals working for nonprofit agencies, such as the National Association of State Alcohol and Drug Abuse Directors, the International Association of Fire Chiefs, or the National Association of Student Financial Aid Administrators. Because of the occupational basis of membership, nonprofit sector associations have very homogeneous memberships, by which we mean that members tend to be highly similar. For example, 258 (or 93.8 percent) of the nonprofit groups reported that their members tend to have similar occupational affiliations, which is further evidence that occupations are at the heart of many groups in America.

Although occupationally based associations have dominated the interest-group system from the beginning, there also is a burgeoning sector of citizen groups operating in Washington, D.C. Membership in citizen groups is not based on occupations, and such groups made up 23.9 percent of our census in 1985. Because citizen groups present no occupational hurdles to membership, they are primarily comprised of individuals who are not members because of their jobs, and the membership of citizen groups is far more heterogeneous than their occupation-based counterparts. The citizen groups category includes almost all the public interest groups organized around ideas or causes, such as Citizens for Clean Air, Young Americans for Freedom, and the Women's International League for Peace and Freedom.

Citizen groups are the kinds of groups that most sharply face the organizational dilemmas pointed out by Olson. Very often their fundamental purpose is to procure broad public goods such as world peace or clean air, and they must somehow identify potential members and recruit them to the cause even though most of those who might wish to join do not engage in daily interaction with one another in the normal course of their occupations. Citizen group members are usually geographically dispersed, and the activities of the groups are marginal to the daily needs and responsibilities of the members. The problems of attracting members across the entire country for groups of this kind are fundamentally different from those facing the American Short Line Railroad Association or the American Bar Association.

Not all citizen groups are entirely divorced from narrow social roles, however. Some of the larger, general purpose veterans groups, such as AMVETS or the Veterans of Foreign Wars, were placed in our typology among the citizen groups, for example, because they do not require members to be veterans and many apparently are not. Groups like the National Association of the Visually Handicapped or other general purpose associations representing the mentally retarded, the aged, or other readily identifiable elements of society also were designated as citizen groups because they regard themselves as general purpose, public interest groups open to all persons, regardless of professional or organizational affiliations. Membership in citizen groups is open to all, even if the goals of the group are narrowly cast.

Citizen groups, nevertheless, sometimes include as members professionals whose occupations have brought them into contact with the issues around which the group is organized. Environmental groups, for example, are naturally attractive to many people who work in the recreation industry, forestry, wildlife management, or some other relevant occupation. However, since an occupational background is not a prerequisite for membership and membership is open to everyone, these groups are in our citizen group category. The data from the survey indicate that most citizen groups have a mixed membership that does not come predominantly from either the public or the private sector. The members of citizen sector groups are almost always drawn from a much broader base of occupations and backgrounds than are members of groups emerging out of the occupations. Most citizen groups (73.7 percent) surveyed in 1985 reported that membership in their association has nothing to do with a member's occupation or other organizational affiliation.

Writing 30 years ago, Schattschneider was right in believing that a great political divide exists in American society between government and business, a divide that provides structure for the world of interest groups in profit and nonprofit sectors. The divide remains today, with over 70 percent of the group system firmly rooted in either the profit sector or the nonprofit sector. But for many groups—especially citizen groups—the lines between profit and nonprofit sectors are blurred, and groups are increasingly successful in straddling the boundary between public and private realms.

## The Recent History of Group Formation

Figure 4-1 provides a portrait of the group structure in the 1980s, but the past three decades represent one of the most unsettled periods in American political history. Newspapers have been full of reports of the formation of new associations, and political leaders have complained loudly about unreasonable pressures from single-interest groups. Despite all the reports in the press, however, there are no comprehensive historical data available that document recent historical trends in group formation. One is forced to rely upon scattered estimates by observers from different periods. Herring (1929, 19) estimated that there were "well over 500 lobbies at work in Washington." A half-century later, *Washington Representatives* estimated that there were approximately 1,300 Washington-based associations by 1977, and in 1980 this estimate was increased to 1,700. By 1984, more than 30 percent of American trade associations were headquartered in Washington, D.C., up from fewer than 20 percent in 1971 (Berry 1989a, 21; also see Aldrich and Staber 1984; Salisbury 1984). These estimates are not strictly comparable because different definitions of groups were being used, and all of them are probably low because of the difficulty of tracking down many of the smaller groups at work in the city that employ part-time staff members or rely heavily upon volunteers, but they lend plausibility to the claim that there are more groups in existence now than there were several decades ago.

There is no doubt that the number of citizen groups has grown rapidly during the past 30 years in several policy areas, including groups organized around the women's movement and the environmental movement (Freeman 1973 and 1975; Carden 1974; Boles 1979, chap. 3; Fox 1981; Gelb and Palley

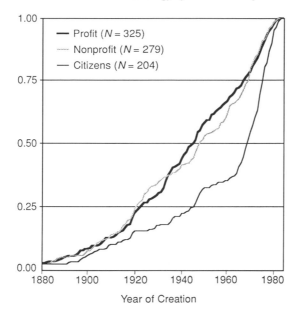

**Fig. 4-2. Cumulative proportion of groups created by date and group type. (Data from 1985 Survey.)**

1973 and 1975; Carden 1974; Boles 1979, chap. 3; Fox 1981; Gelb and Palle 1982, chaps. 2–3 and 8). There is evidence of recent growth from our data as well. All respondents were asked to report the founding dates for their associations, and these data were assembled cumulatively in figure 4-2 for three of the categories in the typology of occupational roles. (Cumulative founding dates for mixed groups [N=50] ranged over time between the founding dates for profit and nonprofit groups.) The data demonstrate that half of the existing occupational groups were founded before the end of World War II. In contrast, half of the citizen groups did not come into existence until 1965; then, during the next 18 years, there was a period of explosive growth during which citizen groups multiplied at twice the rate of all types of occupationally based groups.

Figure 4-2 is a picture of forces active at different times in the interest-group universe. The growth rate of nonprofit sector groups was highest during the Progressive era. Profit sector groups grew most rapidly during World War II and through the 1950s. The 1960s ushered citizen groups into the interest-group universe in unprecedented numbers.

Both the historical evidence and the data from our surveys provide powerful circumstantial evidence of the recent growth in the interest-group structure, but neither constitutes conclusive proof that such growth has actually occurred. It is possible, although unlikely, that citizen groups in areas ignored by historians were declining in numbers during the 1960s and 1970s, thus canceling out the reported gains. If citizen groups have a higher mortality rate than occupational groups, an analysis of founding dates at any period would always indicate that more of the existing citizen groups were founded within the recent past than the longer-lived occupational groups. We estimated group mortality rates by group type and found that 6.9 percent of the citizen groups disappeared over a five-year period in the 1970s. This is contrasted with a 5.6 percent mortality rate among occupationally based groups. This difference in means is small and may be due to the fact that citizen groups in the 1970s were, on average, not as old as occupationally based groups, and older groups are more likely than younger groups to survive another year.

Despite reservations inherent in all data, all available evidence points in the same direction, namely that there are many more interest groups operating in Washington today than in the years before World War II, and citizen groups make up a much larger proportion of the total than ever before. This transformation may not be as large or dramatic as the cross-sectional data suggest, or as some journalists and political leaders have implied, but there are good reasons to believe that far-reaching changes took place during the past 30 years in the system of interest groups in the United States, a conclusion shared by virtually all recent observers (Guinther 1976; McFarland 1976; Heclo 1978; Broder 1980; Wilson 1981; Hrebenar and Scott 1982; Schlozman and Tierncy 1986; Berry 1989a).

### Organizations and Individuals as Group Members

Beyond group differences deriving from the historic emergence of organized interests, groups may represent entirely different types of members. Members are a group's constituents, and the backgrounds and assumptions that members bring to their groups will have an impact on what the groups do and how groups maintain their sources of revenue. As Salisbury warned in 1975, the whole concept of membership is rather vague, and this ambiguity has hampered the discipline's attempts to understand why people become members (also see Baumgartner and Walker 1988 and 1990). Many group members are not individuals seeking some benefit or public policy goal of their own. They have joined the group to represent the interests of a business firm, a university, or a city. The institution is really more the member than its representative. Throughout this discussion and chapter 5, therefore, we distinguish between *autonomous individuals*, whose decisions to join groups are all their own, and *organizational representatives*, who join groups to represent an institution, such as marketing executives joining a marketing policy group on behalf of their company. This is an important distinction because the calculus of joining a group is likely to be much different for autonomous individuals than for employees of an institution who are joining on behalf of or because of their

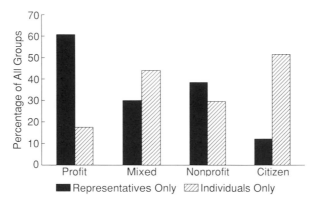

**Fig. 4-3. The occupational roles of interest group members. Bars represent the percentage of groups that are composed of only organizational representatives or only autonomous individuals. (Data from 1985 Survey.)**

business. Even though most recent theory in this field overlooks these differences among members, national interest groups actually are pretty evenly divided between those whose membership is composed primarily of individual citizens (like the Wilderness Society, or the League of Women Voters), and groups that are composed almost entirely of the representatives of large institutions, business firms, or state and local governments (such as the International Hospital Federation, the United States Cane Sugar Refiners Association, or the U.S. League of Cities).

In our 1985 sample of groups, 350 (or 39 percent) of the groups were made up entirely of organizational representatives, while 287 (32 percent) had autonomous individuals who were not representing an organization or institution as members. The remaining groups (29 percent) reported having both types of members, though even here the membership is predominantly composed of either autonomous individuals or organizational representatives.

Figure 4-3 reveals that the type of members that predominate in groups corresponds, to a large extent, with the typology of groups based upon the occupational characteristics of group memberships that was presented in figure 4-1. The figure shows the percentage of groups in each type that report having exclusively one type of member or another. Among groups in the profit sector, 60.7 percent are made up entirely of institutional representatives. Only 17.5 percent of the groups representing the profit sector (mainly professional societies) are composed exclusively of autonomous individuals. This stands in sharp contrast to the citizen groups, where about half (51.5 percent) are composed of autonomous individuals and only 12.1 percent are made up exclusively of institutional representatives. Groups representing the nonprofit sector and those mixed groups that contain substantial numbers of members from both sectors are more nearly evenly divided between those composed of individuals and those made up of institutional representatives.

In the analysis that follows, the composition of a group's membership will be an important independent variable in the explanation of the types of benefits employed by interest groups. As Salisbury (1984) has argued, large institutions and private individuals make fundamentally different calculations of costs and benefits when contemplating whether to join an interest group. For example, one would expect that institutions joining groups are less likely to be enticed into membership by promises of friendship and conviviality than, say, potential members of an Elks lodge. Autonomous individuals and institutional representatives may expect different things from their memberships in groups, and if groups are to be effective, interest group leaders must take these differences into account when deciding on the mix of benefits their groups should offer. Olson pointed out that some business firms are so large that the benefits derived from a change in public policy might make a substantial difference in their financial picture, thus transforming the decision about whether to join in a campaign of collective action from an act of altruism into a hard-headed business decision about the possibilities for private gain (Olson 1965, 29–33).

## Variations in Group Environments

The American interest-group system is no monolith; it is more like a patchwork quilt that covers only parts of society. As background to understanding why some groups exist while others do not, we must confront the tremendous diversity of environments. One begins to grasp the elements of a group's environment by asking questions such as: How decentralized is the potential membership? How much conflict is there over fundamental policy goals? Does the group face competition for members from organizations with similar policy goals? Whether a single potential group thrives or founders is strongly influenced by its environment, and whether clusters or patterns of groups survive reflects the wide variety of environments different groups confront.

*Extent of Decentralization.* It is generally more difficult for potential groups with highly decentralized constituents to organize and speak with one voice in Washington, D.C. Communication among a far-flung membership is difficult, and to the extent that decisions to join a group are influenced by local concerns instead of more national issues, Washington-centered groups are disadvantaged. However, the computer, electronic mailing lists, toll free telephone lines, and other improvements in communications have made it easier for widely dispersed potential members to be contacted by group entrepreneurs. Some national interest groups operate from a single headquarters, while others maintain highly autonomous city or state chapters that have their own sources of revenue and hire their own staff. About 51 percent of the groups in the 1985 survey were centralized in one national headquarters, while 16 percent were at the other extreme of decentralization, with autonomous state or local chapters that maintain their own staffs and have their own sources of revenue. Groups in the profit and nonprofit sectors tend to be more highly centralized than citizen groups, as one would expect given the far-flung nature of citizen group memberships.[2]

*Degree of Policy Conflict.* A high-conflict environment is marked by intense disagreement over fundamental policy goals, by a lack of consensus on the appropriate means for achieving policy objectives, and frequent eruptions of conflict. There is good reason to believe that much of the behavior of interest groups is determined by the amount of conflict they face in their policy area. Most groups do not face a similar interest group bent on destroying them, but conflict can erupt through the efforts of legislators, through the actions of members of the press, or in many other ways. A group engaged in conflict is likely to be successful in attracting members merely by offering its services as a defender of the faith, while one that operates in a settled policy area, where few disputes exist, must offer more tangible benefits in order to attract members. We asked three questions concerning the amount of conflict groups faced.

We asked our respondents whether their associations worked in "a policy area marked by intense conflict or disagreement over fundamental policy goals." Answers were arrayed along a five-point scale ranging from "poor description" (with a score of 1) to "good description" (5). Among citizen sector groups, 51.5 percent checked either a 4 or a 5 on the scale, indicating that they operate in conflictual environments. In contrast, only 23.9 percent of the profit sector groups and 21.5 percent of the nonprofit sector groups described their policy areas as conflictual. An environment of fundamental conflict over policy goals could be detrimental to groups in the nonprofit sector because these groups, like organizations promoting rights for the handicapped and elderly, have few natural enemies. This is because nonprofit sector groups are unlikely to form until there is a consensus among federal

---

2. Our measure of decentralization is arrayed on a four-point scale corresponding to (1) group does not have state or local chapters; (2) group has state or local chapters, but the chapters do not have their own staff and dues go to a central office; (3) group has state or local chapters; their dues go to their own chapters, but they do not have their own staff; and (4) group has state or local chapters; their dues go to their own chapters, and they do have their own staff. Results indicate that 18.5 percent of the citizen groups meet the criteria to be considered the most decentralized, as do 17.2 percent of the profit and 10.3 percent of the nonprofit groups.

bureaucrats or legislators that a social ill warrants governmental attention.[3] Profit sector groups are only slightly more likely to operate in contentious policy areas since the aim of many profit sector groups is to work for an improved business environment. Issues that attract members to groups outside of the occupational sectors, however, are very likely to be highly contentious and ideological.

*Competition for Members.* The decisions by group leaders about what mix of membership benefits to offer will be influenced by the level of competition for new members they experience from groups with similar aims. It stands to reason that competition for members will produce a wider range of benefits and a more aggressive effort to offer benefits that cannot be obtained outside the group. We questioned our 1985 respondents about the degree of competition their group was experiencing and found that 41 percent of the groups faced little competition, while 29 percent reported continuous competition. Groups forming within the occupational sectors are less likely than citizen groups to report facing continuous competition for members because occupational groups are more likely to be specialized in a narrow niche. For example, there is one profit sector group tailored to insulation contractors that, we think, has that part of the interest-group universe wrapped up. Because citizen sector groups often organize around broad issue areas and ideals, it is more difficult for them to carve out a niche to protect themselves from competition. Among citizen sector groups, 35 percent report continuous competition for members, though 28 percent and 24 percent of the profit and nonprofit groups report this high level of competition.

## Group Cooperation and Specialization

For some groups, especially in the citizen sector, policy conflict and continuous competition for members make for a hostile environment in which opportunities to cooperate with other groups are severely limited. Although a few groups employing "outside strategies" (discussed in chap. 6) seem to thrive on conflict and competition, most groups seek out stability, cooperation, and specialization. As Browne (1990) has argued, groups endeavor to carve out their own policy niche through uncentralized coordination with

---

3. Because nonprofit sector groups have fewer natural enemies, when conflict does break out, opponents often come from only distantly related policy areas. Along our "poor" to "good" description" scale, we asked whether each "association repeatedly faces the same opponents on each of the policy issues of interest to it." Only 22.5 percent of the nonprofit groups said this was a good (or the closest rating to good) description of their group. This compares to 56.4 percent of the citizen groups and 41.9 percent of the profit sector groups regularly facing the same opponents.

**TABLE 4-1.  Percentage of Groups Reporting that Members of Their Permanent Staff Previously Held the Following Positions**

|  | Profit | Nonprofit | Citizen |
|---|---|---|---|
| Elected government office | 11.5 | 7.3 | 9.2 |
| Appointed government office | 27.9 | 28.9 | 31.1 |
| Government civil service | 49.7 | 47.0 | 59.6 |
| Legislative staff aide | 47.5 | 30.0 | 49.1 |
| Staff for another association | 73.8 | 65.9 | 77.5 |
| *N* | 326 | 281 | 206 |

*Source:* 1985 Survey.

other groups (Heinz et al. 1990). When we asked groups what types of activities they engaged in, nearly 90 percent claimed to coordinate their activities with other organizations.

This high level of coordination is fostered to the extent that existing groups join together to underwrite the expenses of new organizations, as we will examine in chapter 5. Coordination and communication among groups are also enhanced to the extent that staffers move from group to group. Just as Wilson (1973) speculated that group entrepreneurs learn from the successes and failures of other groups, the daily operations at a staff level may be informed by the successes and failures of similar groups. In our 1985 survey, we asked about the employment history of every group's permanent staff. The results are reported in table 4-1.

About three-quarters of groups employ permanent staff members who have previously held staff positions for another group. This circulating cadre allows groups to improve communication and to share knowledge and expertise. Staff backgrounds may also influence, through remaining contacts and detailed knowledge of bureaucratic intricacies, the relationships a group may have with political parties, Congress, and executive agencies. More than a quarter of the groups employ at least one person who presumably has partisan contacts through a former elective or appointed governmental office. About half of the groups employ at least one staffer who has a background as a legislative staff aide or in governmental civil service.

Staff backgrounds, knowledge, and expertise are usually concentrated around a fairly specific set of issues. A group comprised of public health professionals is not unlikely to hire a staffer with a background in the Public Health Service. Since expertise is the currency of Washington lobbyists, groups tend to specialize within a limited policy domain in order to maintain an edge over similar organizations. In our 1985 survey, we asked how interested a group was in the level of federal government involvement in ten policy areas.[4] In table 4-2, we report the percentage of groups saying that they were either "somewhat" or "very" interested in each issue area.

Most groups report that they are "very interested" in one or two (and rarely more) issue areas. We suspect that groups are further specializing within the ten categories we use, just as Browne (1990) finds that most agricultural interest groups specialize into narrow market niches. When we widen our net to include issues in which groups are "somewhat interested," patterns emerge among the group types. Though all groups pay a relatively high level of attention to federal policies aimed at management of the economy, groups in the nonprofit sector give these policies less attention than education, health and human services, or civil rights and civil liberties. For nonprofit groups, education policy may be a bellwether, warning how well public sector programs will fare in general.

Profit sector groups, most of which count organizational representatives among their members, specialize the most in business issues such as transportation and energy policies. Citizen groups, on the other hand, specialize in the types of issues that have come to the fore since the 1960s, including civil rights, as well as health and human services. These patterns of interest within group types sustain and reinforce policy communities around, for example, civil rights and health issues, or energy and transportation policies. The implications for policy subgovernments are discussed in chapter 7. Policy communities are loose networks of policy professionals and advocates that cluster around substantive areas of government action (see Walker 1981 and 1989; Kingdon 1984; Baskin 1989; Campbell 1989; Campbell et al. 1989; Halpern 1989).

The role of policy communities among American interest groups can be brought into focus comparatively. As Frank Baumgartner (1989a and 1989b) points out, France has made a major commitment to the promotion of nuclear power with remarkably little controversy, while almost every other country in Europe has rejected nuclear power in favor of oil, coal, or other energy sources after much stormy political conflict. Such a stark difference in public policy toward a central policy question stems from differences in the political makeup of Europe, the ease with which opponents of nuclear power can find their way into the center of the policy-making process, and the nature of the cleavages around which the major political parties are structured. It did not stem from differences in the availability of raw materials or the analysis of the pros and cons of nuclear power by the energy policy communities in these countries.

---

4. The question was, "Many associations have an interest in the level of federal government involvement in various areas of public policy. For each of the following policy areas, please indicate whether this association is very interested, somewhat interested, or not very interested in the level of federal government involvement."

**TABLE 4-2.   Issue Specialization and Group Types**

|  | Total | Profit | Nonprofit | Citizen |
|---|---|---|---|---|
| Management of the economy | 69.2% | 80.8% | 58.1% | 63.1% |
| Health and human services | 57.8 | 41.4 | 67.4 | 64.6 |
| Education | 56.8 | 35.5 | 77.1 | 57.9 |
| Structure of government | 55.5 | 52.5 | 55.8 | 56.3 |
| Energy and natural resources | 53.2 | 62.3 | 41.1 | 53.0 |
| Civil rights, civil liberties | 47.0 | 25.6 | 58.8 | 59.5 |
| National security, foreign policy | 44.2 | 39.6 | 40.7 | 57.1 |
| Transportation | 43.2 | 54.5 | 29.2 | 38.9 |
| Housing and urban policy | 35.0 | 27.2 | 32.7 | 27.1 |
| Agriculture | 30.6 | 38.0 | 24.8 | 28.2 |
| *N* | 865 | 316 | 273 | 198 |

*Source:* 1985 Survey.

*Note:* Entries are the percentage of groups that report being either "somewhat" or "very" interested in the level of federal government involvement in each issue area. The column labeled "Total" includes responses from unions and from mixed sector groups, which are not displayed elsewhere on the table.

Interest groups, often at the center of policy communities, foster analysis and creativity to the extent that groups share ideas and personnel across issue areas. Once the role of the policy specialist becomes established within a functioning policy network, an individual can persist in the promotion of an idea, even if that idea is not adopted. Even unadopted ideas can have an impact in that they indicate how disparate issues may be combined into new policy solutions somewhere down the road. Key elements here include interest (partially seen in table 4-2) and communication (enhanced by the relationships shown in table 4-1). The set of potential solutions to policy problems is directly related to patterns of communication and attention within policy communities and among interest groups. Table 4-3 is a snapshot of the interest group portion of several policy communities. The table entries report the percentage of groups that reported that they were "very interested" in the level of federal involvement in related and unrelated issue areas.

Most groups are very interested in only one or two policy areas. Patterns of interest, however, reveal the potential for policy communities and policy cooperation around the combinations of health and human services, civil rights and civil liberties, and education. Other policy communities exist around transportation issues and energy, and around issues concerning the management of the economy. Many groups are very interested in issues such as federal tax policies because changes in policy may directly affect their tax-exempt status. Of 875 groups responding to this question on our 1985 survey, 810 (92.6 percent) reported enjoying tax-exempt status from the Internal Revenue Service. Clearly, an interest in tax policy is shared by groups repre-

**TABLE 4-3.  Percentage of Groups Reporting that They Are "Very Interested" in the Level of Federal Involvement in Both the Row and Column Issue Areas**

|  | Management of Economy | Health, Human Services | Education | Structure of Government | Energy Policy | Civil Rights, Civil Liberties | National Security, Foreign Policy | Transportation | Housing, Urban Policy |
|---|---|---|---|---|---|---|---|---|---|
| Management of economy | — | — | — | — | — | — | — | — | — |
| Health, human services | 13.9 | — | — | — | — | — | — | — | — |
| Education | 11.6 | 17.1 | — | — | — | — | — | — | — |
| Structure of government | 12.0 | 9.2 | 8.2 | — | — | — | — | — | — |
| Energy policy | 12.9 | 8.5 | 7.2 | 5.6 | — | — | — | — | — |
| Civil rights, civil liberties | 10.9 | 14.0 | 14.1 | 10.9 | 6.0 | — | — | — | — |
| National security, foreign policy | 9.4 | 7.1 | 7.2 | 5.9 | 6.6 | 6.7 | — | — | — |
| Transportation | 10.3 | 5.8 | 4.6 | 5.1 | 10.4 | 4.4 | 4.2 | — | — |
| Housing, urban policy | 8.2 | 8.7 | 5.8 | 4.2 | 5.5 | 6.6 | 3.1 | 4.7 | — |
| Agriculture | 7.1 | 5.4 | 3.6 | 2.8 | 6.8 | 2.5 | 3.7 | 3.5 | 2.5 |

*Source:* 1985 Survey.

*Note:* Entries are the percentage of groups reporting that they are "very interested" in the level of federal involvement in both the row and column issue areas. For example, only 2.5 percent of all surveyed groups were "very interested" in the level of federal involvement in housing and urban policy as well as agricultural policy.

senting widely differing members; the presence of this shared interest makes communication and coordination on other issues easier to the extent that the tax policy communities stay in contact.

Patterns of interest in table 4-3 also reveal just how insular some policy communities may be. Agricultural interest groups focus on agricultural policies and little else, even though one could imagine potentially fruitful combinations of interest such as agricultural and transportation policy. The fact that very few groups are jointly interested in agriculture and transportation policy makes it less likely that innovative policy solutions will emerge that may solve problems in both issue areas.

## Summary

Since about the time Martin Luther King, Jr., led a "march on Washington" by thousands of citizens in the civil rights movement in 1963, there has been a march to Washington by interest groups as well. We have witnessed an explosive growth in the number of groups finding voice and redress in Washington, D.C. Nearly two-thirds of the national citizen sector groups that we identified in the middle 1980s were founded since the end of the Kennedy administration, and that rate of growth far outstrips increases in the number of groups that have emerged from the profit and nonprofit interest-group sectors.

Despite convincing evidence of the growth in interest groups, exactly why individuals join groups has remained something of a puzzle to social scientists. One reason for this is that social scientists often take rational (or not-so-rational) individuals as their units of analysis. However, the majority of group memberships are subsidized by institutions such as businesses, foundations, universities, churches, and other patrons. In fact, more often than not, group members are not individuals acting on their own behalf at all. Representatives of organizations comprise about half of the interest-group memberships in our surveys. For these members, decisions whether to join a group are often not entirely their own but are made in conjunction with the organizations they represent, and membership is typically paid for by the organization.

There are form and structure to the interest-group system in that groups have emerged from two broad backgrounds: one affiliated with an occupation, either in the profit or nonprofit sectors, and a second open to all citizens for membership. We have focused on the different backgrounds of profit sector, nonprofit sector, and citizen sector groups. We have seen that the types of federal policies pursued by groups, the amount of conflict and competition among groups, and the extent of group decentralization are all related to how groups have emerged within the broader universe of groups. Nonprofit sector groups, such as those representing employees helping the mentally ill, have few natural enemies. Citizen groups, which may be organized around an ideological position, are much more likely to be in conflict with groups holding antithetical positions.

Most groups try to avoid head-to-head conflict with other, similar interest groups, and they tend to specialize on relatively narrow issue areas and coordinate activities with similar groups. Policy experts that are jointly interested in several issues are an important part of policy communities in which innovative solutions can be bounced off others with shared interests. The presence of policy communities instructs the policy solutions that groups promote to lawmakers, federal bureaucrats, the news media, and their own members.

CHAPTER 5

# The Origins and Maintenance of Groups

*David C. King and Jack L. Walker, Jr.*

In chapter 4 we saw that there has been a rapid growth in the number of national interest groups—especially among groups in the citizen sector. How can these recent changes in the interest-group system be explained? Why would anyone bother to join an interest group? The work of Olson largely undermined David Truman's theory of the spontaneous generation of groups, yet, despite the power of Olson's analysis, the recent increases in the number of groups suggest that Truman has the data on his side. After reading about the many obstacles that must be overcome before groups can be formed, one would not expect to find that so many new ones have been created during the past 25 years, especially citizen groups, the type most affected by the collective goods dilemma. These trends in group formation raise serious questions about the predictive utility of the line of theory founded by Olson.

We will argue that interest groups cannot be organized successfully unless their leaders are able to offer a mixture of benefits that attract members and, particularly, patrons to their cause. The winning formula will not be the same for all groups, and, during the past 25 years, political entrepreneurs have created many new recipes for success, causing a great flowering of both the number and types of interest groups in America. In the Washington of the 1940s, elements of society such as the mentally ill, children in poverty, or the elderly were thought to be much too difficult to mobilize for political action, but in the 1990s all these groups have strong advocates for their interests, as do homosexuals and other people who have been widely despised or even physically suppressed in the recent past.

An increase in the number of groups, by itself, would not disconfirm Olson's theory. Faced with these data, an observer who accepted Olson's analysis might suspect that the citizen groups were offering some new kind of desirable benefit in exchange for membership that was not available to non-members. If these selective benefits were desirable enough, groups might attract large numbers of members and become rich enough to employ a large and talented staff, even though many of their members might actually disagree with the group's goals. The American Association of Retired Persons (AARP) is included in this study and classified as a citizen group, since it has no occupational prerequisites for membership. In 1965, the combined membership of NRTA/AARP stood at approximately 750,000, and by 1990 it had grown to 28 million members, making it one of the largest voluntary associations in the world.[1] Much of this growth was made possible through a wide range of selective material benefits. Is this typical?

As we detail in this chapter, the availability of selective benefits alone will not explain recent changes in the group structure. Observers following Olson might then suspect that group leaders had somehow managed to find ways to coerce new members to join against their self-interest. Olson persuasively demonstrated how legal forms of coercion contributed to the creation and maintenance of American trade unions. Without closed shops and mandatory payment of dues through payroll deduction, union membership would almost certainly plummet as many workers dropped out to become free riders, fully expecting to receive the same benefits from their employers that were granted to union members (Olson 1965, 66–97).

Our surveys of group leaders indicate that a few of the groups in our samples are able to exercise subtle forms of coercion that may inflate their membership rolls. For example, certain trade associations sponsor the creation of codes meant to govern the specifications of goods produced by their industry. Uniform sizes of components or safety standards established in these private codes are often accepted by government or private purchasing agents as minimum requirements and may sometimes be written directly into state or local statutes, thus taking on the force of law. Leaders of small firms often feel compelled to join trade associations to protect their firms from arbitrary changes in such codes that might suddenly render their products unmarketable or require them to make large investments in new tools or equipment (Wines 1981).

Similarly, many associations of professionals in both the public and private sectors have managed to gain significant influence over licensing procedures, and several serve as accrediting agencies for educational programs in their professional specialties. Until a decision by the Supreme Court in 1978 prevented the practice, many associations required any person wishing certification in a field to hold membership in the group—a direct form of coercion—but even now that this practice has been made illegal, many join a professional society as a hedge against decertification.[2]

---

1. The National Retired Teachers Association (NRTA) began as an association of retired teachers and, thus, would have been categorized as an occupational group within the nonprofit sector. After its merger with the AARP, all occupational prerequisites were dropped so that it has clearly become a citizen group. For a description, see Pratt 1976 (119–213).

2. The Supreme Court decision is *National Society of Professional Engineers v. United States* (1978).

These practices are consistent with Olson's theory, but they affect a relatively small number of groups. The fact that some groups use subtle coercion practices is not a satisfactory explanation for the maintenance of most citizen groups. Our conclusion is that neither Truman's nor Olson's theories offer convincing explanations of the changing composition of the group structure in the United States. The political system is beset by a swarm of organizational bumblebees that are busily flying about in spite of the fact that political scientists cannot explain how they manage it.

## The Origins of Groups

There is no single explanation for the increase in the number of groups operating at the national level in American politics. As discussed in chapter 2, long-term improvements in educational levels provided a large pool of potential recruits for citizen movements (McCarthy and Zald 1978). The development of cheap, sophisticated methods of communication, such as the new direct mailing systems and toll free telephone lines, allowed leaders in Washington to reach members in all parts of the country. A period of social protest that began with the civil rights demonstrations of the early 1960s called many established practices into question, created concerns about the future stability of the American political system, and provided a powerful impetus for change. Agencies administering massive new government programs in social welfare, education, health care, housing, and transportation set up in the 1960s (and foundations supporting the programs' goals) began to foster voluntary associations among the service providers and consumers of the new programs. During this period, the new regulatory legislation in civil rights, consumer protection, environmental preservation, pollution control, and occupational health and safety prompted business groups to organize in self-defense—as Truman would have predicted—to protect themselves against the authorities who were charged with enforcing these broad new legislative mandates.

These complex changes in American politics and public policy during the past few decades, and the fundamental transformations in the political environment they generated, go a long way toward explaining recent changes in the structure of interest groups. So many influences have been at work, however, that the fundamental character of the group formation process has been partially obscured. The findings discussed in this chapter show that group leaders learned how to cope with the public goods dilemma not by inducing large numbers of new members to join their groups through the manipulation of selective benefits, but by locating important new sources of funds outside the immediate membership.

The first problem facing would-be interest-group organizers is to bring their groups into being and to keep them going until revenues are large enough

**TABLE 5-1. Percentage of Groups that Received Financial Aid from any Outside Source in Order to Start Operations**

| Sector | $N$ | Percentage Receiving Aid |
|---|---|---|
| Profit | 179 | 33.9 |
| Nonprofit | 190 | 60.0 |
| Citizen | 115 | 89.0 |

*Source:* 1980 Survey.

to meet operating expenses. Profit sector groups that emerge from relatively small and closely knit occupational or industrial communities can usually begin their activities on tiny budgets and can continue operations for several years without a professional staff. In the nonprofit sector, groups often come about at the urging of federal officials who need to have regular contact with administrators of state or local agencies receiving aid from some new federal program. There is a need to share information, develop standard administrative practices, create model bills for adoption by cities or states, and, of course, work to expand support for their programs in Congress. Members of most public and private sector occupational groups are able to charge their travel costs to their firms or agencies and can easily agree to meet together periodically to exchange information and to work out common positions on outstanding questions of public policy.

Citizen groups face an entirely different set of initial circumstances. Their potential membership is extremely large and, in most cases, unknown to one another. There is no ready-made community waiting to be organized, no readily available source of money, and often not even a clearly articulated common interest in creating an organization. Ideally, citizen groups begin with a fairly large staff, or they have little chance of reaching enough of their far-flung potential membership to create a stable organizational base. Improvements in communication have, however, helped citizen groups overcome problems stemming from a decentralized membership base.

Because of the organizational problems facing citizen groups, they must almost always gain financial assistance in order to launch their operations. All respondents in our 1980 survey were asked whether their group had received any form of financial assistance from an outside source at the beginning of its history, and, as reported in table 5-1, 89 percent of the citizen groups reported that they had, whereas only 34 percent of the occupationally based groups from the profit sector had received financial aid.

Not only were the nonprofit and citizen groups more likely to receive aid at the initial stages, but further analysis indicates that access to outside fund-

**TABLE 5-2.  Percentage of Groups Receiving Financial Aid at the Time of Founding from Five Sources**

| Funding Source | Founding Date | | |
| --- | --- | --- | --- |
| | 1836–1929 | 1930–59 | 1960–83 |
| Profit sector groups | | | |
| Foundations | 2.2 | 2.7 | 3.8 |
| Other associations | 13.0 | 17.4 | 14.4 |
| Corporations or businesses | 42.0 | 17.4 | 14.4 |
| Government grants | 3.4 | 3.5 | 11.4 |
| Individuals | 32.9 | 28.8 | 27.2 |
| N | 90 | 111 | 106 |
| Nonprofit sector groups | | | |
| Foundations | 14.1 | 12.9 | 29.9 |
| Other associations | 17.6 | 32.4 | 32.0 |
| Corporations or businesses | 8.6 | 13.0 | 17.3 |
| Government grants | 13.0 | 20.0 | 33.0 |
| Individuals | 32.6 | 32.4 | 29.0 |
| N | 92 | 68 | 107 |
| Citizen sector groups | | | |
| Foundations | 11.8 | 21.2 | 47.7 |
| Other associations | 21.2 | 25.0 | 28.7 |
| Corporations or businesses | 18.2 | 21.2 | 35.5 |
| Government grants | 12.5 | 11.4 | 20.3 |
| Individuals | 80.6 | 67.7 | 77.5 |
| N | 34 | 31 | 130 |
| Total N | 216 | 210 | 343 |

*Source:* 1985 Survey.

ing has increased in recent years. In table 5-2, groups in our 1985 sample are divided into three time periods. The second period brackets the New Deal programs and the expansion of federal programs that attracted interest from groups in the nonprofit occupational sector. The third period was marked by the increasing prominence of citizen groups and the growth of both private foundations and activist administrative bureaus in the national government— two of the most important sources of patronage for political action.

Emerging from table 5-2 is a picture of the evolution of funding sources that have produced the group structure of the 1980s. The entries report the percentage of groups founded in each period that reported receiving start-up funds from five different sources: foundations, other associations, corporations or businesses, government grants, and individuals. Large gifts from individuals have been highly important sources of funds in all three sectors and have been steadily rising in importance, especially for the citizen groups, but the sharpest changes have occurred in the three other funding sources.

**TABLE 5-3.    Timing of Support from Three Types of Patrons of Political Action as a Percentage of All Groups Reporting**

|  | Government | Foundations | Individuals |
|---|---|---|---|
| Start-up funds, patron acting alone | 12.8 | 15.7 | 41.7 |
| Start-up funds, more than one patron | 17.2 | 34.4 | 22.1 |
| Maintenance support | 70.0 | 49.9 | 36.2 |
| *N* | 210 | 189 | 257 |

*Source:* 1980 Survey.

First, the group structure in the nonprofit and citizen sectors has been elaborating itself as associations have helped to spawn new ones in order to build larger networks of groups around volatile issues like civil rights or around constituencies like the elderly or the handicapped.

Second, both government agencies and private foundations have steadily become more important patrons of interest groups in the nonprofit and citizen sectors. Both government agencies and foundations are active in sponsoring groups built around professional specialties in areas such as health care, education, welfare administration, mass transportation, scientific research, and other program areas that depend heavily on federal funds. Government agencies and foundations both made contributions to the founding of a few groups in the profit sector, but their efforts are clearly concentrated in the nonprofit and citizen sectors. During the 1960s, the federal government became increasingly active in providing start-up funds to nonprofit sector groups as these groups became less dependent on individuals for seed money. The period since the 1960s has also brought foundations into the forefront of sponsoring the creation of citizen sector groups.

It requires boldness to provide start-up funds to an untested political entrepreneur or to patronize a cause that might create controversy. Our data demonstrate that, among all the patrons studied, private individuals are the most likely to provide backing for new organizational ventures, far outdistancing foundations and government agencies in their willingness to take risks. Table 5-3 shows that only 13 percent of the groups received government support in the form of start-up money when the government agency was acting as the sole source of patronage. Another 17 percent of the groups received government support as start-up funds when the government agency was acting in league with other patrons, but 70 percent of the groups reporting support from government received it solely for maintenance of their operations, only after they were successfully launched and had established a record of performance. Foundations are more likely than government agencies to sponsor new groups, but the most adventurous patrons are clearly private individuals. Of the groups that reported receiving support from individuals,

42 percent got it to help establish their operations when individuals were acting as their only patrons, and another 22 percent received start-up support when individuals were joined by other types of patrons. Patronage for political action from large institutions has increased in importance in recent years, but wealthy individuals are still a crucial source of the venture capital needed by aspiring political entrepreneurs.

Are American groups peculiar in relying on, or at least in benefiting from, outside patronage? We cannot answer such a question definitively since we rely on an American survey. Still, when a similar study was undertaken with approximately 130 groups and associations in the area of education policy in France, one source of outside support—that from the government— was found to be virtually identical to that among education groups in our sample. The majority of the groups received at least some government subsidies, with some benefiting from hundreds of paid staff at government expense. Decision rules followed by the French and American governments were found to be virtually identical (Baumgartner and Walker 1989). Clearly, groups must rely not only on their immediate members for support. Government agencies have an interest and a well-developed organizational structure, and they are often willing supporters of groups in their fields, according to this and other comparative analyses.

## The Maintenance of Groups

Once a group has been brought into being with the aid of a patron, in most cases, the patron continues to support the group as a going concern. New groups sometimes are weaned from dependence on other associations as a source of continuing support, although there is a positive tau-*b* correlation of .21 between the receipt of start-up funds from other associations and the receipt of continuing support from them. Groups evidently find it even more difficult to become independent of reliance on grants from individuals, private foundations, and government agencies. From the 1980 survey, the tau-*b* correlations between the receipt of start-up funds from a source and the continuing receipt of support for maintenance from the same types of sources are .37 for government agencies, .43 for foundations, and .44 for individuals. These figures indicate that once groups come into being with support from a patron, they tend to maintain financial connections of some kind with these sponsors throughout their existence.

All groups in both the 1980 and 1985 surveys were asked to describe their current budget receipts; results from the 1985 survey are displayed, according to the typology of groups, in table 5-4. The patterns of support that were evident in the data on group origins appear once again in this table. Citizen groups received less than half of their support from routine contribu-

**TABLE 5-4.  Average Percentage of Revenue Obtained by Groups from Each Source in 1984 Budgetary Year, by Group Type**

|  | Profit | Nonprofit | Citizen |
|---|---|---|---|
| Routine contributions |  |  |  |
| Dues | 61.5 | 47.1 | 32.7 |
| Publications | 7.0 | 10.4 | 7.0 |
| Conferences | 14.1 | 10.5 | 3.6 |
| Interest | 4.0 | 3.6 | 3.5 |
| Subtotal | 86.6 | 71.6 | 46.8 |
| Nonrecurring contributions |  |  |  |
| Government contracts, grants | 2.4 | 9.5 | 5.7 |
| Corporate and business gifts | 2.6 | 3.0 | 7.5 |
| Gifts from individuals (not dues) | 0.5 | 1.8 | 11.9 |
| Foundation grants | 0.5 | 4.4 | 10.1 |
| Fund raising events | 0.3 | 0.5 | 5.1 |
| Other associations | 1.5 | 2.4 | 2.8 |
| Sale of merchandise | 1.9 | 1.7 | 3.0 |
| Subtotal | 9.7 | 23.3 | 46.1 |
| Other revenue sources | 3.7 | 5.1 | 7.1 |
| Total | 100 | 100 | 100 |
| N | 326 | 281 | 206 |

*Source:* 1985 Survey.

tions, including membership dues, the sale of publications, conference fees, and interest on endowments. More than a fifth of the revenue for citizen groups came from foundation grants and gifts from individuals. Those two sources of income made up less than 1 percent of the receipts from a typical profit sector group. Routine contributions are more predictable and stable than nonrecurring revenue sources, and this sense of security in funding will affect how group leaders respond to member interests. Profit sector groups received 86.6 percent of their 1984 revenues from these sources, and citizen sector groups received less than half from these stable sources.

The role of government support in founding and maintaining interest groups should not be underemphasized—especially for groups in the nonprofit sector. Nonprofit sector groups receive nearly as much support from government agencies as profit sector groups receive from all nonrecurring sources combined. Government contracts with groups often indicate cooperative relationships between groups and federal agencies, and government-supported groups may serve as constituents and sounding boards for policy entrepreneurs within agencies. In addition to asking how much money groups received from government contracts, we asked how important "administering service programs on contract with government agencies" was perceived to be for a group's financial support, and the results mirror the findings in table 5-4. Most groups, 69.1 percent in the 1985 survey, did not work on government contracts, but this leaves a surprisingly high proportion, 30.9 percent, tuned into finding funds from government contracts. For some groups, 43 of 863 in our 1985 survey (5.0 percent), working on government contracts is "one of the most important" things they do to get money.

Table 5-4 provides much valuable information about the maintenance of interest groups, but it understates two types of patronage. First, membership dues are often subsidized. Dues are an important source of revenue for most groups of all kinds, but they are not, in every case, voluntary contributions from individuals who have made a rational decision to join a group in the hope of advancing some ideological or personal goal (Salisbury 1984). Organizational representatives and some autonomous individuals are allowed (by their employers) to charge the cost of their dues, publications, and travel to association meetings to their agency budgets. Without such subsidies, many of these individuals would not participate in group activities. The data reported in table 5-4 on the support from dues for both private and public sector groups, therefore, include an unknown, but probably substantial, amount of indirect patronage from the budgets of government agencies or private corporations.

Many large private corporations provide a second form of patronage by making extraordinary contributions that are labeled dues, and when we consider member patronage as well as outside patronage, the levels are even higher than they appear in table 5-4. Most trade associations employ a sliding scale or "split" dues schedule under which a small number of large firms contribute much larger amounts than the rest of the members, much as Olson suggested they would in his discussion of "the exploitation of the great by the small" (Olson 1965, 3, 27–32, 34–36; Hardin 1982, chap. 5). McKean (1949) reported that in the 1940s, 5.0 percent of the membership of the National Association of Manufacturers contributed approximately 50.0 percent of the funds needed for the group's maintenance. The average dues payment in 1981 from the 215,000 members of the U.S. Chamber of Commerce was approximately $265, based on a sliding scale that ranged from $100 for the smallest members to more than $75,000 for a handful of major corporations. Most of the chamber's member firms are small—91.0 percent have fewer than 100 employees—yet the chamber's board of directors is overwhelmingly dominated by the large national and multinational corporations that make the maximum dues payments (Richman 1982). Arrangements of this kind apparently are typical in cases where a single firm (such as Ralston Purina in the feed manufacturing business) or a small number of large firms (as in the production of agricultural chemicals) account for most of the sales in the industry. A small proportion of the groups in our 1985 survey (8.0 percent) reported that a single member (typically an organization) paid more than 10.0 percent of the total annual revenues for the group in 1984. This form of private member-patronage is especially common among profit sector groups, where 11.8 percent of the groups had single member-patrons. One major trade association, for example, reported dues ranging from $1,000 for the smallest corporate members to $4 million for the largest. Among nonprofit sector groups, 5.1 percent had such large patron-members, and among citizen groups, just one (1.2 percent of the total) had a single private member contributing over 10 percent of the total yearly revenues (and this contribution was only $3,000). With a certain level of organizational maintenance assured by a small core of patron-members, groups can afford to ignore mass memberships all together, or groups can afford to subsidize additional members at rates far below costs.

Sliding dues scales are often used even when there is no single dominant industry, and these dues scales are one way that groups cope with asymmetries in the desirability of collective goods (Hardin 1982, chap. 5). Over three-quarters of the groups responding to our 1985 survey reported that they had some form of sliding dues schedule. Sliding dues were especially common among groups operating in the profit sector (87.2 percent reported differential dues) but were common among citizen groups as well (61.5 percent of which reported sliding scales). Most groups are composed either entirely of organizational representatives (39.2 percent of our 1985 survey) or of some mix of organizational representatives and autonomous individuals (28.6 percent). This preponderance of organizational representatives helps explain the prevalence of split dues schedules, since the organizational members may differ greatly in size. Among those groups that charge all members the same dues, 73.1 percent are composed entirely of autonomous individuals.

Most groups continually struggle for funds, and the group system has developed some fairly sophisticated ways of keeping afloat financially. Membership dues are only part of the picture, and these dues include sliding scales and hidden patronage through subsidized memberships. Even using the generous way we have defined membership dues, less than a third of the revenues for citizen groups come from these sources. In 1991, for example, Common Cause budgeted for only 31.3 percent of its revenues to be raised by membership dues, with much of the remainder coming from sustaining donors and special appeals (Common Cause 1990). Foundation grants and private patrons are essential for many groups, and the federal government indirectly supports these patrons by making donations to many groups tax deductible. Federal bureaucracies directly support almost a third of all groups, and more than 75.0 percent of nonprofit sector groups, through grants and contracts.

A group's financial contributors are a group's constituents whose interests are purportedly represented, and we should understand that dues-paying members are only one part of the constituency. The size of this constituency—

the membership—waxes and wanes regularly, and group leaders have devised strategies for expanding their memberships. Like other political entrepreneurs, group leaders claim credit and advertise. They claim credit for policy successes even when the group's effort was of little consequence to the outcomes, and they advertise these policy successes to current and potential group contributors. Groups also offer current and potential members a variety of membership benefits, which may include private benefits, such as a glossy magazine, or collective benefits, such as clean air. Ongoing with the search for funds, then, is a search for membership benefits that will maximize the size or power of the membership.

## The Provision of Benefits by Groups

Why do people join groups? We reviewed Mancur Olson's answer—people join if they are coerced or if they receive "selective incentives"—in chapter 3. Most studies of what motivates people to join groups have been limited in scope, but it seems certain that collective benefits have a more potent attraction than Olson understood. Empirical studies have repeatedly chipped away at Olson's thesis (Mitchell 1979; Moe 1980; Knoke 1988 and 1990; Rothenberg 1988). However, such studies of group members usually rely upon reports from individuals, and respondents may be confused about the reasons for their decision to join a group. For most people, joining voluntary associations requires relatively few resources, and their decisions may have been made in the distant past. It is difficult to assemble data to test hypotheses arising from the theoretical debate in this area, and a definitive answer to many questions probably would require a massive panel study of potential group members stretching over several years.

Our approach was to ask the leaders of groups what benefits they provide their members and how important (or unimportant) different benefits are in attracting members. Group leaders have been engaged in a form of trial and error for years. They search for the best bundle of benefits that works for their potential membership. Even though they might be laboring under mistaken impressions, ultimately these group leaders decide which inducements actually will be offered to the public, thus strongly determining the choices individuals can make.

In table 5-5, data on sixteen benefits are reported by group type. Ten of the benefits listed along the left side of the table are grouped into four categories that include the frequently used typology of purposive, solidary, and material benefits—along with a category we call *professional benefits*.[3] We

3. Three of the categories reflect the typology first developed by Clark and Wilson (1961). The fourth category grows out of our attention to the occupationally based groups that are so

**TABLE 5-5.  Percentage of Groups Providing Benefit by Group Type**

| Benefit | Profit | Nonprofit | Citizen |
|---|---|---|---|
| Professional benefits | | | |
|    Conferences | 99 | 97 | 92 |
|    Professional contacts | 98 | 97 | 79 |
|    Training | 91 | 92 | 86 |
| Purposive benefits | | | |
|    Advocacy | 96 | 96 | 97 |
|    Representation before government | 93 | 88 | 92 |
|    Participation in public affairs | 86 | 82 | 91 |
| Solidary benefit | | | |
|    Friendship | 97 | 94 | 92 |
| Personal material benefits | | | |
|    Trips, tours | 41 | 40 | 36 |
|    Insurance | 36 | 37 | 22 |
|    Discount on consumer goods | 15 | 18 | 18 |
| Other benefits and services | | | |
|    Publications | 98 | 98 | 99 |
|    Coordination among organizations | 93 | 89 | 88 |
|    Research | 76 | 77 | 81 |
|    Legal help | 51 | 33 | 28 |
|    Maintain professional codes | 40 | 41 | 13 |
|    Collective bargaining | 14 | 11 | 9 |
| $N$ | 326 | 281 | 206 |

*Source:* 1985 Survey.

intend the professional and personal benefits categories to capture what Olson means by "selective incentives." Perhaps the most striking finding is that so few groups provide many of the personal material benefits that Olson thought necessary to attract members. For example, only 22 percent of the citizen groups say that they offer insurance policies, yet, since their far-flung members have so little in common outside of their enthusiasm for a cause, one might expect such groups to offer more in the way of personal material benefits as inducements to join.

Almost all groups claim to be providing some purposive (or collective) benefits such as advocacy, representation before government, and participa-

---

prominent in our sample. From the list of sixteen benefits, we selected ten benefits to populate the four categories. As confirmation that these types of benefits tend to go together, see Knoke's factor analysis (1988). While a factor analysis of this type is not definitive, it does provide evidence that groups that provide one of the benefits (for example, trips and tours) are more likely than other groups also to provide other personal material benefits (such as discounts on consumer goods).

tion in public affairs. We cannot tell from the data in table 5-5, however, whether these benefits are being provided as an afterthought once the selective benefits are paid for or if these purposive benefits are the group's reason for existence. The group leaders may also be projecting their own wishes onto the survey, thereby overestimating the importance of collective benefits to the organization.

## The Relative Importance of Benefits in Attracting Members

We not only asked respondents whether each of the benefits was supplied by their groups; we also asked them for their assessment of the importance of each benefit as a device for attracting members.[4] Data on the relative importance of benefits are displayed in table 5-6, with higher numbers indicating greater importance. A value of 20 indicates that a group leader considers a benefit to be "one of the least important" benefits provided, while a value of 100 means that the benefit is "one of the most important" for attracting and maintaining members. The average assessment of the importance of merchandise discounts given by the leaders of citizen groups is only 40. Seen another way, 18 percent (37 out of 206) of the citizen groups provide discounts on consumer goods, and most of those groups think that the selective incentive is not very important. This finding runs directly counter to Olson's predictions, as do the results on trips, tours, and insurance.

One striking finding shown in table 5-6 is that purposive or collective benefits consistently receive high rankings by the leaders of all types of groups. Conversely, personal material benefits are not only provided by relatively few groups, but they also are considered the least important class of benefits in attracting members among the groups that do provide them. For the overwhelming majority of groups, collective benefits are considered to be more important than the solidary benefit, friendship, that has received attention from social scientists as a solution to Olson's collective goods dilemma.

Professional material benefits such as conferences and job contacts likely serve the role that Olson ascribed to incentives like insurance discounts.

---

4. Respondents were asked whether their groups provided a given benefit and how important they considered the benefit to be as a means of attracting members. The question was: "For each of the following factors, please indicate on the scale provided your best estimate of the importance of that factor for attracting members to this association." Respondents were presented with a list of sixteen benefits, and, for each benefit, they were given six choices along a scale ranging from "This benefit is not provided" to "One of the most important benefits or activities provided." This question provided data, therefore, on whether the group offered a particular benefit and, if so, on how important its executive director considered the benefit to be as a means of attracting members.

TABLE 5-6.  Importance of Benefits in Attracting Members,
by Group Type

| Benefit | Profit | Nonprofit | Citizen |
|---|---|---|---|
| Professional benefits | | | |
|    Conferences | 82 | 86 | 66 |
|    Professional contacts | 82 | 88 | 68 |
|    Training | 74 | 76 | 61 |
| Purposive benefits | | | |
|    Advocacy | 88 | 84 | 94 |
|    Representation before government | 90 | 78 | 80 |
|    Participation in public affairs | 66 | 64 | 74 |
| Solidary benefit | | | |
|    Friendship | 68 | 70 | 62 |
| Personal material benefits | | | |
|    Trips, tours | 38 | 34 | 42 |
|    Insurance | 52 | 50 | 54 |
|    Discount on consumer goods | 32 | 36 | 40 |
| Other benefits and services | | | |
|    Publications | 85 | 89 | 85 |
|    Coordination among organizations | 67 | 69 | 68 |
|    Research | 61 | 62 | 61 |
|    Legal help | 60 | 56 | 55 |
|    Maintain professional codes | 65 | 65 | 45 |
|    Collective bargaining | 60 | 35 | 46 |

Source: 1985 Survey.

Note: Entries are self-reported estimates of how "important" each benefit is in attracting new members to the group. The lowest entry is 20, corresponding to "one of the least important benefits provided," and the highest entry is 100, corresponding to "one of the most important benefits provided." Groups not providing the benefit are scored zero; entries are averages for all groups of the type indicated.

Almost all groups provide at least one of the professional or personal benefits, though the relative importance of these incentives varies widely from group to group. Leaders of citizen sector groups, for example, place only moderate emphasis on the importance of professional benefits, which is not surprising given that these groups are open to members regardless of occupational badges. For attracting members, citizen sector groups emphasize purposive benefits—which is to say collective goods—more than any other class of benefits. The preeminence of collective benefits among profit sector groups comes through as well, with "representation before government" seen as a more important membership lure than any other benefit listed, including potentially lucrative professional contacts.

One could argue that, in filling out our 1985 survey, group leaders overestimated the importance of purposive benefits in a self-congratulatory way while more truthfully reporting the importance of other benefits such as trips and tours. We doubt that misreporting was widespread, but it may well have happened, and the effect would be an overemphasis (by us) on the extent to which individuals and institutions join groups in order to pursue public goods. Even with an unknown amount of upward bias, however, there is a great deal of variance on answers to the purposive benefits questions. After exploring some reasons why certain benefits are provided, we will present a multivariate test of Olson's by-product theory. The multivariate technique will exploit the variance in the responses, and, for our purposes, the unknown amount of upward bias in responses will not affect our conclusions. A tendency to overestimate the importance of purposive benefits will not alter our subsequent conclusions.

## Determinants of Benefit Provision

The key to understanding the mix of benefits provided by an interest group lies in the characteristics of its organizational structure, its financing (especially its reliance on patrons), and the amount of policy conflict it is experiencing. More precisely, a group's emphasis on any particular type of benefit is some function of its organizational form, membership composition, financial structure, and policy environment, along with the influences that arise from its evolution within one of the several group types that we have identified. We expect the variance in benefit provisions to be largely related to the following influences.

*Extent of Decentralization.* As we discussed in chapter 4, groups vary by how decentralized their operations are, and groups with active local chapters can provide much more in the way of solidary benefits than a group managed by a few professionals from an office in the nation's capital. We also expect autonomous individuals to be more interested in solidary benefits than organizational representatives who join a group because of their professional backgrounds or affiliations.[5]

*Group Size.* Mancur Olson argued that the problems of organizational maintenance change as the size of a group's membership increases. A large group with members scattered across the country would almost be forced into providing frequent publications to its members or making other efforts to increase their sense of belonging. Also, because of economies of scale, large

---

5. The possibly different ways that individuals and organizational representatives respond to solidary benefits will be handled through an interaction term in our multivariate analysis, reported in table 5-7.

groups may more easily afford selective material benefits.[6] In our 1985 survey, we found that groups that included organizational representatives averaged about 950 organizational members, and groups that included autonomous individuals averaged more than 100,000 members. For groups of autonomous individuals, however, this average reflects the weight of a few very large groups, such as the American Association for Retired Persons.

*Membership Composition.* We expect that individuals are more likely to be induced to join interest groups by merchandise discounts or other personal material benefits than would officers of large corporations or government agencies acting as representatives of their organizations. Organizations might regard professional training or recognition as an important benefit for their employees, but they are also likely to be concerned about the effectiveness of the group in advancing the long-range interests of their industry or policy area. We use a variable measuring the proportion of a group's membership composed of autonomous individuals.

*Group Resources.* The more resources an interest group commands, the more benefits it can provide to its members—especially those benefits that require the efforts of a large staff. Questions about the size of interest-group budgets often were left blank by our respondents, but almost all groups were willing to supply information concerning the size of their staffs. Since there is a very close relationship between the size of a group's staff and the size of its budget, staff size can serve as a reasonable indirect measure of total group resources. Following this reasoning, our measure of group resources is based upon the number of full-time equivalents (FTEs) in the group's staff. Since there surely is a diminishing impact of increases in the size of an interest group's staff, the variable reported in the analysis is the natural log of staff size, rescaled to range from zero to one.[7]

---

6. Even though it is clear that group size is an important variable, it also is difficult to measure because, as demonstrated in fig. 4-3, some groups are made up of individuals while others are made up of representatives of large institutions or companies. A group with only 50 members might still be considered large if all fifty members represented huge, multinational corporations that employed thousands of people. In order to capture the significance of the fact that all group members are not the same, we employ two measures of group size. One is based upon the natural log of the number of autonomous individuals that the group claims to have, while the second is based upon the natural log of the number of organizational representatives who are members of the group. We use natural logs because we expect that the impact of additional members decreases as the size of the group increases.

7. One might expect that the measures for a group's size correlates highly with staff resources—which would decrease the efficiency of our estimates. Actually, these correlations are quite low (.22 for individual members size and .04 for organizational representatives size). Several groups with small memberships are able to employ relatively large staffs with sizable budgets because they receive financial support from outside sources, such as governmental grants, foundations, and other interested patrons.

*Influence of Patrons.* A group's decisions about which benefits to provide depend to a large degree upon the principal sources of its revenue and the kinds of activities that appeal to the individuals or patrons who support them. Groups in the 1985 survey received an average of 18.4 percent of their revenue from patrons, but some groups receive as much as 100.0 percent from sources other than membership dues or payments, and patronage is heavily concentrated among the citizen groups. We have measured the degree of patronage in a group's budget by adding up the resources it receives from sources other than dues or conferences fees, or from revenues generated by the staff or through interest payments or royalties.

Following our discussion in chapter 4, environmental influences, such as the degree of policy conflict and the competition for members, should have a powerful impact on the types of membership benefits provided by groups. When programs cherished by individuals or institutions are under attack in a contentious policy environment, a call to rally around the issue may be enough to induce members to join an organization. At the same time, when two or more groups operate in the same policy area so that they compete for the same pool of members, we expect that groups will be more likely to provide selective incentives.

*Membership Composition Interaction Effects.* One of the most important characteristics of interest groups is the nature of their memberships. Some groups, as we have shown, are made up almost exclusively of the representatives of large, complex organizations, while others comprise mainly autonomous, individual citizens. Most scholarship on the rationality of joining interest groups has employed only autonomous individuals as the unit of analysis despite the obvious possibility that these two different types of members might very well react to some of the influences affecting interest groups in fundamentally different ways.

Individuals, for example, might react strongly to the development of a sharp political conflict over issues that directly affect them, while organizational representatives might find the same type of conflict less threatening, since they presumably keep the long-range interests of their institutions in mind when evaluating the daily flow of political events. Individuals, who do not possess the resources required to follow public policies in detail, may only realize that some cherished program is threatened at the time when sharp conflicts arise. We also expect that decentralized groups will have an easier time of engendering friendship among members, thereby more easily providing solidary benefits.

*Learning from Similar Groups.* As we argued when we presented the classification of American interest groups in fig. 4-1, the group system has emerged from two principal sources: occupational groupings and a series of broad social movements. As the American interest-group system has evolved, groups of the same general type have emulated each other as they have grown. Trade unions look to other trade unions to find which tactics and which mixes of benefits seem to achieve the best results, and, in the same way, trade associations tend to emulate other trade associations, professional societies copy other professional societies, and citizen groups look to other citizen groups to discover which fund-raising gambits or benefit packages to adopt. Groups thought to be successful will be imitated, and within each of the broad categories we have identified, a consensus emerges concerning the standard operating procedures that groups of a certain type should follow if they expect to thrive.

Is there evidence to support the speculations we have just marched through? Our subsequent discussion expands on results from multivariate tests presented in King and Walker 1989. Membership benefits that groups provide are strongly influenced by the circumstances in which they find themselves. If the group is involved in intense conflict over public policy, it is likely to conclude that members can be attracted mainly through the group's efforts to act as an effective representative of its members' interests. If a group is heavily supported by individual donors or private foundations, it is likely to place a heavy emphasis upon the importance of purposive benefits and to pay much less attention to solidary, personal, or professional benefits. In a way, patrons are paying for the collective benefits that others may consume. If members are mainly organizational representatives rather than individual citizens, group leaders will be tempted to place greater emphasis upon professional and purposive benefits.

In the opinion of group leaders, members are attracted to their associations mainly by the opportunities they find to advance themselves in their professions and by the role groups play as advocates and representatives in the political process. Most group leaders do not believe that solidary or personal material benefits are nearly as important as inducements for group membership. The leaders of citizen groups stand out because the purposive benefits they provide are the principal reasons people join their groups. These leaders clearly believe that the maintenance of their organizations depends on their success as representatives for their members or as advocates for a cause.

A few of the larger interest groups that operate in areas of low conflict and have high proportions of individuals as members are able to offer a wide array of selective material benefits, but few groups believe that these inducements are the key to their organizational viability. Oft-studied groups such as the AARP may fit Olson's predictions, but the overwhelming majority of interest groups in America solve their maintenance problems in ways Olson did not foresee.

While personal material benefits are not important for most groups, many associations provide extensive professional benefits (conferences, training seminars, and opportunities to make contacts with other professionals) as an important element in a strategy of group maintenance. These benefits cannot be obtained easily outside of the groups that provide them, and so they play the same functional role in group maintenance that Olson sketched out for personal material benefits. Professional benefits are available through groups of all types, but they are most likely to be employed by those groups that are based upon preexisting occupational communities in the profit and nonprofit sectors.

Professional benefits are useful mainly to groups made up of organizational representatives (rather than autonomous individuals) and to groups operating in a policy environment characterized by very little conflict. It is wrong, however, to conclude, as Olson does, that collective benefits are provided as a by-product of professional incentives, because groups can and do represent collective interests while offering no material incentives at all. Perhaps these professional benefits play the same functional role in organizational maintenance that Olson specified for personal material benefits, but support for Olson's by-product theory would have to show that purposive benefits are provided in conjunction with these material benefits (we will examine evidence on this point later in this chapter). Citizen groups, presumably the ones most in need of selective benefits to offset the costs of collective action, do not regard the professional, solidary, or personal material benefits as very important inducements for their members.

Groups emphasizing the importance of purposive benefits are mainly those in the profit and citizen sectors that are heavily engaged in conflict over public policies. As Hansen (1985) and Hardin (1982) have argued, when persons face a threat to their livelihood or to rights they already enjoy, they are more likely to engage in collective action to protect these gains despite the problems posed by the public goods dilemma. Groups that emphasize the importance of purposive benefits also typically are made up of organizational representatives presumably taking a long-range view of the interests of their organizations. If one holds the view that citizen sector groups pursue public goods while profit sector groups pursue private goods, that view is simply wrong. Groups of both types typically advance public policies with consequences that go well beyond their memberships.

Citizen sector groups supplying purposive benefits are very likely to rely heavily upon outside patrons rather than their members for financial support. Presumably, the patrons make investments in groups precisely because they are effective advocates for a cause or because they do a good job of representing the interests of a constituency that the patron wishes to see protected or promoted.

It is important to understand that not all members of interest groups are individual citizens deciding whether to send off small checks in response to appeals received through the mail from the Washington headquarters. Some group members are acting as representatives of large departments of city or state government or of business firms such as Ford Motor Company or Sears and Roebuck, which control billions of dollars worth of assets and employ hundreds of thousands of people. These huge organizations join interest groups in order to further the collective interests of their institutions. Such large firms are constrained by a complex web of legal rules, tax laws, and accounting practices, and their leaders clearly make different calculations about the costs and benefits of group membership than do individual citizens when determining whether to participate in collective action. Our findings suggest that institutions are often more concerned than individual citizens with gaining representation, having an opportunity to play a role in public affairs, and in the attainment of broad collective goals. In order to wield influence in Washington, one often must conduct campaigns in the mass media that are meant to transform public opinion, or one must engage in a program of intensive lobbying that lasts over a period of years.

Though the general tendency is that institutions and institutional members underwrite the provision of collective goods, there are several groups made up almost exclusively of autonomous individuals (rather than institutional members) that place strong emphasis upon purposive benefits. In almost all cases, however, their budgets are very heavily subsidized by patrons (foundations, wealthy individuals, or government agencies) who, like the institutional members of other groups, are dedicated as organizations to the long-term promotion of certain public goods. On average, nearly 40 percent of the budgets of the citizen groups in our sample is supplied by patrons—a level of support four times higher than the average received by groups in the profit sector whose memberships are most heavily made up of institutional representatives.

### A Challenge to Olson's By-product Theory

Mancur Olson's by-product theory of benefit provision asserts that interest groups able to engage in the pursuit of collective goals will be those "that obtain their strength and support because they perform some function in addition to lobbying for collective goods" (Olson 1965, 132). Groups must attract and hold their members by providing them with benefits that they could not obtain outside the group, thus freeing the leadership to engage in the pursuit of collective goals as a by-product of their successful use of selective benefits. One unsatisfying aspect of the by-product theory is that Olson fails to explain why groups would ever decide to provide collective goods if their organizations are doing so well by simply providing material incentives. If Olson is right, and rational actors are joining groups just to get the selective enticements they are offered, then why would a group ever do something as economically taxing as taking on the concentrated costs of providing the by-product collective good?

We do not doubt that some people join groups such as the Sierra Club in order to participate in the hikes and canoe trips it sponsors, even though they disagree with the association's position on water pollution controls or exploration for oil. There also are cases when policy entrepreneurs may literally capture a group originally designed to pursue an entirely different, apolitical goal. Hardin refers to certain environmental lobbying groups where staff members piggybacked their public policy concerns onto groups that originally "were just conservation and nature appreciation organizations whose infrastructures have since been borrowed by environmentalists" (1982, 43).

If organizations arc, indccd, bcing piggybacked by entrepreneurs to provide collective goods, then one might say that the purposive benefits are a by-product of these other activities. But to say that making collective benefits a by-product of other activities is possible is not the same as saying that it is common or even likely. The central findings of our analysis point to the conclusion that the by-product theory may not be generalizable. Our findings suggest that there are situations in which interest groups not only seek to attract members by promising collective goods, but they also choose, at the same timc, to dccmphasize or even eliminate most other benefits.

In order to discover whether groups that emphasize purposive benefits decide to deemphasize other forms of inducements at the same time—a finding that would run directly counter to the by-product theory—we employ a dependent variable that reflects the ratio of purposive benefits to total benefits emphasized. For example, if a group leader answered "one of the most important benefits provided" to all three questions making up our index of purposive benefits (see table 5-6) and answered "not provided" to every other member benefit, then our "trade-off ratio" would be 1 to 1. We calculated trade-off ratios for every group and then rescaled the measure to range from 0 to 100. The higher the value, the more a group emphasized purposive benefits above and beyond all others.[8]

Groups that emphasize purposive benefits over and above other incentives may serve a diverse set of constituencies—not just the citizen sector groups that have received most of the scholarly attention. Among the groups scoring highest on the trade-off variable are Common Cause, the National Association of Railroad Passengers, and the National Association of Manufacturers, a very diverse set of associations. Near the bottom of the scale are

---

8. Construction of the variables presented in table 5-7 are discussed in King and Walker 1989. All of the independent variables range from 0 to 1, and, except for the group type intercepts, the variables were constructed to be as nearly continuous as possible.

**TABLE 5-7.  Model Estimates Reflecting a Trade-off between an Emphasis on Purposive as Opposed to Other Membership Benefits**

|  | Trade-off for Purposive or Collective Benefits |
|---|---|
| Structural influences | |
| Group decentralization | 2.24 |
| | (4.07) |
| Group size—autonomous individuals | 1.07 |
| | (8.99) |
| Group size—organizational representatives | −22.27*** |
| | (7.08) |
| Membership composition | |
| Percent autonomous individuals (PAI) | −27.85*** |
| | (6.47) |
| Interaction of PAI with policy conflict | 5.93 |
| | (6.99) |
| Interaction of PAI with group decentralization | −0.31 |
| | (5.79) |
| Financial variables | |
| Group resources | 10.49* |
| | (5.57) |
| Percentage of budget from patrons | 17.54*** |
| | (4.69) |
| Environmental influences | |
| Policy conflict | 15.03*** |
| | (5.05) |
| Competition for members | 0.49 |
| | (2.41) |
| Group-type intercepts | |
| Profit sector groups | 30.26 |
| Mixed sector groups | 21.99 |
| Nonprofit sector groups | 22.36 |
| Citizen groups | 41.40 |
| Unions | 39.72 |
| Standard error of estimate | 26.19 |
| $R^2$ | 0.20 |
| df | 780 |

*Source:* 1985 Survey.

*Notes:* See text for descriptions of the variables. The independent variables are scaled to range from 0 to 1. The dependent variable ranges from 0 to 100. Entries in the table are unstandardized regression coefficients with standard errors in parentheses. For example, a one unit increase in policy conflict (from low conflict to high conflict) is associated with an increase of 15.03 in the trade-off in favor of purposive benefits against material benefits.

*$p < .05$.     **$p < .01$.     ***$p < .001$.

several professional organizations, including the American Production and Inventory Control Society and the American Society of Pharmacy Law. What kinds of circumstances foster the provision of purposive benefits within such a varied set of groups?

The patterns of coefficients in table 5-7 provide powerful evidence that interest groups clearly attempt to solve Olson's collective goods dilemma without making their efforts a mere by-product of other activities. Groups that are engaged in conflict, are composed mainly of organizational representatives rather than autonomous individuals, and are receiving a large proportion of their budgets from outside patrons often trade off purposive against all forms of material and solidary incentives. Olson's by-product theory may fit some groups, but it is clear that it does not describe all groups, otherwise the coefficients shown in table 5-7 would not be so striking. Groups in the American system can and do provide collective benefits regardless of the selective material incentives offered.

Three major influences conspire to undermine Olson's by-product theory: (1) members representing institutions are more likely than autonomous individuals to value the pursuit of collective goods; (2) group patrons and large donors who subsidize associations place a high value upon representation before government and are not interested in paying for benefits that are distributed to individual group members; and (3) once a threatening environment of conflict emerges, autonomous individuals are more likely to realize that cherished rights, programs, or group goals are threatened and are increasingly willing to join and support groups in exchange for only purposive benefits. Though there undoubtedly are groups that provide purposive benefits only as a by-product of other activities, our data show that there are many groups featuring collective goods as *the* major inducement to their members. If groups such as People for the American Way or the Federation for American Immigration Relief felt the need to provide other membership benefits to maintain their organizations, we believe that they would, but it is clear that many groups in our sample maintain their organizations by promoting collective goods while promising little else. Patrons stand at the center of a common solution to Olson's collective goods dilemma. Financial support is usually provided to groups for a purpose, and patrons expect to receive benefits in return for their aid. Those benefits often revolve around the pursuit of collective goods.

## Patrons and Public Policy

Beginning with efforts to improve agriculture at the turn of the century and continuing through the War on Poverty in the 1960s, most American social policies have been highly elaborate cooperative efforts involving many levels of government in the federal system and both private and public corporations. Federal agencies have an interest in encouraging coordination among the elements of these complex service delivery systems and in improving the diffusion of new ideas and techniques. Groups like the American Public Transit Association or the American Council on Education, both of which receive extensive patronage from federal agencies and private foundations, serve as centers of professional development and informal channels for administrative coordination in an otherwise unwieldy governmental system.

Besides their administrative and professional functions, however, groups obviously also play an important political role, and most patrons are fully aware of this role when they agree to provide financial aid. There are many types of patrons, each with a distinctive interest in public affairs. One of the chief reasons that business firms join trade associations, for example, is their desire to secure sympathetic public policies or to mount effective defenses against government regulation.

Government agencies organize their constituents not only to improve coordination in the federal system, but also to lobby Congress and the presidency on their behalf. The social movements and political upheavals of the 1970s prompted many individuals and foundations to act as patrons for a variety of challenging groups. Several of the country's largest foundations only began serious operations in the 1950s and were in search of a meaningful role in American life (see Commission on Foundations and Private Philanthropy 1970; Goulden 1971; Nielson 1972). Foundation officials believed that the long-run stability of the representative policy-making system would be assured only if legitimate organizational channels could be provided for the frustration and anger being expressed in protests and outbreaks of political violence during the 1960s and 1970s (see Marris and Rein 1973). Another important form of patronage came from already established interest groups, which assisted in the creation of new groups in their fields, especially if these new organizations promised to perform services or reach constituencies that had not yet been exploited by existing organizations. Public policy concerns may not always be the primary consideration when assistance is granted, but patrons are not likely to support groups that do not share their general approach to social policy.

A graphic illustration of the close match between the interests of patrons and the general attitudes of the groups they patronize is provided by the data in table 5-8. All respondents in the 1980 survey were asked whether, in general, they favored more, less, or the present level of government provision of social services. They were also asked whether the policy of their associations called for more, less, or the present level of regulation of business and industry. The responses to these two questions were combined to produce a

**TABLE 5-8.   Relationship between Receipt of Government Financial Aid and Support for Increased Government Intervention in Society, in Percentages**

| Receipt of Government Funds | Desired Level of Government Intervention | | |
| --- | --- | --- | --- |
| | More | Present Level | Less |
| Yes | 46.1 | 30.9 | 32.0 |
| No | 21.4 | 16.6 | 62.0 |
| | $N = 319$ | Tau-$b$ = .32 | |

*Source:* 1980 Survey.

three-point scale measuring the respondent's overall preference for governmental intervention in the society. The findings in table 5-8 are from the 1980 survey, and our 1985 survey yielded almost identical results.

The strong relationship shown in table 5-8 speaks for itself. Groups receiving money from government agencies are much more likely than those not receiving funds to believe that an expansion of governmental activity would be desirable. Government agencies make grants or issue contracts to improve the training of professionals, to increase citizens' understanding of public policies, or to encourage local bureaucracies to employ the most effective administrative practices. While carrying out these more-or-less neutral programmatic and administrative tasks, the agencies are also furthering their own political objectives.

### Patrons of Political Action and the Theory of Groups

Patrons of political action play a crucial role in the initiation and maintenance of interest groups. This does not mean that Olson's emphasis on the incentives facing likely group members is misplaced, or that Salisbury's ideas about the importance of entrepreneurial leadership are wrong. Our attention certainly should not shift entirely away from groups toward the motives and activities of patrons. This analysis, however, points to another important method, beyond the provision of selective benefits and the use of coercion, that groups have employed to cope with Olson's dilemma of collective action.

Efforts to form new groups and associations have occurred in every decade of the past century, but David Truman was surely correct in arguing that the propensity to form groups increases during periods of general social upheaval, as in the 1930s and 1960s, when challengers to the established order may ride upon great outbursts of protest and the political leadership is divided (Gamson 1975; Jenkins and Perrow 1977; Goldstone 1980). No matter what propensities exist, however, large amounts of capital are needed to form most interest groups. The key to success in these efforts usually is the ability of group organizers to secure both start-up funds and reliable sources of continuing financial support from patrons of political action. Furthermore, now that two decades have passed since the turmoil of the 1960s, it is clear that most of the groups founded in the wake of the civil rights and peace movements that were unable to secure adequate patronage have disappeared. The much-publicized effort during this period to organize college students, for example, failed in large part because no patron could ever be attracted who was willing to back the effort; or, as in the case of the National Student Association, one of the patrons that was secured proved to be so unpopular with the potential membership that its sponsorship seriously damaged the group's credibility. The NSA almost collapsed in 1967 after revelations that it had been receiving financial aid for years from the Central Intelligence Agency (Meyer 1980).

The stormy history of Students for a Democratic Society (SDS) illustrates the importance of patronage in the maintenance of challenging groups. The SDS started in 1959 as an effort to challenge the conservative political consensus prevailing on American college campuses during the Eisenhower years. The group began as an affiliate of the League for Industrial Democracy (LID), a small, socialist organization that had itself been supported for several decades mainly by private gifts. After a bitter controversy in the early 1960s in which the LID threatened to withdraw its support over supposed communist infiltration, SDS quickly grew from the dedicated band of 150 activists who gathered in Port Huron, Michigan, in 1962 to ratify its manifesto into a vigorous organization with over 20,000 dues-paying members in 1966. Besides its campus activities, SDS employed more than 300 full-time field workers engaged in grass roots community organizing in several large, industrial cities. Dues and private gifts were important sources of funds during this period, but the principal income of SDS was a series of grants from the United Auto Workers to conduct the SDS campaign of community organization and much of the group's publishing and issues research.

Factional infighting intensified in the late 1960s as the group became a kind of revolutionary vanguard rather than a broadly based student movement. Despite warnings from some of its leaders, SDS soon took itself beyond the ideological reach of the UAW, which finally terminated its grants. This withdrawal of patronage led almost immediately to a collapse of the group's staff and organizational center. Having drifted beyond the normative boundaries of the political system as defined by the values of its principal patrons, SDS soon disintegrated, first into brawling factions of extreme radicals and finally into the terrorist fantasies of the Weathermen, whose activities eventually were primarily financed by robbing banks.[9]

Changes in the structure of the interest-group system cannot be understood only through the study of shifts in public opinion or the clever tactics of innovative leaders. The success of efforts to create and maintain political interest groups also depends upon such legal and institutional factors as the provisions of the tax code governing the ability of business firms to claim deductions for the expenses of lobbying, subsidies in the form of reduced postal rates for nonprofit groups heavily dependent upon direct mail solicitation, the availability of financial support from regulatory agencies for groups that wish to testify at administrative hearings, the rules concerning the registration of lobbyists and the financial disclosures they are required to make, legal restraints on the accessibility of foundations, and many other policies and actions by government or other patrons that either stimulate or inhibit the process of political mobilization. The number of interest groups and their rate of growth are heavily influenced by the incentives, supports, and opportunities created through public policies and legal provisions, and most governments, naturally enough, choose to promote the mobilization of their allies, as the Johnson administration did through the War on Poverty, Model Cities, VISTA, the Older Americans Act, and many other programs of social reform; or to frustrate or demobilize their antagonists as the Reagan administration seems to have done through budget cuts in the discretionary programs of the Great Society, raises in postal rates, and challenges to the nonprofit status of several groups and publishing enterprises (Mackenzie 1981; Peterson 1981; Stanfield 1981; Babcock 1982; Seaberry 1982).

The energy that drives the process of group formation may come from below in the form of social movements arising out of widespread popular discontent, or from individual political entrepreneurs operating largely on their own. Initiative may also come from above in the form of efforts by trade unions, government agencies, private corporations, churches, and other large organizations in the public and private sectors sponsoring groups that they believe will further their interests. Wealthy individuals and private foundations often take the lead in promoting groups designed to mobilize large segments of the public in support of controversial causes. Without the influence of patrons of political action, the flourishing system of interest groups in the United States would be much smaller and would include very few groups seeking to obtain broad collective or public goods. If all sources of patronage suddenly disappeared, the interest-group system would immediately shrink

---

9. For the history of the SDS, see Newfield 1966 (83–108); Adelson 1972; Barbrook and Bolt 1980 (274–89); for a similar account of the Student Nonviolent Coordinating Committee, see Carson 1981.

until it included only a small set of highly unstable insurgent groups that would remain in existence only as long as they were able to command the loyalty of some aroused segment of the public and another set of more stable associations that represented only small, tightly knit, commercial, occupational, ethnic, or religious communities, those groups able to draw successfully upon the resources of their members to meet their operating expenses.

Our findings lead to the principal conclusion that the number of interest groups in operation, the mixture of group types, and the level and direction of political mobilization in the United States at any point in the country's history will largely be determined by the composition and accessibility of the system's major patrons of political action. The American system of political patronage has grown dramatically and become more diversified during the past three decades, so that many new opportunities have arisen for aspiring political entrepreneurs of both liberal and conservative persuasions. As the patronage system has grown, so have the number and variety of interest groups. The key to the origins and maintenance of interest groups in the United States lies in the ability and willingness of the patrons of political action to expand the representative system by sponsoring groups that speak for newly emerging elements of society and promote new legislative agendas and social values.

CHAPTER 6

# Pathways to Influence in American Politics

*Thomas L. Gais and Jack L. Walker, Jr.*

There are many pathways to influence in the American political system and some of the largest interest groups carry out several kinds of activities at once, but in order to bring pressure upon government officials most groups concentrate either on an "inside" strategy of conventional lobbying or an "outside" strategy meant to shape and mobilize public opinion. Inside activities are designed to convince public officials to take some form of action or to modify an established policy by means of close consultation with political and administrative leaders, relying mainly on financial resources, substantive expertise, and concentration within certain congressional constituencies as a basis for influence. Outside activities may sometimes be merely an indirect effort to exert influence upon the outcome of a specific policy decision—only a supplement to a campaign based mainly upon inside strategies—but they are often intended to build support within the general public for an entirely new set of values that may eventually be manifested in public policy many years in the future.

The choice between these political strategies is a fundamental one usually made early in a group's history that orients the organization's tactical decisions throughout much of its life. This stability grows out of the strong roots of these strategic choices, which are intertwined with the group's constituency and resources, as well as with crucial aspects of its political environment. The political strategies of interest groups, like the financial strategies discussed in the previous chapter, are not adopted or changed by interest group leaders at will but, rather, depend on previous decisions and the particular institutional and political environments they face.

The correlates of these strategic choices are important because they tell us a great deal about our political system and the problems of institutional design. If groups representing different types of interests also adopt distinct political strategies, then any institutional reforms or other changes that restrict a particular strategy may have a biased impact on how well various interests are represented. More subtle implications would arise if we find certain conditions to be critical in the adoption of a particular strategy—such as the availability of patronage or the ease of setting up federated structures within associations—since regulations affecting those conditions would also affect the nature and scope of interest-group advocacy. Questions about interest-group strategies become particularly significant when we consider their aggregate effects. A political system in which inside strategies are predominant is likely to be quite different from one in which outside strategies are common or even the primary method of advocating interests—different in the interests represented, in the systems' capacities for comprehensive change, in the autonomy of elective and executive institutions, and in the precision and types of political issues raised.

In this chapter we seek to explain the choice of strategies by interest groups in their search for influence. We ask why some groups confine themselves to inside strategies of legislative lobbying while others go outside with broadly targeted campaigns of political education. To put the question more precisely, what are the principal factors in the organizational structure and environment of interest groups that determine their operational priorities? And more broadly, what implications are there for the political system in the way interest groups cope with the financial, social, and organizational realities prevailing in America during the 1980s and 1990s?

## The Choice of Strategies by Interest Groups

The first priority for group leaders is to find an organizational strategy that will ensure the continued existence of their group, and their choice of tactics usually arises out of this search (Wilson 1973, 30–32). It is a rare group leader who, out of devotion to principle, knowingly adopts tactics that will lead to the group's destruction. Interest groups, in an effort to attract resources, search for strategies that will appeal to their members or their principal patrons.

The most important factor determining the level of political activity engaged in by interest groups is the amount of conflict they experience in their immediate political environment.[1] Some policy areas are fraught with conflict and supply the central topics of controversy that divide the national political parties, while other policy areas long ago settled down into virtual consensus and continue to operate with little change, no matter what the election results and the comings and goings of presidents and legislators.[2] The interest groups

---

1. See Schattschneider 1960 on how private conflicts lead to group politicization. Policy conflict also plays an important role in political activation within pluralist thought (Dahl 1961; Truman 1971). For an empirical study that finds that, in a local setting, conflict explains patterns of group mobilization better than social structure, see Crenson 1983.

2. See, for example, Ripley and Franklin's discussion of the different kinds of politics associated with distributive, redistributive, and regulatory policies (1980). For an earlier statement of this general theme, see Lowi 1964.

that operate within these different political worlds adjust their strategic priorities to the degree of conflict or consensus existing in their immediate environments. If a group is operating in a policy area marked by conflict, one in which many organized groups are advancing different political interests and policy alternatives, both members and patrons will increase their demands for political or purposive benefits in return for group support, and the conflictual environment will produce incentives for interest groups to increase their involvement in all kinds of political action.

Once political activity begins, the choice of whether to adopt an inside or outside strategy depends on the organizational resources under a group's control, the character of its membership, and its principal sources of financial support. Organizational resources are important because they determine how much a group can accomplish. A small group with an inexperienced staff must restrict its activity to a narrow range of activities, no matter how much conflict it experiences. Once the group's organizational resources begin to increase, it may adopt different kinds of political tactics. A decentralized organization composed of many local or regional subunits whose staff members are involved in political and civic networks at the city and state level all over the country may seriously consider launching a national campaign of political education or grass roots mobilization. A large central staff headquartered in Washington, on the other hand, permits the group to engage in policy research if it wishes, place staff members on the advisory committees of federal agencies, and otherwise nurture the connections between the group and sympathetic public officials through an inside political strategy.

The character of a group's membership is another determining factor in the choice of strategies, because the members determine the goals of the association. The survival of the organization is assured only as long as it is able to maintain the approval of its members, so its leaders normally must direct all the efforts to advancing those values and policies that are of direct concern to the membership. Groups that draw their membership and most of their financial support from a closely knit professional or occupational community, for example, must be careful to choose political tactics and issues that seem to advance or protect the immediate collective interests of that group. Groups with a far-flung membership united only by their dedication to a cause, on the other hand, are naturally drawn toward controversial issues and tactics that will capture the attention of their diffuse membership and demonstrate that they are a consequential group, worthy of continued support.

The character of group membership is captured in our typology of groups based on members' occupational roles. Groups organized around occupational communities in the profit sector can be expected to have a relatively narrow policy focus built around the professional or commercial interests of their members. The representatives of prestigious professions or businesses are usually granted privileged access to government officials (Lindblom 1977) and typically prefer to restrict the scope of the conflict surrounding the policy questions that concern them. It is to their advantage to operate within the smallest and most exclusive governmental forums, as far out of public view as possible, and thus they usually prefer inside to outside strategies.

Groups based upon occupational communities in the nonprofit sector—such as social workers, health-care providers, educators, or social service professionals—are often closely associated with government agencies operating in their policy areas. Sometimes these groups were actually started at the suggestion of federal officials or even with their assistance, and these officials remain in close contact with the leaders of the groups after the associations are launched. Social service professionals often act as advocates for their clients and, thus, sometimes engage in campaigns of public education or agitation. For the most part, the desires of their members to protect their professional standing and the requirements of organizational maintenance arising from their close association with federal agencies encourage groups with members from the nonprofit sector to avoid controversy and seek influence through inside political strategies. Citizen groups based upon a cause or idea and open to anyone have members scattered across the entire country who normally are not tied together through routine contacts within occupational communities. Members of citizen groups often participate only by contributing small amounts of money or, on rare occasions, by contacting a legislator at the group's request. The loyalties of group members in citizen groups must be continually reinforced. Much of what they know about the achievements of their group they learn through reports in the mass media, so that citizen groups are almost forced into an outside strategy of public persuasion and political mobilization.

Another factor that we rely upon to explain the choice of group tactics is the nature of the financial support received by groups. Many groups depend almost entirely upon membership dues to meet their expenses, while others rely heavily upon sympathetic patrons who sponsor the group's activities with gifts, grants, or service contracts. Most groups rely upon several different sources of funding and are not entirely beholden to any single patron, but group leaders cannot ignore the political goals or preferences of their patrons any more than the needs of their dues-paying members. The choice of political strategies is intimately connected to the group's prospects for organizational maintenance. For example, government agencies, like most established bureaucracies, prefer that their political environments be both supportive and predictable. Open partisan struggles, provocative public debates, and protest demonstrations are avoided whenever possible. Given these fundamental objectives, government agencies are not likely to support most citizen groups, especially those that are dedicated to raising controversial issues and mobilizing dissatisfied people. Government agencies may be expected, instead, to favor groups that engage in supportive activities, such as policy research, demonstration projects, direct service provision, and conventional forms of legislative lobbying. Most support from government goes to groups based upon public service occupations that are disposed toward an expansion of government services, groups that are seldom engaged in the kind of political activities that would expand the scope of the conflict in unpredictable ways. Some government support goes to citizen groups, and even to a small number of trade associations and business groups in the profit sector, but, as we demonstrated in chapter 5, government patronage is concentrated in the non-profit sector.[3]

We also would expect groups based upon occupational or commercial communities that support themselves primarily through membership dues without help from external patrons to concentrate mainly upon inside strategies of political influence. Such groups are under pressure to address the personal, immediate, professional, or financial concerns of their membership rather than vague collective goals that might eventually benefit many individuals who have made no contribution toward the maintenance of the group. Citizen groups that depend for support upon membership dues or private foundations and individual philanthropists, on the other hand, are most likely to employ outside strategies of political influence. Members that join groups of this kind do so in order to demonstrate their support for certain collective values, and they expect the group to advance these concerns as vigorously as possible. Private patrons that support citizen groups often show a pronounced affinity toward broad efforts to reshape public attitudes or values—activities that can be regarded as legitimate expressions of opinion in a free society—rather than specific lobbying campaigns that might stimulate an angry legislative backlash against the patrons themselves. The factors we have identified are most consequential in determining the choice of group tactics early in the history of an association, but once members are attracted, a staff is recruited, and administrative routines are established, it is not easy to change course. A group that begins its life dedicated to campaigns of grass roots agitation and political mobilization, for example, will find it very difficult to shift its strategy toward intensive negotiations with officials in regulatory agencies or congressional committees, even if circumstances call for such a change in

---

3. A tendency for government agencies to subsidize the more supportive, predictable professional associations rather than the more volatile citizen groups was found in a related comparative study of education policies in France and the United States (Baumgartner 1989a; Baumgartner and Walker 1989). Many education groups in both nations received financial support from government: 50 percent of the education groups in the United States, and 60 percent in France. Most of these groups had memberships in the nonprofit sector, and the grants generally went to the oldest, richest, and largest groups in both countries. Government subsidies tended to go to groups that followed inside strategies and that reinforced the existing group structures.

tactics. Their members have not joined the group to support this kind of activity, and the group's staff lack the knowledge or experience needed to pursue such tactics. Because of this form of organizational inertia, choices about strategies by established groups result from their efforts to cope with the political environments they face and the needs and inclinations of their members and patrons, moderated by the tactical styles adopted early in their histories.

Our explanation of the choice of strategies by interest groups accounts for organizational inertia and for both external and internal influences upon group decisions. Our aim in this chapter is to test several hypotheses derived from our theory empirically. We are limited in our analysis by data from a cross-sectional sample of interest groups operating at the national level of government, so we will not be able to provide evidence for some of the dynamic elements of our explanation. Nevertheless, the analysis in this chapter identifies some of the most important factors that determine the choice of strategies and individual tactics by interest groups and provides a sound basis for further elaboration of our theory.

## Measures of Inside and Outside Strategies

We seek to explain why groups engage in one form of political action rather than another, so the first step in our analysis must be to develop measures of our dependent variables: inside and outside political strategies. Our measures of these two strategies are based on our 1980 survey respondents' estimates of the importance to their organizations of 22 different activities normally engaged in by interest groups, including such things as conducting or organizing research, applying for grants or contracts, and answering questions or handling requests for service or aid from the membership of the association. Respondents were asked to determine the "relative importance" of each activity for the "work of this association" by indicating whether the activity was very important, important, not very important, or not engaged in at all.[4]

Eight of our questions concerned political tactics or activities intended to affect political institutions or politically significant outside groups. These included working for the passage of needed legislation, working to improve the administration of government programs, insuring the election of political leaders sympathetic to the goals of the association, engaging in litigation of class action lawsuits, organizing conferences and meetings for interested lay-

---

4. Chapter 6 relies only on data from the 1980 survey because the analyses based on the 1985 survey were still underway at the time of Jack Walker's death. The chapter is based on material originally written in 1983. Rather than try to guess Jack's final interpretations of any differences between the 1980 and 1985 survey results, we chose to restrict this analysis to the earlier survey.—Editors.

**TABLE 6-1.  Percentage of Interest Groups Reporting That Each of Eight Political Tactics Is Important to Their Organization**

| Activity | N | Percentage Reporting That Activity Is Important or Very Important |
|---|---|---|
| Administrative lobbying | 559 | 80.1 |
| Legislative lobbying | 559 | 78.0 |
| Working with mass media | 557 | 71.6 |
| Providing speakers | 561 | 67.9 |
| Sponsoring lay conferences | 552 | 35.5 |
| Litigating | 560 | 31.6 |
| Electioneering | 559 | 22.9 |
| Protesting or demonstrating | 557 | 6.5 |

*Source:* 1980 Survey.

men, citizens or other nonspecialists, developing publicity or otherwise drawing the attention of the mass media to important developments in this field, providing speakers or other program materials for other groups and associations, and carrying out public demonstrations or protests.

Of these eight activities, administrative and legislative lobbying were the most widely viewed as important tactics. Table 6-1 shows the perceived significance of direct lobbying activities by displaying the percentage of groups that reported a tactic was "important" or "very important" to their organizations in the 1980 survey. Just below these lobbying activities in importance were three methods of communicating with outside publics: working with the mass media to increase publicity and public attention for certain developments, providing speakers or materials for other groups, and, though much lower in importance, organizing lay conferences. Litigation activities were important to less than a third of the groups in the sample, while electoral activities were significant to less than a quarter.[5] As might have been expected, protests and demonstrations were important tactics to only a small proportion of the associations.

5. The relatively small percentage of groups reporting involvement in elections was not an artifact of sampling associations rather than their affiliated political action committees or, to use the legal term, "separate segregated funds." In a related study, U.S. federal election records for the 1979–80 election cycle were examined to determine whether the membership associations in the 1980 Michigan Survey had separate segregated funds: only 17 percent did, most of them trade associations in the profit sector (Gais 1983). A few membership associations reported that electioneering was important to them, even though they did not sponsor PACs. Informal interviews suggested that most of these groups were communicating with their members through internal publications, activities usually not viewed as political expenditures or contributions under federal regulations and, thus, not requiring a PAC.

**TABLE 6-2.   Inside and Outside Strategies as Factors Underlying Specific Activities of Interest Groups**

| Activity | Factor 1 (Inside) | Factor 2 (Outside) |
|---|---|---|
| Legislative lobbying | 0.83 | 0.10 |
| Administrative lobbying | 0.73 | 0.06 |
| Litigating | 0.67 | 0.13 |
| Electioneering | 0.53 | 0.10 |
| Working with mass media | 0.39 | 0.55 |
| Protesting or demonstrating | 0.18 | 0.55 |
| Providing speakers | 0.13 | 0.75 |
| Sponsoring lay conferences | −0.13 | 0.82 |

*Source:* 1980 Survey.
*Note:* Entries are factor weights after varimax rotation.

These eight political tactics allow for many different combinations of priorities by groups. Our explanation is based, however, on the assumption that underlying these eight measures of political activity are two dimensions: one representing the inside strategy and the other the outside strategy. The existence of these two dimensions was confirmed by a factor analysis of the correlation matrix of the eight measures.[6] There were two steps in the analysis. First, a principal-axes analysis yielded two uncorrelated factors, and then the axes were rotated according to the varimax criterion, a solution that maximizes the variance of the loadings. The results of this analysis are displayed in table 6-2, where two clearly identifiable factors appear, one made up of the measures of lobbying, litigation, and electioneering; and the other composed of the efforts to generate publicity and mold public opinion.[7] Efforts to draw "the attention of the mass media to important developments" in a group's policy area load on both factors, indicating that this activity is often engaged in even by groups that follow a predominantly inside strategy, but our results indicate that interest groups usually employ mixtures of two fairly distinct clusters of political tactics in their efforts to seek influence.[8]

6. Each measurement variable is a four-point scale ranging from one (activity not engaged in) to four (activity is very important).

7. For excellent discussions of the subtle ways in which a group's electoral activities might supplement or strengthen an inside strategy, see Hall and Wayman 1990 and Wright 1990.

8. The close correlation between litigation and other inside tactics diverges somewhat from the findings in chap. 9, which show that some uses of litigation are related to inside strategies while others are related to outside strategies (see, in particular, table 9-3). Unfortunately, the 1980 survey, which is used in this chapter, did not ask respondents to make distinctions between the different aspects of their litigation activities, as did the 1985 survey used in chap. 9. We would guess that many of the litigation activities measured in the 1980 survey derived from suits filed on behalf of members.

Our factor analysis shows that it is reasonable to combine the responses of groups into two linear combinations, one containing the four measures that loaded on the inside strategy factor, and the other containing the four measures that loaded on the outside strategy factor. We constructed each of the two indices by standardizing the four original measurement variables, calculating their sum, and then restandardizing the resulting score. The sample mean of each index, in other words, will be equal to zero and its sample standard deviation will be equal to one.

## Factors Determining Interest Group Strategies

We believe that the choices of political strategies by interest groups are largely a function of four factors: (1) the degree of conflict in the political environments they face, (2) the groups' internal organizational resources, (3) the character of their memberships, and (4) the principal sources of their financial support.

*Political Environment.* We have employed two measures that capture the most important aspects of the political environments of interest groups. First, we asked our respondents whether there were any "associations or groups" with whom they found themselves "in disagreement or opposition." About 59 percent of our respondents were able to identify an organized opponent, but 41 percent could not. Our second measure of political environment was based on a question about changes in the relationship between groups and the government brought about by the 1976 election in which President Gerald Ford, a Republican, was replaced by Democratic President Jimmy Carter. Groups that reported either an important or moderate increase in cooperation (about 20 percent of the total) or those that reported an important or moderate decrease in cooperation (about 15 percent of the total) were indicating that they had a larger stake in the outcome of the partisan struggle than other groups and, thus, were more likely to take action to compensate for or take some advantage of the outcome of national elections. The important impact of increased conflict upon the operational priorities of interest groups is clearly portrayed in table 6-3, which reports the relationship between the amount of conflict existing in a group's political environment and the emphasis it places on either inside or outside political strategies. When there is no organized opposition for a group and it experienced no change in its relationship with government as a result of the 1976 election, it is much less likely than the sample (as a whole) to engage in either inside or outside strategies, but as

---

Also note that the measures of inside and outside strategies used in this chapter differ in other ways from their construction in chap. 9, but these other differences are not substantive. In fact, we believe that these inside and outside dimensions are general enough to underlie many variations in construction and specific survey items.

**TABLE 6-3.  Conflict and the Importance of Political Activities**

| Level of Conflict | N | Inside Strategy | Outside Strategy |
|---|---|---|---|
| Organized opposition and sensitive to party shifts | 138 | 0.42 | 0.32 |
| Organized opposition or sensitive to party shifts | 196 | 0.23 | −0.06 |
| Neither organized opposition nor sensitive to party shifts | 148 | −0.54 | −0.41 |

*Source:* 1980 Survey.
*Note:* Entries are means of standardized activity indices.

conflict increases, groups begin to report a greater emphasis upon both types of political activity. These data reveal the strong impact of conflict on the propensity of groups to engage in political activity. Conflict seems to propel groups into political activity, where they employ either an inside or outside strategy, whichever is compatible with their requirements for organizational maintenance.

*Organizational Resources.* We are aware that any single measure fails to capture all the subtle features of interest-group operations and contains a certain amount of error, but we believe that the two items we have chosen, the size of a group's central staff and the existence of local chapters or subunits, provide a rough approximation of the organizational resources at the command of interest-group leaders. Staff size was chosen as an indicator of a group's organizational resources rather than its revenues or expenditures because political activities are generally labor intensive—often depending more on the number of persons working for the group than the size of their salaries or the group's capital expenditures. In any case, the choice of measure will have little impact on our findings, since, as we point out in chapter 5, most interest groups spend over 80 percent of their budgets on personnel and the correlation between staff size and budget size for groups in our sample was $r = .90$.

Our second indicator of organizational resources is based upon whether a group maintains local offices, chapters, headquarters, or other such organized bodies below the level of the central staff and headquarters. About 48 percent of our 1980 respondents maintain organized subunits. The existence of subordinate units may constrain group leaders, in some cases, or require the use of scarce resources simply to maintain the structure, but groups that operate subunits are better equipped to mobilize their membership for political action, and, for this reason, we regard the more elaborate organizational form as an important internal resource.

Evidence of the importance of organizational resources as determinants of the choice of tactics is reported in table 6-4. The pattern of relationships between our two measures of organizational resources and group strategies

**TABLE 6-4. Effect of Organizational Resources on the Choice of Political Strategies by Interest Groups**

| Size of Group Staff | N | Inside Strategy | Outside Strategy |
|---|---|---|---|
| Large[a] | | | |
|   Subunits | 154 | 0.26 | 0.37 |
|   No subunits | 109 | 0.16 | −0.33 |
| Small[b] | | | |
|   Subunits | 93 | −0.23 | 0.25 |
|   No subunits | 157 | −0.23 | −0.46 |

*Source:* 1980 Survey.
*Note:* Entries are means of standardized activity indices.
[a]Twelve or more FTEs.
[b]Fewer than 12 FTEs.

displayed in this table shows that the larger the size of a group's staff, the more likely it will be engaged in inside strategies, while the presence of subunits is clearly related to a preference for outside strategies. These findings suggest that inside strategies require a larger, and presumably more specialized, central staff operating in Washington, while outside strategies require more decentralized organizational structures that facilitate contact with members located beyond the nation's capital.

*Group Membership.* Powerful evidence of the importance of the character of group membership in determining the choice of tactics is contained in figure 6-1. The bars in this graph represent the balance between the use of inside and outside strategies by groups with different types of members. We determined this balance by subtracting a group's score on the inside strategy index from its score on the outside strategy index, creating a measure of the group's relative emphasis on these two strategies. The higher the score, the more a group relies on outside rather than inside strategies. Lower scores show that the group focuses its efforts on inside strategies. We then calculated the mean of the resulting outside-inside index for each of the four types of groups. The data clearly demonstrate the sharp differences in tactical priorities between citizen groups, whose preference overwhelmingly is for outside strategies, and those groups whose members come mainly from the profit sector, which lean heavily toward inside strategies, with those in the nonprofit sector falling somewhere in between.

*Sources of Financial Support.* Empirical evidence of the importance of the relationship between interest groups and their patrons is shown in figure 6-2, where groups are classified according to their pattern of financial support. In this figure, "dependence on patrons" is coded as follows: "None" means that the group reported receiving no financial support from government agen-

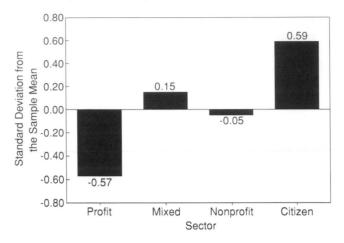

**Fig. 6-1. Relationship of interest groups' membership and choice of strategy. (Data from 1980 Survey.)**

cies, from private foundations, or from gifts from individuals. "Some" means that the organization received financial support from one or more of these patrons, but that more support came from member dues than from patrons. A group is "high" on this variable if its financial support from patrons is equal to or greater than the revenues it receives from member dues. The figure reveals that groups that rely exclusively upon membership dues are less likely to engage in outside strategies than the sample as a whole, and more likely to engage in inside strategies. At the other extreme, groups that receive more support from patrons than from their members display an equally pronounced tendency to adopt outside, rather than inside, strateiges. These data suggest that there are powerful incentives for groups to keep the goals and values of their members and patrons firmly in mind when choosing to engage in any type of political strategy.

## A Multivariate Analysis of Interest Group Strategies

We have presented evidence that the conflictual character of an interest group's political environment, its organizational resources, its membership characteristics, and the sources of its financial support all are related to its choice of political tactics. The next step in our analysis is to estimate a model predicting interest group strategies.

The fundamental relationship in our model is between the form of political activity engaged in by an interest group—whether some form of inside or outside strategy—and a linear combination of the amount of conflict in its environment, its organizational resources, and its dependence upon govern-

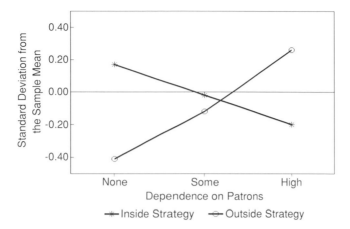

**Fig. 6-2. Effects of reliance on patron support on the choice of political strategies by interest groups. (Data from 1980 Survey.)**

mental rather than private sources of financial support. Since we believe that the impacts of these variables are independent of each other, we also presume that their effects are additive. Our model of the choice of tactics by interest groups, therefore, can be described as:

$$\text{ISI}_i \text{ (or OSI}_i) = A + B(\text{STAFF}_i) + C(\text{LOCAL}_i) +$$

$$D(\text{CONFLICT}_i) + E(\text{PATRON}_i) + U_i$$

where:

$A$ = the intercept term

$\text{ISI}_i$ = the inside strategy index score of the $i$th group (standardized);

$\text{OSI}_i$ = the outside strategy index score of the $i$th group (standardized);

$\text{STAFF}_i$ = the number of full-time equivalent persons employed by the headquarters of the $i$th group (log 10 transformed);

$\text{LOCAL}_i$ = a dummy variable indicating whether the $i$th group has local officers, chapters, or other subunits;

$\text{CONFLICT}_i$ = a variable that indicates whether the $i$th group perceives organized opposition on policy issues, significant organized opposition on policy issues, significant policy differences between the national political parties, or both (the variable may take on the values 0, 1, or 2);

$\text{PATRON}_i$ = the percentage of a group's total revenues obtained from government, foundations, and private gifts minus the percentage obtained from member dues; the variable ranges from $-100$ (all revenues obtained from patrons) to 100 (all revenues obtained from member dues); and

$U_i$ = a disturbance term.

Membership characteristics were included in the analysis by making separate estimates of the slope and intercept coefficients for each of the four types of groups in our sample. The parameters were estimated separately because we believe that different types of interest groups respond differently when they are confronted by political conflict and they are likely to make different kinds of investments of their organizational resources. Citizen groups are likely to respond to a conflictual environment by increasing their emphasis upon various outside strategies, while groups that draw members from the profit sector are more likely to attempt to manage political conflict through the use of inside strategies. Groups with mixed memberships or with members coming predominantly from the nonprofit sector can be expected to engage in complex mixtures of inside and outside strategies. Since interest groups of different types respond differently to the same kind of stimuli, they must be treated separately in our analysis.

Estimates for the slope and intercept terms for each group type were obtained by the following equation:

$$\text{ISI}_i \text{ (or OSI}_i) = A_p P_i + B_p P_i \text{STAFF}_i + C_p P_i \text{LOCAL}_i +$$

$$D_p P_i \text{CONFLICT}_i + E_p P_i \text{PATRON}_i + A_m M_i +$$

$$B_m M_i \text{STAFF}_i + \ldots + E_m M_i \text{PATRON}_i + A_n N_i +$$

$$B_n N_i \text{STAFF}_i + \ldots + E_n N_i \text{PATRON}_i + A_c C_i +$$

$$B_c C_i \text{STAFF}_i + \ldots + E_c C_i \text{PATRON}_i + U_i$$

where:

$P_i$ = a dummy variable which equals one if the $i$th association belongs to the profit sector category, and equals zero otherwise;

$M_i$ = the same as $P_i$, but for the mixed category;

$N_i$ = the same as $P_i$, but for the nonprofit category; and

$C_i$ = the same as $P_i$, but for the citizen group category.

**TABLE 6-5.  Regression of the Choice of Outside Political Strategy on Organizational Resources, Perceived Conflict, and Source of Revenue**

| Explanatory Variable | Type of Group | | | |
| --- | --- | --- | --- | --- |
| | Profit | Mixed | Nonprofit | Citizen |
| Membership type (intercept) | −.367 | −.921 | −.844 | −.562 |
| Staff size (Log 10) | .093 | .258 | .163 | .151 |
| | (.113) | (.187) | (.112) | (.144) |
| Subunits | .414 | .396 | .685 | .777 |
| | (.154) | (.261) | (.134) | (.190) |
| Conflict | .141 | −.036 | .283 | .306 |
| | (.101) | (.174) | (.085) | (.122) |
| Patronage | .00378 | −.00322 | .00391 | −.00149 |
| | (.00210) | (.00283) | (.00148) | (.00149) |
| | $df = 418$     $F$-ratio $= 8.68$     $R^2 = 0.30$ | | | |

*Source:* 1980 Survey.

*Note:* Entries are unstandardized regression coefficients; standard errors are in parentheses.

This equation produces parameter estimates that are equivalent to those generated by running separate regressions for each type of group. By estimating one equation rather than four, we obtain a single measure of the variance explained by the effects of all variables and their interactions within each group type. Table 6-5 contains OLS estimates for the equation dealing with outside strategies, while table 6-6 reports the result for inside strategies.

Our analysis reveals that interest groups tend to choose strategies that are compatible with their organizational form. Table 6-5 shows that decentralized organizations that maintain local chapters or subunits are likely to increase their use of outside strategies, no matter how large their central staffs in Washington may be. Groups with members from the profit or mixed sectors show little tendency to adopt outside strategies under any circumstances, but citizen groups or those with members from the nonprofit sector are much more likely to respond to conflict with outside strategies.[9]

---

9. Our findings roughly parallel those drawn from Schlozman and Tierney's analysis of a smaller sample of Washington interest groups. They found, for example, that citizen groups were more likely than trade associations (which, in their sample, were generally though not exclusively affiliated with profit sector firms) to engage in or spend considerable time and resources in mounting grass roots lobbying efforts, in conducting protests or demonstrations, in publicizing voting records, and in talking with the press and media, all of which were clearly outside strategies. On the other hand, their trade associations were more likely than the citizen groups to participate in or spend resources on planning legislative strategies, shaping the implementation of policies, alerting Congress to the effects of bills, helping to draft legislation and regulations, and other inside strategies (1986, 431–32).

**TABLE 6-6. Regression of the Choice of Inside Political Strategy on Organizational Resources, Perceived Conflict, and Source of Revenue**

| Explanatory Variable | Type of Group | | | |
| --- | --- | --- | --- | --- |
| | Profit | Mixed | Nonprofit | Citizen |
| Membership type (intercept) | −.503 | −1.324 | −.980 | −1.44 |
| Staff size (Log 10) | .257 | .376 | .442 | .501 |
| | (.114) | (.189) | (.113) | (.145) |
| Subunits | .091 | .097 | −.032 | .099 |
| | (.155) | (.264) | (.135) | (.192) |
| Conflict | .313 | .513 | .421 | .592 |
| | (.102) | (.175) | (.085) | (.123) |
| Patronage | −.00319 | −.00569 | −.00311 | −.00351 |
| | (.00211) | (.00286) | (.00150) | (.00151) |

$df = 418$     $F$-ratio $= 9.33$     $R^2 = 0.32$

*Source:* 1980 Survey.

*Note:* Entries are unstandardized regression coefficients; standard errors are in parentheses.

It is striking that groups in the profit and nonprofit sectors—the types that are most likely under most circumstances to adopt inside strategies—are induced to engage in outside strategies when they rely upon patrons, while citizen groups—the type most likely, under most circumstances, to engage in campaigns of protest or propaganda—are discouraged by patrons from engaging in outside strategies. These findings suggest that patrons have a moderating effect on the behavior of citizen groups, encouraging them to seek influence through the established channels of representative government, while at the same time they encourage the profit and nonprofit sector groups they support to invest more energy in campaigns designed to influence public opinion.

Table 6–6 shows, even more consistently than did table 6-5, how important group perceptions of conflict are in inducing political action. Conflict is strongly associated with the choice of inside strategies, although once again it affects citizen groups and those in the nonprofit sector more strongly than those in the profit sector. While the existence of subunits encourages groups to engage in outside strategies of political mobilization and the size of a group's staff had little impact on this choice, the opposite is true where inside strategies are concerned. The data in table 6-6 show that the existence of a large, central staff is a powerful influence encouraging a group to engage in inside strategies, while the existence of a decentralized structure of local chapters has little or no impact.

It is important to note, however, that the impact of internal resources varies with the group's membership. The association's own resources appear to be less important in accounting for the political activities in the two categories of groups with at least some members in the profit sector, while staff size and subunits are critical for citizen groups and those in the nonprofit sector. Note, for example, that groups in the profit and mixed sector categories, when compared to citizen groups and nonprofit sector groups, show smaller coefficients for staff size in predicting the importance of inside strategies. The same pattern appears among the estimated coefficients for organizational subunits in the equation for outside strategies. This intriguing asymmetry suggests that the political activities of citizen groups and associations based in the nonprofit sector depend more on the resources they are able to mobilize than do interest groups with ties to the business sector, perhaps because of the enormous institutional resources available to profit sector interests for informal subsidies and patronage, such as the ability of a trade association to call upon executives in the industry to visit Washington or make individual campaign contributions.

As all the other parts of our analysis would lead one to expect, groups with members from the profit sector show the greatest overall predisposition to adopt inside strategies. This can be seen by comparing the estimated intercepts for the profit sector category with the intercepts associated with the other three group types. To summarize, the groups most likely to adopt inside strategies are those in the profit sector that maintain large staffs and perceive high levels of conflict in their environment, while the groups least likely to follow the inside pathway to influence are those citizen groups with few organizational resources that experience little or no conflict with other groups and do not feel that they are affected by the outcome of national elections.

**Summary and Conclusion**

The assertion that interest groups adopt a dominant operating style early in their histories cannot be given a definitive empirical test with data from our cross-sectional survey, but we do not wish to create the impression that interest groups constantly shift their tactics as circumstances change. Established groups do sometimes alter their dominant strategies, but only after much discussion, and usually after their standard approach has proved unsuccessful time and time again. Most groups adopt a preferred style of political action early in their histories, and, when these early choices are being made, group leaders naturally emulate the tactics being employed at that time by the most successful groups. Once either an inside or outside strategy becomes the association's dominant approach, it is very difficult to move in a new direction.[10] Choices made early in the history of a group establish a strategic style

---

10. The claim that group strategies are stable finds some support in Schlozman and Tierney's survey of Washington interest groups, most of which reported that they became more politically active during the late 1970s and early 1980s—a period of considerable political

that restricts innovation, largely because political strategies are so intertwined with other basic organizational decisions. Yet, within the boundaries established by past decisions, group leaders choose new tactics in response to the incentives and opportunities that are presented by the desires and inclinations of the group's membership and by the influences of the broader political system. The most important factors determining whether interest groups will engage in political action and the type of tactics they will adopt are the conflictual character of their political environment, the nature and extent of their internal resources, the character of their memberships, and the sources of their financial support. At one extreme, groups that are based upon occupations in the profit sector that depend primarily upon dues from their members for financial maintenance and are heavily engaged in conflict with opposing groups are most likely to adopt a vigorous inside political strategy based upon legislative or other institutional lobbying. At the other extreme, groups engaged in conflict that are organized around a cause or idea and depend heavily upon small financial contributions from large numbers of members scattered across the country are most likely to adopt an outside strategy based upon various forms of mass political persuasion. Patrons—such as government agencies, foundations, and wealthy individuals—act as moderating forces, encouraging occupationally based groups to engage in activities directed toward broader publics and leading citizen groups to enter into conventional policy-making forums, rather than acts of protest or campaigns of political mobilization.

The tactics adopted by interest groups are part of a general strategy of organizational maintenance, as much a part of the organization's character as its choice of issues. There is nothing inherently desirable about inside or outside political strategies—each results from efforts by interest-group leaders to cope with the incentives produced by their organizational history and environment. Those who fear that American institutions are becoming seriously fragmented and yearn for a new era of national consensus will not be able to persuade group leaders to confine their activities to inside strategies out of concern for overall political stability, but it might be possible to affect the choice of strategies by interest groups by changing the incentives or opportunities facing interest-group leaders. This might be done, for example, by changing the rules allowing grass roots lobbying by groups with tax-exempt status, changing the regulations governing political activities by government contractors (as the Reagan administration tried to do with little success), restricting the rights of foundations to make grants for programs of

---

conflict—but that they had not changed their general strategies toward those resembling some of our outside activities (1986, 157). The primary effect of partisan and group conflict or other characteristics of the political system is to change a group's stress on political activity in general, not its relative emphasis on inside or outside strategies.

political action, or making it more difficult for interest groups to achieve standing in the courts for the purpose of filing class action lawsuits. As our analysis has shown, however, many factors that determine the choice of political tactics by interest groups are beyond the reach of government regulations. Groups will not alter their political strategies unless their fundamental social or political circumstances are changed, and this usually would require significant changes in the substance of public policy, not simply the rules of the political game.

Our analysis also raises some intriguing questions: How do these strategic differences of advocacy groups affect the types of interests represented before different political institutions? What do the differences in strategies imply for the general modes of interest representation available in the American political system? And what do these strategies—and their close connections to the broader political system—suggest about the relations between interest groups and the dynamics of the party system? It is to these questions that we now turn.

CHAPTER 7

# Interest Groups, Iron Triangles, and Representative Institutions

*Thomas L. Gais, Mark A. Peterson, and Jack L. Walker, Jr.*

President Carter will perhaps be remembered most for his perceived incompetence, an impression produced largely by his inability to forge coalitions in Congress and by his failure, as an "outsider," to intervene effectively in the established policy-making processes in Washington. Carter believed the source of his troubles to be the fragmentation of power and decision making exploited by influential special interests. He believed that his administration was trapped in a web of organized groups allied with well-placed congressional and bureaucratic sympathizers seeking to protect their narrowly defined interests and frustrating his own broader vision of the public good. Looking back on his experiences in Washington, Carter found that even his liberal supporters were major obstacles because "when you don't measure up one hundred percent to those so-called liberal groups, they demand a gallon of blood. There's no compromise with them. If they get ninety percent of what they want, that's not important. It's the ten percent that they didn't get that becomes a driving political force."[1]

Jimmy Carter was not alone among chief executives in experiencing such frustration. Triangular relationships among interest groups, Congress, and the bureaucracy "came as a rude shock" to President Nixon and his White House staff. Their desire to fracture those relationships in order to gain control of the bureaucracy was the primary motive behind their plans for extensive governmental reorganization (Seidman 1980, 116). Indeed, many scholarly commentators have complained about the pernicious influence of "cosy little triangles" of private, congressional, and administrative actors more durable than any single presidential administration (James 1969, 126; Lowi 1969; Dodd and Schott 1979; Lammers 1979, 19–20, 146–47, 258–60; Cronin 1980, 177–78, 335–39). Studies of interest group–congressional–bureaucratic rela-

---

1. Jimmy Carter, interview with Mark A. Peterson, Plains, Ga., June 20, 1984.

tions are filled with references to subgovernments, policy subsystems, iron triangles, or "whirlpools of special social interests and problems" ("subgovernments" in Cater 1964, 17; "policy subsystems" in Freeman 1965, 11; "whirlpools" in Griffith 1939, 182.)

But just as this vision of the American system as a frustrating maze of autonomous and impermeable iron triangles became popular with journalists and departing presidents, several scholars began to question its utility as a guide to understanding the policy-making process. In Hugh Heclo's view, fluid, new "issue networks" that were made up of technical specialists, journalists, administrators, and political entrepreneurs began emerging. Most recent changes in public policy have been fashioned within these networks, which also are the seedbeds for coalitions advocating new legislation. In Heclo's words:

> Based largely on early studies of agriculture, water, and public works policies, the iron triangle concept is not so much wrong as it is disastrously incomplete . . . the conventional view is especially inappropriate for understanding changes in politics and administration during recent years . . . . Looking for closed triangles of control, we tend to miss the fairly open networks of people that increasingly impinge upon government. (Heclo 1978, 88)

Because this "kaleidoscopic" new system of issue networks lacks the structure and internal homogeneity of subgovernments, Heclo believes it serves to "complicate calculations, decrease predictability, and impose considerable strains on those charged with governmental leadership" (Heclo 1978, 105). Other observers go further, viewing the decline of subgovernments as part of a pronounced atomizing trend in American political life that makes the task of creating majorities, in the words of Anthony King, "like trying to build coalitions out of sand" (1978, 391).

Occupants of the White House might find themselves frustrated as much by a fluid, permeable system prone to surprising shifts in policy as by a decentralized system of entrenched special interests. In both systems, the will of presidents may often be thwarted and extensive bargaining is necessary in order to achieve even the simplest policy goals. Even though there are similarities in the operational requirements of the two systems, there are also many important differences. The classic system of iron triangles would be more sympathetic to the desires of large, vested interests in the society and its policy outputs would be more predictable. Budget shares would be more nearly fixed and lines of authority, even though decentralized and complicated, would be clear and understandable to the system's insiders. In a shifting, conflictual, accessible system of the type described by Heclo, authority would be fleeting. Insiders would often be surprised by the rapid mobilization of new coalitions and the unexpected enactment of legislation thought to have had little chance of passage. Conflict would suddenly flair up in policy areas that had been stable for years. A system of subgovernments has strong built-in barriers against all efforts at redistribution. New programs could be added as long as the established system was not disturbed, but efforts to eliminate programs or change budget shares in order to free resources could be successful only if political leaders were willing to make extremely large investments of energy and prestige. In a more amorphous system, redistribution and shifts in budget shares are more likely, but also less controllable. Initiatives for change may begin with the president or congressional leaders, or they may begin with an ambitious first-term senator or a crusading political activist.

We believe that during the three decades ending with 1980 just this kind of conflictual, permeable, unpredictable system evolved in the United States. Many iron triangles remained in operation, but their influence was less pervasive than in the 1940s and 1950s, and the governmental system could no longer accurately be characterized as a loose collection of subgovernments.

Such broad generalizations cannot be fully substantiated by evaluating the empirical contours of any single component of the political system, such as interest groups. Indeed, part of the argument presented here is that the fundamental outlines of American politics have been altered in a variety of respects. Nevertheless, the study reported in this book thus far has provided ample evidence that one of the primary causes of the transformation in this country's politics has been the rapid expansion in the number and, more important, the variety of interests that have achieved formal representation in the American system.

In this chapter, we describe the group basis and policy context of American politics and government as they were configured at the end of the 1970s. Our purpose is to investigate the programmatic goals of different types of groups, the implications of their contrasting strategies for seeking to influence the government in pursuit of their goals, and the response of the policy-making system to their efforts. The changes in the structure and behavior of interest groups led to important adjustments in the operation of both Congress and the presidency. We outline several important ways in which the incentives and opportunities facing the president and members of Congress were redefined at the outset of the last decade. The stage will then be set to evaluate, in the next chapter, the unusual efforts instigated by President Ronald Reagan to capture control of the policy-making process by taming the much elaborated interest-group community.

## The Widening Scope of Conflict

Under a regime of subgovernments, national policy-making would be controlled by an elaborate pattern of interest communities, each capable of developing and administering public policy within its narrow realm without significant opposition from elsewhere in the governmental system and without much internal dissension. These arrangements could be altered slowly as personalities came and went or when economic or social changes undermined their foundations, but such changes typically would occur over many years. The participants would remain the same through several different presidential administrations and their fortunes would not be materially affected by the shifting partisan balance in Congress. Interest groups in a mature subgovernment would enjoy an intimate, cooptive relationship with government and would seldom be directly challenged by hostile groups fundamentally opposed to their interests.[2]

According to J. Leiper Freeman, Henry Kariel, and Grant McConnell, structural decentralization and a vigorous tradition of local control, often constitutionally sustained or reinforced, were the primary institutional features of the American political system that led to the development of subgovernments (Kariel 1961, 11; Freeman 1965, 22; McConnell 1966, 6–7, 244–339). In their view, the resulting fragmentation of authority in Congress and administrative autonomy of bureaucratic agencies allowed private interests to cultivate relationships with relatively small sets of governmental actors who possessed the authority necessary to resolve most policy issues. While the constitutional structure of the American system has not changed, there has been a vast transformation of the size and scope of the federal government since World War II. Hundreds of new programs have been inaugurated and the federal government has been thrust into many new policy areas, such as elementary and secondary education, urban mass transportation, health care, and pollution control, that were once considered primarily matters of state or local concern. These developments, of course, might simply have expanded the number of opportunities for the creation of subgovernments and need not have altered the decentralized structure of policy-making.

The growth of the welfare state, however, accentuated the ideological content of the public-policy debate and challenged the domination of established commercial interests in the policy-making process. Many of the new programs enacted during the postwar surge in the growth of government were intended either to constrain business or to redistribute wealth. One of the principal arguments of Randall Ripley and Grace Franklin in their classification of the variations in subgovernment influence is that subgovernments

---

2. The development of this concept of subgovernments began when Freeman (1965) studied the Bureau of Indian Affairs from 1928 to the late 1940s; Arthur Maass (1951) investigated the Army Corps of Engineers in the 1940s; Grant McConnell (1966) concentrated on business, agricultural, public works, and public lands groups operating up to the end of the early postwar period; and Henry Kariel (1961) summarized the literature from the prewar and early postwar period.

thrive best in areas where policies begin or can soon come to be regarded as distributive in nature, where program benefits can be disbursed widely without obvious cost to any one sector of society (Ripley and Franklin 1980, 8–20, 90, 212; also see Lowi 1972, 298–310). Subgovernments require the kind of policy that allows for accommodative bargaining. Distributive policies continue to be introduced, but it is not an overstatement to describe the years from 1960 to 1980 as a regulatory and redistributive revolution in American public policy. There was an important upsurge of redistributive policy-making during the Kennedy-Johnson years, and an expansion of the regulatory powers of the national government continued well into the Nixon administration. The costs of the new regulations would be borne largely and explicitly by businesses, while the redistributive programs threatened to pit minorities and the disadvantaged against both working-class whites and more affluent citizens.

If Ripley and Franklin are correct, these new regulatory and redistributive policies should have produced a quite different system of conflict resolution than that found within subgovernments. Redistributive and regulatory issues prompt the formation of coalitions of interests in opposition to one another, and decisions are made not in subcommittees or bureaus, but more often by the full Congress and in the White House, frequently with the direct involvement of the president (Ripley and Franklin 1980, 123–24, 152–56, 212).

The enactment of new legislation in civil rights, environmental protection, consumerism, and safety brought narrowly focused, occupationally based interests into contact with many more decision makers in diverse parts of the government. An interview with the president of the National Agricultural Chemicals Association, for example, revealed that environmental laws increased the number of agencies with which his association communicates. The organization's research division continues its ties with the Department of Agriculture, but the more recent relationship established with the Environmental Protection Agency, which regulates chemicals, may be of even greater importance. In addition, regulations governing the conveyance of chemicals brings the group into contact with the Department of Transportation. In short, by 1980, single subgovernments were no longer capable of handling the range of issues with which these associations must concern themselves, thus contributing to the complication of the subgovernment picture, if not to its fundamental alteration.

Once the president and congressional leaders become directly involved in debate over an issue, the controversy naturally attracts the attention of larger numbers of people. The mass media begin to transmit information about the policy questions and personalities involved, and members of the public are tempted to make their preferences known to their elected representatives. In Schattschneider's terms, possibilities increase for a widening of the scope of conflict to include groups and citizens outside subgovernments and outside Washington itself (Schattschneider 1960).

## The Significance of the Emergence of Citizen Groups

The pronounced emergence of citizen groups in the 1960s and 1970s, discussed in earlier chapters, lent organizational vitality to all of the forces that were reshaping the practice of governance. Their entry as stable participants in the policy-making process, facilitated by the support of outside patrons, is important because these groups had distinctive objectives and strategies that threatened the quiescence of subgovernments. The differences between citizen and other groups became plain when respondents to our 1980 survey were asked two questions about their general ideological preferences concerning the role of government in society. The responses to these questions are displayed in table 7-1, with the groups classified according to the typology of occupational roles. Systematic differences appear with respect to both ques-

**TABLE 7-1.  Relation between the Type of Group and Their Political Demands**

|  | Profit | Mixed | Nonprofit | Citizen |
|---|---|---|---|---|
|  | Percentage of Interest Groups Preferring Various Levels of Government Regulation of the Economy[a] | | | |
| More regulation | 7 | 15 | 13 | 46 |
| Present level of regulation | 5 | 13 | 33 | 26 |
| Less regulation | 88 | 72 | 54 | 28 |
| Total | 100 | 100 | 100 | 100 |
| N | 158 | 39 | 138 | 70 |
|  | Percentage of Interest Groups Preferring Various Levels of Government Provision of Social Services[b] | | | |
| Greater provision of services | 13 | 40 | 69 | 66 |
| Present level of service | 19 | 22 | 18 | 17 |
| Less provision of services | 68 | 38 | 13 | 17 |
| Total | 100 | 100 | 100 | 100 |
| N | 120 | 37 | 141 | 72 |

Source: 1980 Survey.

Note: Ns vary because all surveyed groups did not respond to both questions.

[a]"In general, do the policy positions of this association tend to call for: Much more government regulation of business and industry? Some additional government regulation of business and industry? Present level of regulation? Less government regulation of business and industry? Much less government regulation of business and industry?"

[b]"In general, do the policy positions of this association tend to call for: Much more government provision of social services? Some additional government provision of social services? Present level of social services? Less government provision of social services? Much less government provision of social services?"

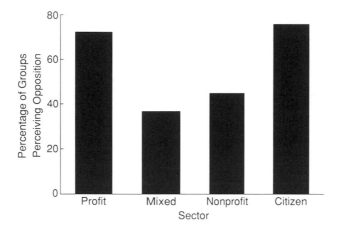

**Fig. 7-1. Perceptions of group opposition. (Data from 1980 Survey.)**

tions, but with interesting contrasts. It is clear that, in 1980, interest groups in general expressed much less support for government regulation than for the government's provision of social services. Profit sector occupational groups were solidly opposed to expansions of either regulations or services and, in fact, showed heavy majorities in favor of the contraction of each. On the opposite side, citizen groups solidly favored an expansion of government activity in both realms, establishing a distinct line of ideological cleavage within our sample of associations. Between the two opposing sides, the groups that mix profit and nonprofit members and the pure nonprofit sector groups shifted first to one side and then the other. Both types favored the expansion of government services—the mixed groups by only the slimmest of margins—but a majority of both types expressed opposition to the government's recent infringements on occupational self-regulation.

There has been little discussion about ideological cleavages within the interest-group structure in the literature on subgovernments, but fairly clear expectations about the patterns of conflict one might expect to find emerge from the literature. According to the subgovernment thesis, decentralization reduces overt conflict by delegating policy-making authority to virtually independent, segmented communities of like-minded participants. These communities might be afflicted with factionalism or might be thrown into conflict with each other, but one would not expect to see a consistent pattern of group conflict of the kind reported by the groups in our study. Figure 7-1 shows the percentage of groups within each group type that reported the existence of another group working in direct opposition to its interests in 1980. What emerges is an unambiguous U-shaped pattern of conflict perception, with the profit sector groups and the citizen groups perceiving the most overt opposition to their views.

We cannot necessarily infer that the conflicts reported in figure 7-1 are uniformly the result of direct confrontations between the profit sector and citizen groups. Unfortunately, our data do not allow precise monitoring of patterns of conflict, but it is certain that citizen groups are involved on both sides of the intense struggles over such issues as abortion and nuclear disarmament. It is also certain that conflicts exist between groups representing different kinds of industries, or between occupational groups in both the profit and nonprofit sectors. Yet even though such intrasectoral conflicts are common, it is also apparent that much of the group conflict of the 1960s and 1970s over expanding the welfare state, cleaning up the environment, advancing the rights of minorities, protecting unwary consumers, or promoting a greater emphasis upon occupational health and safety involved direct clashes between business interests on the one side, who preferred minimal government intervention, and citizen groups on the other, most of whom favored an expansionist state. Much of the conflict being reported by our sample of groups, in other words, matches the ideological differences reported in table 7-1. A set of groups seeking to remedy presumed deficiencies in the operation of the market economy were often directly opposed, during this period, by organizations representing the business firms whose behavior the citizen groups were attempting to constrain.

The existence of stable citizen organizations with distinctive sources of financial support and contrasting ideologies could, thus, present a challenge to the iron triangle or subgovernment thesis. If, however, these new groups were willing to resolve their differences through bargaining and compromise with other participants in established subgovernments, without appeals either to higher political authority or to the general public, the integrity of the system of subgovernments could be maintained. As long as citizen groups were willing to be accommodating, there is no reason why they could not eventually be made a functioning part of a segmented, decentralized, and predictable system of conflict resolution.

One test of whether citizen associations were being integrated into a system of subgovernments by 1980 might be whether they were gaining any form of routine access to the decision-making process. Three indicators of institutional access are available from the 1980 survey, which asked the respondents if one or more members of the organization's permanent staff held positions on any official government advisory commissions or committees, if the association was regularly consulted by federal agencies on legislative or policy matters, and if a "very important" or "important" activity of the organization was to serve as consultants or advisers to federal, state, or local government agencies. For purposes of our analysis, we decided that any group

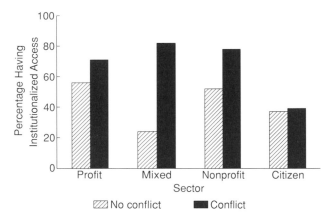

**Fig. 7-2. Percentage of interest groups that have institutionalized access to administrative decision making. (Data from 1980 Survey.)**

experiencing at least two of these various forms of ongoing interactions with government agencies could be described as having institutional access.

Looking again at perceptions of conflict, we found that groups of all types that reported that they were engaged in conflict with opposing groups were much more likely to enjoy institutionalized access, and that formal efforts at consultation were more prevalent in settings where there was conflict among groups. Occupational groups of all kinds, however, were more likely to enjoy higher levels of institutionalized access than citizen groups when conflict was present, as illustrated in figure 7-2. In addition, a higher percentage of the occupational organizations than the citizen groups enjoyed all three attributes of institutionalized access. Citizen groups were more likely to report no access at all, and considerably more of the groups in the occupational sectors reported actively being approached by federal agencies.

By 1980, a significant minority of citizen groups reported achieving some access to agencies of the federal government, and we have no way of knowing whether citizen organizations in general were gaining greater access during the years just before the 1980 survey. The system of subgovernments may have been slowly absorbing these recent arrivals, but, at least in 1980, the process of digestion was not complete and important differences remained in how occupational groups and citizen associations interacted with the government.[3]

Even if a degree of institutionalized access is attained, citizen groups will

_____

3. Although some of the question wording was changed in the 1985 survey, the responses to that survey nevertheless suggest that, between 1980 and 1985, there was little change in the nature of perceived conflict or access enjoyed by citizen groups.

never fit easily into a system of subgovernments unless they are ultimately willing to cooperate in the process of bargaining and consultation upon which such arrangements are based. Access does not necessarily generate consensus. The 1985 survey, in fact, provided many indications that most citizen associations had not adopted such cooperative, inside strategies, due to reasons that derive directly from the very nature of these organizations. The significance to subgovernments of the analysis of group strategies presented in chapter 6 makes this point quite apparent. Citizen groups, once they experienced conflict, were twice as likely as all types of occupational groups to appeal to the public through the mass media and to engage in various forms of grass roots mobilization at the local level. Citizen organizations were also much less likely to engage in lobbying administrative agencies than were all types of occupational groups, although we found no appreciable differences among groups in their willingness to lobby Congress. As shown previously in figure 6-1, dramatic differences were found between the types of groups in their balance of political activities comprising inside and outside strategies. The occupational associations, both in the profit and nonprofit sectors, concentrated their efforts on institutional lobbying, while the citizen groups tried to expand the scope of conflict through use of the media and other forms of publicity rather than allow policy to be established within the network of subgovernments.

Business organizations were not immune to the changes introduced by the emergence of citizen groups. Indeed, the expansion of policy conflict brought about by such groups may have helped to ignite the institutional manifestation of the countermobilization by American business that we have discussed. Since the beginning of the period of enhanced conflict over redistributive and regulatory policy, associations in the profit sector were especially likely to move their headquarters to the nation's capital. Of groups in our sample established before 1961, 28 percent of the profit sector organizations moved their headquarters to Washington by the end of the 1970s, while 19 percent of the associations representing the nonprofit sector and only 4 percent of the citizen groups had made the same move. The most important response to the changing circumstances in Washington, however, did not come from trade associations. In the 1970s there was a rapid growth of direct action by large firms themselves. Individual corporations increased the amount of representation they maintained in Washington, and corporate political action committees were established at a rate far greater than committees associated with any other institutions (Cantor 1982, 62; Sabato 1984).[4]

This countermobilization notwithstanding, citizen groups were still more

---

4. See the estimates of growth summarized in the introduction to Close, Bologna, and McCormick 1989, 3–8; also see Heclo 1978; Shabecoff 1979, 134–46; Wilson 1981.

**TABLE 7-2.   Percentage of Groups Reporting Change
in Levels of Agency Cooperation Due to the 1977 Change
in Administration**

| Group Type | Level of Cooperation[a] | | | |
| --- | --- | --- | --- | --- |
| | Increase | No Change | Decrease | *N* |
| Profit | 11 | 62 | 27 | 171 |
| Mixed | 10 | 79 | 10 | 58 |
| Nonprofit | 20 | 68 | 12 | 181 |
| Citizen | 46 | 46 | 8 | 109 |

*Source:* 1980 Survey.

[a]"How did the change in 1977 from Republican to Democratic control of the presidency affect the amount of cooperation and consultation between this association and federal agencies? Important increase in cooperation? Moderate increase in cooperation? No change in the relationship? Moderate decrease in cooperation? Important decrease in cooperation? This association had no contact with federal agencies at that time."

sensitive to ideological issues than were groups in the profit sector, and they made greater efforts to mobilize people into their policy networks. They were also more sensitive than occupational groups to shifts in partisan control of the presidency. For example, when the representatives of the organizations in our study were asked whether they had experienced any change in cooperation with government agencies as a result of the transition from Republican President Gerald Ford to Democratic President Jimmy Carter, consistently different evaluations were reported by the different types of groups. These two administrations did not advance radically different positions on many issues, but they contrasted enough to create divisions in the group system. As illustrated in table 7-2, 46 percent of the citizen groups reported an increase in cooperation from the Carter administration while, in contrast, 27 percent of the profit sector associations indicated that cooperation had decreased. Twenty percent of the nonprofit groups also noted an increase in cooperation, while most of the organizations in the mixed membership category identified no change in their relationship with government.

These judgments about cooperation are correlated with differences in the ideologies of the groups. Answers from groups on an index of ideology— based on responses reported in table 7-1 to questions about increased social services and government regulation—were related to the groups' reports about the changes in cooperation experienced after the transition from the Ford to the Carter administration. This relationship appeared for all types of groups, although it was much stronger among citizen groups (Kendall's tau-*b* = 0.60) than among profit sector groups (tau-*b* = 0.26) or groups in the nonprofit sector (tau-*b* = 0.14). Profit and nonprofit groups, enjoying a high degree of institutionalized access and relying mainly upon an inside strategy of influence, were able to insulate themselves from the relatively mild ideological shift engendered by Carter's election and to protect their policy interests. Citizen groups, however, heavily engaged in the tactics of an outside strategy and enjoying less institutionalized access, were much more in tune with changes in the partisan or ideological character of the new presidency.

As the 1980s dawned, the American system was acquiring the capacity, due to the rise of a distinctive new element in its leadership structure, to sustain a virtually continuous confrontation between the representatives of private commercial interests and, for lack of a better term, representatives of the public interest (citizen groups) backed by private foundations, wealthy individuals, and sometimes the government itself. These challenging groups were highly sensitive to ideological issues and were not able to achieve as much routine access to government agencies as the occupationally based associations. They were also more likely to make attempts to expand the arena of conflict by appealing to new participants outside of the nation's capital. These data indicate that the decentralized system of subgovernments was definitely being threatened. A new set of groups was available as willing participants in coalitions working for broad-scale social reform. These citizen groups provided much of the organizational base for sustained attacks initiated by political entrepreneurs who challenged the system of subgovernments.

## The Widening Scope of Conflict and Representative Institutions

The 1980 survey of interest groups uncovered the basis for a higher level of conflict in American politics, anchored by ideological differences between commercial interests and newly established citizen groups attempting to obtain broad public goals.[5] This new pattern of politics threatened previously stable policy communities. In the process, the expansion of the representative system and the greater emphasis being placed upon ideological questions created enduring pressure for change in the country's principal representative institutions, Congress and the presidency.

### Congress

The emergence of organized representation of citizen interests and the countermobilization of business injected many new conflictual issues into legisla-

---

5. Although some changes in question wording make direct comparisons between the 1980 and 1985 surveys difficult, there is nothing in the group responses to the 1985 survey that suggests that these patterns of conflict changed during the first part of the decade.

tive deliberations. Citizen groups search constantly for issues and new policy proposals. Their goal is to attract the attention of their members, justify themselves before patrons, and appeal to entrepreneurial members of Congress who are trying to build national reputations as protagonists for new policies (Walker 1977, 423–25). As citizen groups gained organizational stability and became recognized elements in the interest-group system, congressional leaders making committee assignments felt compelled to recognize their concerns by accepting, as members on committees, some legislators who did not embrace the narrow preferences that had dominated subgovernments in the past. Representatives of consumer interests joined the agriculture committees, and members with preservationist sentiments were added to the House Interior Committee.[6] Dissension within congressional committees caused by their new composition was broadcast to the rest of the membership and to the public at large. Even the House Appropriations Committee, which always valued consensus among its members, was unable to maintain its tradition against dissent in committee reports (Schick 1980, 432) and dissidents on the Ways and Means Committee exploited rule changes to carry their tax reform proposals to the House floor or to the Democratic caucus (Rudder 1977, 126–27). Although high turnover in Congress, changing social values, and slow economic growth were important causes of the decay of committee autonomy, the emergence of the citizen groups was also a significant contributing factor.

The openness of Congress to the political conflicts raised by the citizen groups does not mean that it was or will be able to resolve these disputes. Citizen groups are organized in many congressional districts and in most states, thus their enhanced activity increases the potential for conflict within most members' constituencies and increases the problems that legislators must face in devising successful strategies for reelection (Fiorina 1974). Faced with this difficulty, legislators are tempted to divert these controversies into other policy-making forums. The struggle over women's rights, for example, was diverted into state legislatures by way of the constitutional amendment process. Authority to make potentially controversial rules or regulations can be delegated to the federal bureaucracy or passed on to state or local governments along with grants-in-aid (Lowi 1969; Hayes 1981). By avoiding the electoral risks posed by an increasingly representative system of interest

---

6. Change in the range of interests represented within the House Agriculture Committee was manifested in the establishment of the Subcommittee on Domestic Marketing, Consumer Relations, and Nutrition, chaired by Representative Fred Richmond, a Democrat from Brooklyn, New York. Indeed, the House Agriculture Committee changed from its position as the most conservative of all House committees in the 1960s to one whose central ideological tendency did not diverge much from that of the parent chamber (see Bibby, Mann, and Ornstein 1980, 110). On change in the House Interior and Insular Affairs Committee, see Fenno 1973, 285.

groups, Congress participates in the diminution of its own influence over policy.

But even when Congress has attempted to make choices on the new regulatory and redistributive issues, the committees are often unable to achieve a consensus, and disputes spill out onto the floor, where numerous amendments are offered (see Bach and Smith 1988; Davidson 1988; Smith 1989). New ideas and a wide range of opinions surface in floor debates, but these often lead to the defeat of the amended legislation or to a reduction in the influence of detailed, programmatic expertise on the legislative product, expertise that perhaps can only be applied in deliberations of the substantive committees (see Austen-Smith and Riker 1987; Gilligan and Krehbiel 1987). The movement of the locus of congressional policy-making from the committees to the floor also suggests that coalition builders, be they members of Congress or the administration, must invest greater resources in order to ensure the passage of legislation. The strain on legislative leadership may be so great that passage cannot be attempted for more than a few major bills during any single Congress (see Sinclair 1983). The number of bills introduced and enacted dropped dramatically after the mid-1970s, and a significant portion of the major programs that did pass in the 1980s were incorporated in what became the ritualistic, mammoth, omnibus budget reconciliation bills compiled at the end of each session of Congress.

Ironically, the loosening grip of the committees and the increasing conflict among broad coalitions of groups may reinforce some of the more parochial tendencies of Congress. When ideological questions are being debated, the conflict generated by the issues creates incentives for congressional leaders to manipulate the geographical distribution of policy benefits in order to stabilize policy coalitions and to compensate members for the electoral risks that accompany stands on controversial matters (see Arnold 1979). Similarly, individual members of Congress may seek greater electoral security in the face of uncertain political circumstances through an emphasis on casework, aided by growing staffs and a cooperative federal bureaucracy. Legislators demand pork barrel benefits and constituency services in an effort to recoup the electoral losses they incur from policy struggles on polarizing issues (Fiorina and Noll 1979, 1081–1101; see also Cain, Ferejohn, and Fiorina 1987). Though some commentators consider congressional behavior to be increasingly particularistic, others believe there are tendencies toward a more ideological style of legislative politics (compare, for example, Dodd and Oppenheimer 1977 or Maass 1983 with Fiorina 1989). It is possible that both of these seemingly contradictory interpretations are correct because growing congressional particularism may be, in fact, a result of increased congressional openness to ideological conflict, at least partially engendered by the changes in the group system.

An expanded range of permanently organized interests, therefore, weakens the control of a collective Congress over policy outcomes. Responsiveness to majorities in the parent chambers is enhanced as group conflicts shift a greater amount of discretion onto the floors. Decision making on the floor does not allow for coherence, attention to detail, or control by substantive experts, and, thus, leaves many important choices to be made by the executive branch (witness President Reagan's success with the massive tax and budget reconciliation bills in 1981). In addition, when group conflict intensifies and member participation expands, it becomes more costly to make decisions, both in leadership resources and electoral security for members. The changing group structure may transform Congress into a more sensitive and accurate reflector of the fundamental issues that divide the American people, but it may also reduce its authority over the resolution of these issues and make it even more dependent on the presidency for direction and coordination.

## The Presidency

Critics of the system of subgovernments complain about the constraints that such a decentralized system places upon the president (see, for example, James 1969, 126–27; Hardin 1974, 135; Lammers 1979, 20, 146–47, 258–61; Cronin 1980, 177–78, 335–39; Cutler 1980; Seidman 1980, 38, 162, 164). They have argued that presidents wishing to place their own stamp upon policy have had to break the hold of subgovernments, a task that often required a prohibitively heavy expenditure of political capital. Presidents must bargain within the framework and on the terms established by subgovernments. Consequently, where subgovernments have flourished, difficult negotiation has replaced the normal means of persuasion as a presidential instrument of bureaucratic control (see Neustadt 1980); presidential objectives, especially those involving domestic policy, have often been frustrated; and symbolic actions have taken the place of substantive policy initiatives. Further, these observers have charged that the system has isolated the process of policy formation from the normal mechanisms of democratic accountability, such as political parties, presidential nominations, and elections.

Although a system of subgovernments has several shortcomings, it should be remembered that this system has worked to protect the presidency from a potentially unmanageable flood of disputes and technical policy questions that must be resolved somewhere within the government. A system of subgovernments insulates the presidency from more subdued conflicts in many policy areas that may otherwise demand intervention, forcing the chief executive to take positions on issues that might best be left to others. These protective and insulating functions permit presidents to shape the agenda of the highest levels of government, choosing issues that will enhance their reputations and increase their future influence. A system of subgovernments can be allowed to run itself, while presidents concentrate their time and resources upon a more manageable set of central policy concerns. Further, in the absence of other significant institutional links, such as strong political parties, subgovernments may create informal ties between the legislative and executive branches, providing mechanisms that skillful presidents might employ in order to achieve their own favored policy outcomes (King 1978, 391).

As the decentralized system of conflict resolution organized around distributive policy issues is displaced by a process characterized by programmatic disputes over mainly redistributive or regulatory issues involving more elaborate coalitions of groups, the presidency itself often emerges as the focus of conflict.[7] Each executive decision becomes a threat to some element of the president's electoral or governing coalition as the administration struggles to resolve disputes that were either ignored in the past or settled out of public view behind the walls of insulated subgovernments. As the White House intervenes in a wider range of issues, presidents, historically viewed as central policy actors, are seen by most citizens as bearing even greater responsibility for the outcome of government policies, linking their popularity and chances for reelection more closely to events over which they have little effective means of control (see Peterson 1990a). The presidential agenda becomes cluttered with all sorts of issues that are unable to be resolved at lower levels of administration. The danger arises that the president will lose control over what to decide as the expanding number of policy issues that confront a modern government are thrust upon the relatively small circle of presidential assistants and advisers, forcing them to deal with questions that require considerably more expert knowledge and careful analysis than they can possibly supply (Hess 1967, 159).

As presidents have grown in importance as conflict managers, their staffs have expanded, described by Thomas Cronin as "the swelling of the presidency" (1980, 243–47). The presidential establishment has ballooned through the addition of numerous special advisers and councils, and through the development of direct channels of communication between the president and interest groups maintained by the Office of Public Liaison (OPL; see Wehr 1981, 975–97; Pika 1982 and 1983; Peterson 1990b). Indeed, these relatively recent efforts by presidents to cultivate direct ties with interest organizations reveal, according to Joseph Pika, "much about the political and social pressures acting on the presidency over the last several decades" (1982, 6). Pika's

---

7. The problem faced by presidents was further aggravated in the 1970s and 1980s by the change in issues toward those that create many more enemies than potential supporters, such as energy or welfare reform (Light 1982, 206).

research has shown that most of the associations with formal and enduring access to the White House are citizen groups—the type that has enjoyed the greatest growth in the 1960s and 1970s (Pika 1982, 50).

Formal contacts with a wide range of interest groups increased the potency of the chief executive in the political struggles of Washington, as exemplified by the successful efforts in the Carter administration to mobilize support for the Panama Canal Treaty, and by the cooperation businesses and trade associations extended to President Reagan during congressional action on the fiscal year 1982 budget (Pika 1982, 15, 20; see also Keller 1981, 1740–41; Peterson 1990b). Orchestrated campaigns joining interest-group strategies with the president's rhetorical influence on the public may have been especially fruitful (Kernell 1986; see also Lowi 1985; Tulis 1987). These dramatic success stories, however, probably exaggerate the effectiveness of efforts at presidential alliance building. The increase of routine contacts between the presidency and interest groups may encourage the groups to appeal more of their policy disputes directly to the highest levels of government (Light 1982, 95), thus furthering the president's involvement in conflict resolution. Presidents may then be led in one of two possible directions, either acquiescing to additional growth in the already swollen White House establishment or, as chapter 8 explores in the case of President Reagan, launching an assault on the group system itself.

## Interest Groups and Iron Triangles in the 1980s

There may never have been a period when the American political system was organized around a pervasive set of politically autonomous iron triangles. Since no systematic historical data exist, we must rely upon the insights provided by case studies written mainly in the 1930s, 1940s, and 1950s, and by our own surveys of interest groups conducted many years later (see also Schlozman and Tierney 1986; Salisbury et al. 1987). In our 1980 survey, we detected a higher level of group conflict than would have been anticipated after reading the literature on subgovernments. Newly invigorated occupationally based groups from the profit sector, backed by corporate patrons and focused on immediate commercial interests, were being confronted by a set of organizations claiming to represent broad collective interests backed by a diverse set of patrons, including private foundations, wealthy individuals, and the permanent government bureaucracy.

The citizen groups were also not following the same tactical path to political influence traveled by most profit and nonprofit sector groups in the past. They advocated proposals for the redistribution of resources and for increases in government regulation that would not lend themselves to resolution through logrolling, long-term agreements or through exclusive, face-to-face negotiations. By mobilizing supporters and making efforts to move conflicts into broader political arenas whenever possible, the citizen groups diminished the autonomy of subgovernments, made policy outcomes less predictable, and forced the policy debate into forums open to public view (see Berry 1989a). Because most of these organizations now have the capacity to remain on the scene, there will no longer naturally be periods of political repose when the traditional interests can reestablish secure subgovernments.

The changing structure of the policy-making system in America and the new modes of conflict resolution that are emerging are creating changes in the country's representative institutions (Berry 1989a and 1989b). Many new controversial issues are being pushed onto the agendas of both Congress and the presidency, requiring action even though the political system does not often furnish the tools for successfully resolving these disputes. Political leaders sometimes respond by dodging these difficult decisions and passing them on to lower levels of government, the bureaucracy, or other representative bodies in the system, thus protecting their political livelihoods by reducing the power of the institutions they control. At other times, representatives strive to create more opportunities to distribute individualized benefits and services to constituents, which they hope will compensate for the opposition they are sure to engender when they take stands on highly controversial, ideological issues.

While elected representatives often seem about to be overwhelmed, the elaboration of the interest-group structure and the rising concern with ideological issues also create new opportunities for political leaders to expand their power and influence. By the 1980s it was even possible that a new, national, ruling coalition could be brought into being by leaders skillful enough to attract some of the new patrons of political action, build alliances with clusters of sympathetic interest groups, create the right mixture of ideological appeals, and devise new mechanisms for coordination of these forces that would help to recruit leaders, aggregate demands, and carry out the crucial agenda-building functions of a national political party—even if the new organizational creation were called by some other name.

As Ronald Reagan entered the Oval Office in 1981, it would have been impossible to predict the direction of American politics or the direction of the evolving relationship between the new group system and national representative institutions. It seemed unlikely that a decentralized system of autonomous subgovernments would or could be reestablished, but it was also not clear the extent to which a new president could wrest some degree of control over the increasingly complex policy-making process. Nevertheless, solidifying the Republican party's ideological base and challenging the institutional vitality of his interest-group opponents, discussed in chapter 8, were in fact primary instruments of Reagan's efforts to reorder American government.

CHAPTER 8

# Interest Groups and the Reagan Presidency

*Mark A. Peterson and Jack L. Walker, Jr.*

As bargaining concluded between members of President Ronald Reagan's White House staff and congressional leaders over the massive tax cut that was the first-year legislative hallmark of "Reaganomics" in 1981, David Stockman, budget director and one of the chief architects of the administration's political and economic strategy, was dismayed. He was shocked at the lack of regard by Washington lobbyists for equity or fairness in the tax system. The bill's central purpose was to provide incentives for individuals to save and invest, but once serious bargaining began in the Congress, representatives of special interests—the "piranhas" as Stockman called them—demanded amendments that would provide millions of dollars of privileges for their clients in exchange for their support. The bill had not originally been designed to all but eliminate the corporate income tax or to provide the many other exemptions for business and industry that the final version contained. "Do you realize the greed that came to the forefront?" Stockman asked, almost in wonder, in a conversation with a reporter. "The hogs were really feeding. The greed level, the level of opportunism, just got out of control" (Greider 1981, 58).

President Reagan, of course, preferred that liberal groups in particular receive as little as possible of what they wanted, especially in the form of direct support from the federal government. While Jimmy Carter had shared the widespread criticism of single-interest groups and publicly announced his frustrations with group politics, Ronald Reagan took direct action. The Reagan administration launched a campaign to "defund the left" that was designed to reduce the number and diminish the influence of interest groups in Washington. To shrink permanently the size of the federal establishment—the president's fundamental, overriding goal—the Reagan administration believed that the "iron triangles" still thought to bind congressional committees, federal bureaus, and interest groups into close-knit, impenetrable policy communities had to be broken. To achieve this goal, the Reagan administration sought to inhibit the growth and reduce the financial resources available from government for interest groups operating in Washington. Strenuous efforts were made to prevent federal agencies from providing grants, contracts, or consultancies to organizations unfriendly to the administration. In collateral moves, the Office of Management and Budget (OMB) maneuvered to change regulations concerning the political activities of federal contractors and the Internal Revenue Service (IRS) altered the bases under which tax exemption was granted, making it more difficult for nonprofit groups to engage in anything resembling partisan political activity (Mackenzie, 1981; Peterson 1981; Stanfield 1981; Babcock 1982; Seaberry 1982; Barringer 1983).

For the political scientist, Reagan's presidency offers a rare opportunity to study the reaction of our governmental system to an unusually determined effort by a partisan leader to effect a sharp change in the programmatic thrust of public policy. Acting in the name of the presidency and the Republican party, President Reagan challenged the representative system that had set the policy agenda in Washington for over 30 years. In this chapter, we seek to measure the success of one aspect of this challenge. Was the Reagan administration able to reduce the number of interest groups operating at the national level, especially among its opponents, or force major changes in the way they are maintained? How did the interest-group system respond to this strong thrust from the partisan political leadership? Did the central target of the Reagan budgetary strategy—the social welfare policy community—suffer especially serious policy setbacks or have the number of interest groups working in this area been reduced? Did the Reagan administration represent a dramatic shift in the way public policy is made in Washington, or were the organized advocates able to roll with the punches and continue operating much as they had before Ronald Reagan was elected?

By assessing the impact of the Reagan "revolution" on the Washington political establishment, we also have a unique opportunity to examine some of the fundamental characteristics of the relationship between political parties and interest groups. Reagan played a central role in transforming the national party system into a more centralized, ideologically based instrument of mass persuasion (Schlesinger 1985). Each party is coming to resemble some of the larger interest groups that emerged from the civil rights, environmental, and other social movements. We will show that, because of the general political forces linking the party and group systems, the Reagan administration, with its potent partisan base, in many respects reinforced rather than weakened the interest-group system.

## Growth in the Number of Groups under Reagan

All administrations try to reward their friends and frustrate, if not punish, their political enemies. Democratic administrations during the 1960s used

**TABLE 8-1.  Growth in the Number of Membership Associations, 1980 and 1985**

| Sector | 1980 | | 1985 | |
|---|---|---|---|---|
| | *N* | Percentage of Groups Ten Years Old or Younger | *N* | Percentage of Groups Ten Years Old or Younger |
| Profit | 140 | 15 | 325 | 14 |
| Mixed | 44 | 11 | 50 | 14 |
| Nonprofit | 151 | 12 | 279 | 12 |
| Citizens | 75 | 27 | 204 | 30 |
| Total | 412 | 16 | 858 | 17 |

*Source:* 1980 and 1985 Surveys.

several methods to funnel financial support to liberal political entrepreneurs who were endeavoring to create interest groups that would promote new social welfare programs and support the Democratic legislative agenda. The Carter administration revised the provisions in the tax code concerning nonprofit organizations to foster grass roots lobbying campaigns, and, using an invigo-rated Office of Public Liaison in the White House, it encouraged contacts between those organizations and Congress (Peterson 1990b and n.d.). The Reagan administration differed from these earlier efforts only in that it placed far greater emphasis on directly challenging its liberal opposition. While Democrats did not threaten the organizational base of their opponents, Reagan's administration made such efforts a significant part of its policy agenda. The first question we must ask in assessing the impact of Reagan upon the group system, therefore, is whether the system's growth was affected in any significant way.

Our data indicate that the Reagan administration's strategic attack on opposing organizations did almost nothing to reverse the steady expansion of the group system. As shown in table 8-1, 16 percent of the total number of groups in our 1980 survey were founded during the 10 years prior to the survey, compared with 17 percent of the groups responding to the 1985 questionnaire. We also have been able to determine that fewer than 5 percent of the groups responding to the 1980 survey had left the scene in 1985 either by merging with other organizations (1.4 percent) or ceasing their activities (3.2 percent). These data suggest that the rate of growth in the number of groups probably leveled off during the 1980s, but the system still seems to be expanding briskly. There were significantly more interest groups operating in the nation's capital in 1985 than there had been five years before.

Not only did the group system continue to expand during the Reagan years, but that growth took place in much the same way as it had in the recent past, as shown in table 8-1. The data presented in chapter 4 revealed that the citizen groups were the fastest growing segment of the group system. Through the Reagan years the trend progressed unabated. In both the 1980 and 1985 surveys, only 12 percent of the groups made up of nonprofit professionals were created in the ten years immediately before the survey was conducted, but 27 percent of the citizen groups were ten years old or less in 1980, and that number increased to 30 percent in the 1985 study. Citizen groups are more likely than those based in the occupational sectors to go out of operation, but their five-year death rate of 6.9 percent is not high enough to entirely counteract their vigorous overall rate of growth. The surge in the formation of citizen groups begun in the early 1960s, with the appearance of boisterous newcomers leading to increasing conflict and polarization within the American system of representation, was largely unperturbed by Reagan's assault.

## Ideological Polarization in the New Group System

This study has provided ample evidence that the new groups founded during the past 30 years have not simply reinforced the interests that were already represented in Washington. The consequences for executive branch politics produced by the increasing political polarization stemming from the elaboration of the group system is clearly illustrated by the evidence presented in table 8-2. Just as the 1980 survey queried groups about the effects of Carter's election on their relations with federal agencies (reported in chap. 7), groups participating in the 1985 survey were asked whether they had experienced an increase or decrease in cooperation and consultation with federal agencies as a result of the Reagan presidency. [1] For both new and old groups, we present the results of this question for the entire 1985 sample (sec. A), and for several subsamples based upon the reported policy interests of the associations (secs. B–F).

Table 8-2 illustrates, first of all, that many of the groups founded since 1965, in the years after the Kennedy-Johnson administrations and the mobilization engendered by the expanding Great Society programs, experienced a decline in cooperation from federal agencies under the Reagan administration. In section A of the table, where the total sample is described, 26 percent of the groups founded before 1965 reported increased cooperation, and about the same proportion—22 percent—indicated a decrease in cooperation. Among those founded in 1965 or after, however, only 14 percent reported more federal agency cooperation under the Reagan presidency, while 37 percent, almost three times as many, experienced a reduction in cooperation. The 1985 survey shows that the group system as a whole was about evenly balanced

---

1. The question was: "How did the change in 1981 from Democratic to Republican control of the presidency affect the amount of cooperation and consultation between this association and federal agencies?"

**TABLE 8-2. Perceptions of Changes in Federal Agency Cooperation Produced by the Election of Ronald Reagan**

| Founding Date | N | More Cooperation | No Change | Less Cooperation | No Contact Prior to 1980 | Row Total |
|---|---|---|---|---|---|---|
| | | A. Total Sample | | | | |
| Up to 1965 | 493 | 26% | 44% | 22% | 8% | 100% |
| Post-1965 | 292 | 14 | 34 | 37 | 15 | 100 |
| | | B. Agriculture | | | | |
| Up to 1965 | 78 | 33 | 38 | 26 | 3 | 100 |
| Post-1965 | 37 | 11 | 35 | 38 | 16 | 100 |
| | | C. Economic Development | | | | |
| Up to 1965 | 254 | 35 | 39 | 24 | 2 | 100 |
| Post-1965 | 137 | 20 | 37 | 34 | 9 | 100 |
| | | D. Social Welfare | | | | |
| Up to 1965 | 270 | 21 | 48 | 28 | 3 | 100 |
| Post-1965 | 166 | 11 | 28 | 48 | 13 | 100 |
| | | E. National Security | | | | |
| Up to 1965 | 94 | 33 | 44 | 19 | 4 | 100 |
| Post-1965 | 59 | 17 | 29 | 32 | 22 | 100 |
| | | F. Government Management | | | | |
| Up to 1965 | 86 | 40 | 37 | 23 | 0 | 100 |
| Post-1965 | 54 | 15 | 22 | 54 | 9 | 100 |

*Source:* 1985 Survey.

between those who perceived greater access under the Reagan administration and those who reported a decline in their relationship with government agencies, but it is clear that the newer groups that arose during an era when a liberal political consensus prevailed in Washington were the ones whose collective position declined most dramatically. It is also worth noting that the Reagan administration was not shooting at phantoms when it initiated its attack on the expanded group system. The associations founded since 1965 were more likely to desire an increase in federal social services than those created in earlier years.

Sections B through F in table 8-2 provide evidence that the polarization created by the influx of new interest groups since 1965 has taken place in all areas of American public policy. The patterns discovered for the full sample are repeated in all policy areas.[2] It comes as no surprise that the groups expressing an interest in social welfare policy (sec. D) experienced declines in cooperation with federal agencies under Reagan, given the Reagan administration's efforts to curtail expenditures for social programs sharply. The most extensive declines in cooperation, however, actually appear among groups interested in the management and accountability of the federal government (sec. F), presumably because of the Reagan administration's efforts to limit regulatory procedures and reduce public access to decision making. The modern system of interest representation is highly polarized, and becoming more so as the system grows.

The trend reflected in these data is toward increased ideological differences within the group structure underlying the two political parties. Interest groups, as they struggle to advance their own programs, are steadily being drawn into the orbit of one of the two major parties, thus experiencing the consequences of electoral politics and conflict within policy communities. The analysis presented in chapter 7 showed the degree to which these changes, by 1980, had disrupted established patterns of group, legislative, and executive interactions typically characterized as iron triangles or autonomous subgovernments. The continuing evolution of the group system in the 1980s, combined with the actions of the Reagan administration, further eroded these relationships. Even as issue networks had grown more complex by the end of the 1970s, 63 percent of the respondents to the 1980 survey reported that they saw no change in their governmental relationships when President Jimmy Carter replaced President Gerald Ford. Only about 40 percent of the groups responding to the 1985 survey, however, made a similar claim about the limited impact of Reagan's rise to the presidency. A somewhat larger proportion of younger organizations found their relationships with federal agencies less insulated from presidential politics, as shown in section A of table 8-2. Of groups that formed in years up to 1965, 44 percent reported no change in the level of cooperation they experienced with agencies during the Reagan administration; the proportion is only 34 percent for those organizations that emerged after 1965.

It is important to recognize, however, that the activities and relationships of a large number of groups are still largely impervious to the outcomes of partisan elections. Many of the newer groups have not established any contacts with federal agencies, so they have no relationships that can be affected by the outcomes of partisan elections. Some of these unaffected groups have

---

2. Respondents were asked to indicate the level of interest their groups had in ten policy areas. The results of a factor analysis were used to reduce the number of policy areas to five.

objectives and engage in activities that are inherently nonpartisan, or even apolitical. Approximately 8 percent of the groups in the 1985 survey, for example, did not engage in any of the electoral, lobbying, legal, or public relations activities asked about in our questionnaires. Groups like the Naval Historical Society, the American Genetics Association, or the American Home Economics Association confine themselves to standard setting, information exchanges, specialized midcareer training, or other purely technical functions for the professions they represent. Other organizations that are unaffected by changes in the partisan control of the White House are highly political and well connected with the federal executive and congressional establishments but continue to operate within the remaining subgovernments that are largely isolated from the pressures of partisan politics. There are still many groups who are able to conduct business as usual, no matter who is in the White House, but their numbers seem to be declining rapidly and the broader political contexts in which they operate are under more persistent challenge.

### Ideology and Response to the Reagan Administration

It is a group's ideology, not the policy area with which it is concerned, that best explains the degree of cooperation it experienced with federal agencies during the Reagan administration. Evidence from the panel data set substantiates this generalization. The results displayed in table 8-3 clearly show the strong relationship between group responses to the general questions about ideology posed in 1980 and the groups' perceptions five years later, in 1985, concerning the effect of the Reagan administration on the degree of cooperation and consultation they experienced with agencies of the federal government.[3] In the upper panel of the table, the positions taken by groups in 1980 on whether they desired increases in social services correlate strongly ($\gamma = -.55$) with 1985 reports of cooperation with federal agencies under Reagan. Those who desired higher levels of social services in 1980 reported that they experienced declines in cooperation with federal agencies once the Reagan

---

3. There may be some concern that the question about federal agency cooperation is merely tapping a group's ideological position in another way rather than its actual behavior. In other words, liberal groups may have reported declines in cooperation simply because they disliked and distrusted Ronald Reagan, not because of a real change in their relationship with federal agencies. Our data suggest, however, that this concern is unfounded. For example, in both surveys we asked the groups whether they were regularly consulted by federal agencies when policy changes were being considered. For the groups wanting much more social services provided by the government, the proportion reporting that they were consulted on policy issues declined from 87 percent under Carter to 53 percent under Reagan, while the proportion for their ideological opposites increased from 73 percent to 85 percent. In the 1985 survey, conservative groups consistently reported more frequent and more cooperative interactions with federal agencies than did their liberal counterparts.

**TABLE 8-3.   Relationship between a Group's 1980 Ideological Positions and 1985 Perceived Changes in Federal Agency Cooperation**

| Desired Level in 1980 | N | Perceived Level in 1985 | | | Row Total |
| | | More Cooperation | No Change | Less Cooperation | |
|---|---|---|---|---|---|
| Social Services | | | | | |
| Much More | 46 | 4% | 30% | 66% | 100% |
| Somewhat More | 98 | 8 | 43 | 49 | 100 |
| Present Level | 51 | 20 | 54 | 26 | 100 |
| Somewhat Less | 47 | 34 | 38 | 28 | 100 |
| Much Less | 43 | 53 | 40 | 7 | 100 |
| Federal Regulation | | | | | |
| Much More | 17 | 0 | 6 | 94 | 100 |
| Somewhat More | 46 | 4 | 30 | 66 | 100 |
| Present Level | 51 | 6 | 43 | 51 | 100 |
| Somewhat Less | 124 | 25 | 55 | 20 | 100 |
| Much Less | 74 | 58 | 28 | 14 | 100 |

*Source:* Panel data set.

administration came to power. In the lower panel, a group's 1980 position on the desirability of further federal regulation was an even better predictor of cooperation with the Reagan administration ($\gamma = -.67$). Groups that expressed a preference for greater federal regulation in 1980 tended to experience declines in cooperation in 1985.

These empirical manifestations highlight the stable and enduring ideological commitments of interest groups and demonstrate that, for many groups, these commitments determine the amount of access they enjoy with the administrative agencies of government. In 1980, the relationships between these ideological commitments and reports of cooperation with the Carter administration were also strong ($\gamma = .53$ and $.55$), although in these cases, groups that expressed a preference for more social services or regulation enjoyed *greater* cooperation with federal agencies. The sharp swings in the experiences of interest groups caused by changes in administrations provide further confirmation of the importance of ideology and the outcome of partisan elections in structuring the relationships between interest groups and the executive establishment.

The ideological positions of interest groups are closely related to the elements of society they represent. Trade associations and professional societies emerging from occupational communities in the profit sector of the economy are more likely, as a general proposition, to call for a reduction in the size and influence of the federal government. Groups advocating an en-

**TABLE 8-4.  Distribution of Ideology and Partisan Sensitivity of Groups**

| Ideology/Partisan Sensitivity | *N* | Profit | Mixed | Nonprofit | Citizen | Row Total |
|---|---|---|---|---|---|---|
| | | \multicolumn{4}{}{Type of Group} | | |
| | | \multicolumn{4}{}{Effect on Cooperation Due to Carter's Election} | | |
| Liberal/increased cooperation[a] | 46 | 13% | 7% | 33% | 78% | 100% |
| Conservative/decreased cooperation[b] | 28 | 75 | 0 | 14 | 11 | 100 |
| | | \multicolumn{4}{}{Effect on Cooperation Due to Reagan's Election} | | |
| Conservative/increased cooperation[c] | 39 | 69 | 3 | 15 | 13 | 100 |
| Liberal/decreased cooperation[d] | 70 | 7 | 6 | 41 | 46 | 100 |

*Source:* Panel data set.

[a]Groups that called for an increase in the provision of federal social services in 1980 and perceived an increase in federal agency cooperation as a result of the election of President Carter.

[b]Groups that called for a decrease in the provision of federal social services in 1980 and perceived a decrease in federal agency cooperation as a result of the election of President Carter.

[c]Groups that called for a decrease in the provision of federal social services in 1980 and perceived an increase in federal agency cooperation in 1985 as a result of the election of President Reagan.

[d]Groups that called for an increase in the provision of federal social services in 1980 and perceived a decrease in federal agency cooperation in 1985 as a result of the election of President Reagan.

hanced regulatory role for government and an expansion of social programs usually are either citizen groups with financial backing from foundations, wealthy individuals, churches, or trade unions, or they emerge from occupational communities within the society's growing nonprofit realm that often service or administer government programs. The contrasting organizational foundations of the group system are revealed in table 8-4, in which the types of groups most opposed to the Carter and Reagan administrations and those that are most supportive are compared.

In the upper panel of table 8-4, groups who strongly supported an increase in social services at the federal level (described as liberals in the table) in 1980—the last year of the Carter administration—and also enjoyed more cooperation from federal agencies during the Carter administration are compared with those that both called for reductions in federal social services (designated as conservatives in the table) and experienced less cooperation from federal agencies during the Carter years. In the lower panel of the table, the contrast is between the conservative groups who wanted to reduce social services and experienced greater cooperation from the Reagan administration—presumably the president's strongest supporters—and those liberal groups who stood for an increase in social services in 1980 and experienced a *decrease* in cooperation from federal agencies under Reagan.

Table 8-4 shows quite dramatically that the strongest opponents and supporters of the two administrations come predominantly from different parts of the interest-group world. Seventy-five percent of President Carter's conservative critics came from the business-oriented groups in the profit sector, while his liberal supporters were among the citizen groups (48 percent) and groups made up of social service professionals in the nonprofit sector (33 percent). Five years later, the situation was completely reversed. The conservative interest groups that were Reagan's strongest organizational allies came predominantly from the business-oriented, profit sector (69 percent), while his most determined liberal opponents were to be found among groups in the nonprofit (41 percent) and citizen (46 percent) sectors. These distinctions also have a partisan component to them. Two-thirds of all groups reporting an increase or decrease in the cooperation they received from federal agencies as a result of Reagan's election said (earlier in the 1985 survey) that they perceived differences between the Democratic and Republican parties that were relevant to their policy objectives ($\gamma = .61$).[4]

When Ronald Reagan replaced Jimmy Carter in the White House, there was a virtual revolution in the access or denial of access experienced by different segments of the interest community represented in Washington (see Peterson 1990b). In the past, many groups, regardless of their philosophical or policy orientation, may have been able to maintain their contacts with the bureaucratic agencies of the federal government through politically isolated subgovernments or iron triangles no matter what the outcome of the election. By 1980, it was increasingly difficult to build such safe enclaves around a group's favorite programs as at least some subgovernments gave way to less autonomous issue networks. With Reagan's election, the potential for isolation from electoral fortunes deteriorated even further, and ideological compatibility with the administration in power became more significant than ever before. When candidates for the presidency employ broad ideological themes in their campaigns, as Reagan did, and threaten to alter fundamentally the direction of public policy, almost no governmental program is entirely secure. Even some of the groups with the most narrow commercial, occupational, or professional focus may find themselves being drawn into alliances with one of the two major political parties in order to protect their futures, whether they like it or not.

---

4. In response to the statement, "This association perceives an important difference between the two major political parties on those issues most relevant to its goals," group respondents were asked to place the organization on a five-point scale ranging from 1, a "poor description of the association," to 5, a "good description of the association." Groups that marked 3, 4, or 5 on the scale were treated as being sensitive to partisan concerns.

## The Maintenance of Interest Groups under Reagan

The Reagan administration's campaign to restrict the resources and influence of interest groups that receive financial aid and comfort from the federal government was a logical extension of its unusually sharp, confrontational style. The policymakers in the White House were well aware that groups in the nonprofit and citizen categories were likely to be unsympathetic with the policy goals of President Reagan. The administration may have failed to reduce the total number of interest groups operating at the national level, but our data reveal that it was successful in significantly reducing the amount of government funding being used to maintain the types of groups most likely to oppose the administration's principal goals. Using data from the panel study, table 8-5 presents the sources of revenue for all four types of groups—profit, mixed, nonprofit, and citizen—in 1980, just prior to the beginning of the Reagan administration, and in 1985, during the first year of President Reagan's second term.

Each type of group was affected by the policy changes of the Reagan administration in slightly different ways. The groups in the profit sector— mainly trade associations and professional societies that were sympathetic to the Reagan administration—received most of their revenues in recurring payments from their members in the form of dues, publication subscriptions, and conference fees in both 1980 (82.9 percent) and 1985 (81.3 percent). These groups changed their mix of support slightly by relying less upon annual dues in 1985, and increasing the revenues they secured from conferences, trade shows, and seminars. These business oriented groups also increased the proportion of their revenues coming from nonrecurring sources, such as grants, contracts, and gifts from other associations and business firms, and, interestingly enough, they maintained their small level of financial support from government agencies in the Reagan administration.

Government support was down substantially for other types of groups in 1985, however, and this caused the nonprofit and citizen groups to seek out several new sources of revenue. Table 8-5 reveals that groups in the nonprofit sector, unlike the other groups, maintained the same level of revenues from dues, while citizen groups received perhaps even less of their financial support from their members in 1985 than they had in 1980. Citizen groups obtained only 31.3 percent of their support in 1985 directly from annual dues, down from 34.9 percent reported five years before.

There was an uneven pattern of gains and losses in memberships among the citizen groups that opposed the Reagan administration. Many of the groups from the environmental, peace, and women's movements reported sharp increases in the size of their memberships, but, overall, groups that

**TABLE 8-5.  Mean Percentage of Total 1980 and 1985 Revenues Received from Various Sources**

| Revenue Source | Profit | | Mixed | | Nonprofit | | Citizen | |
|---|---|---|---|---|---|---|---|---|
| | 1980 | 1985 | 1980 | 1985 | 1980 | 1985 | 1980 | 1985 |
| Routine contributions from members and associates | | | | | | | | |
| Dues | 67.9 | 63.1 | 58.1 | 47.6 | 47.7 | 48.2 | 34.9 | 31.3 |
| Publications | 6.2 | 6.4 | 10.2 | 9.6 | 10.3 | 11.2 | 5.7 | 7.7 |
| Conferences | 8.8 | 11.8 | 11.1 | 11.4 | 8.3 | 10.3 | 4.3 | 3.9 |
| Subtotal | 82.9 | 81.3 | 79.4 | 68.6 | 66.3 | 69.7 | 44.9 | 42.9 |
| Nonrecurring contributions from nonmember institutions and persons | | | | | | | | |
| Individual gifts | 1.8 | 0.6 | 2.1 | 4.2 | 3.1 | 1.8 | 16.2 | 11.2 |
| Private foundations | 0.4 | 0.4 | 1.2 | 0.8 | 3.6 | 2.8 | 10.8 | 8.1 |
| Government | 3.4 | 3.2 | 4.1 | 6.0 | 12.2 | 7.8 | 11.9 | 8.0 |
| Business firms[a] | — | 2.3 | — | 5.9 | — | 2.4 | — | 7.2 |
| Churches[a] | — | 0.0 | — | 0.0 | — | 1.2 | — | 1.1 |
| Unions[a] | — | 0.0 | — | 0.0 | — | 0.0 | — | 2.3 |
| Other associations | 2.1 | 1.8 | 0.4 | 0.5 | 3.1 | 2.1 | 3.0 | 3.2 |
| Subtotal | 7.7 | 8.3 | 7.8 | 17.4 | 22.0 | 18.1 | 41.9 | 41.1 |
| Miscellaneous recurring and nonrecurring contributions Investments, sales, fees, commissions, events, rent, interest, etc. | 7.4 | 10.4 | 7.3 | 12.1 | 9.5 | 10.8 | 10.3 | 15.1 |
| Loans | 0.3 | 0.1 | 0.4 | 1.9 | 0.6 | 0.2 | 0.6 | 0.8 |
| Other | 1.6 | 0.8 | 5.1 | 0.0 | 3.0 | 0.5 | 0.9 | 0.1 |
| Subtotal | 9.3 | 11.3 | 12.8 | 14.0 | 13.1 | 11.5 | 11.8 | 16.0 |
| Total[b] | 99.9 | 100.9 | 100.0 | 100.0 | 101.4 | 99.3 | 98.6 | 100.0 |
| N | 155 | 156 | 25 | 28 | 151 | 155 | 96 | 103 |

*Source:* Panel data set.

[a]In the 1980 questionnaire, there were no specific categories for funds from business firms, churches, or unions. Respondents may have included these sources in the categories for individual gifts, other associations, or other.

[b]Totals may not equal 100 percent due to rounding.

were the strongest critics of the Reagan administration, those that supported increases in the level of social services in 1980 and reported a decline in cooperation with federal agencies in 1985 as a result of Reagan's election, lost on the average about 10 percent of their members between 1980 and 1985 (see Waterman 1989, 134).

Gifts and contracts also were down for citizen groups as sources of revenue, not only from the government, but also from individuals and foundations. In order to compensate for these losses, the citizen groups were able to increase significantly the revenues they received in 1985 from business firms,

**TABLE 8-6.   Mean Percentages of Total 1980
and 1985 Revenue Received from Various Sources
for Nonprofit Sector Groups That Received 30 Percent
or More of Their 1980 Funds from Government**

| Revenue Source | 1980 | 1985 |
|---|---|---|
| Routine contributions from members and associates | | |
|   Dues | 23.1 | 32.6 |
|   Publications | 3.6 | 3.9 |
|   Conferences | 4.9 | 3.6 |
|     Subtotal | 31.6 | 40.1 |
| Nonrecurring contributions from non-member institutions and persons | | |
|   Individual gifts | 4.7 | 2.4 |
|   Private foundations | 5.0 | 7.0 |
|   Government | 49.8 | 33.4 |
|   Business firms[a] | — | 6.3 |
|   Churches[a] | — | 0.3 |
|   Unions[a] | — | 0.0 |
|   Other associations | 1.0 | 0.5 |
|     Subtotal | 60.5 | 49.9 |
| Miscellaneous recurring and nonrecurring contributions | | |
| Investments, sales, fees, commissions, | | |
|   events, rent, interest, etc. | 5.6 | 8.3 |
|   Loans | 0.6 | 0.3 |
|   Other | 1.6 | 0.9 |
|     Subtotal | 7.8 | 9.5 |
| Total[b] | 99.9 | 99.5 |
| *N* | 43 | 43 |

*Source:* Panel data set.

[a]In the 1980 questionnaire, there were no specific categories for funds from business firms, churches, or unions. Respondents may have included these sources in the categories for individual gifts, other associations, or other.

[b]Totals may not equal 100 percent due to rounding.

churches, and unions, and were also able to earn more by selling the services of their staffs, gaining greater return on investments, and staging other fundraising events. Government support for most interest groups was reduced by the Reagan administration, but the data in table 8-5 indicate that the types of groups most vulnerable to these reductions were able to diversify their sources of revenue, and thus stay in operation, even if some of the administration's strongest critics suffered membership losses and were forced to reduce the size of their staffs.

The data in table 8-5 report average revenues for all the groups in our sample, but the Reagan administration's efforts to reduce the flow of government grants and contracts to interest groups fell most heavily upon a relatively small number of groups that were the most heavily dependent on government financial support, mainly associations of social service and public service professionals in the nonprofit sector. These groups suffered significant setbacks during the first term of the Reagan administration, and many were forced to dismiss large numbers of staff members and substantially reduce their activities. Their operations became smaller, but this study indicates that most of these groups managed to remain in existence by finding new sources of revenue. This process of diversification is illustrated in table 8-6, which shows the financial status (in 1985) of the 43 groups from the panel study that received 30 percent or more of their revenues from government sources during the last year of the Carter administration.

The groups shown in table 8-6 garnered, on average, 50 percent of their revenues from government agencies in 1980, but by 1985 that proportion had been cut significantly to about 33 percent. Almost all of these organizations were required to reduce their staffs, and they also tried to fall back upon their members by increasing revenues from dues, publications, and conference fees. These efforts raised the proportion of their revenues coming from recurring contributions from members to 40 percent in 1985, up from only 31 percent in 1980. The groups also made vigorous efforts to find new sources of funds from private foundations and business firms and, like most of the groups in the study, devised many new ways to raise money through benefits, social events, the sale of services from their staffs, and the short-term investment of their cash balances. The Reagan administration succeeded in reducing funding for groups that were heavily dependent on support from sympathetic government agencies, but the administration was not able to completely eliminate all funds flowing to these organizations or to force very many of them out of existence.

### Interest Groups, Iron Triangles, and Partisan Politics under Reagan

The Reagan administration's effort to break the ties between government agencies and sympathetic interest groups met with mixed results. To begin with, our data show that the interest-group system continued to expand during Reagan's time in office. Some citizen groups in areas like international peace and security, environmental protection, and women's rights challenged the central tenets of the Reagan program in an effort to polarize issues and draw sharp distinctions between themselves and the administration. In those cases where the President responded with ideological broadsides of his own, he brought these groups to center stage and aided them in attracting new members and patrons. Ironically, the groups most vulnerable to the administration's challenge were not the publicity oriented, contentious citizen groups of the political left, but, rather, the relatively staid professional societies in the nonprofit sector, which had always claimed to be nonpartisan prior to President Reagan's arrival. Rather than defeating the vocal critics of his agenda, Reagan politicized professional organizations that had previously placed a premium on political neutrality and quiescence.

Ronald Reagan had a much larger impact on the interest-group system than Jimmy Carter did, but in both cases many interest groups were able to continue with business as usual, regardless of who was in the White House. A small number of groups, about 8 percent of those in our sample, are virtually apolitical and hardly ever make an effort to exert influence. Business and trade associations—the largest segment of the interest-group system—were not targets of the Reagan administration's campaign, and numerous groups in the nonprofit sector were able to remain aloof because of their ties with the remaining independent subgovernments. The Reagan administration managed to affect the operations of a much higher proportion of the interest groups than the Carter administration, but even so, about 40 percent of the groups still were able to maintain their relations with government agencies without being affected by Reagan's actions as president, at least where the programs and issues of vital importance to them were concerned.

Some of the groups that were able to insulate themselves from the effects of partisan elections supported the Reagan administration's policies and were useful political allies, but almost half of the unaffected groups supported an increase in the social services provided by the federal government and clearly were not in tune with the administration's principal policy goals. The determined effort by the Reagan administration to change the relationships between interest groups and the agencies of the executive branch revealed how complex and mutually supportive these relationships are. It would take years of consistent pressure and the expenditure of enormous amounts of political capital to cut all the ties that bind group representatives with committees of Congress and the permanent agencies of government.

Even though the interest-group system underwent no fundamental changes in its size and scope, there is no doubt that President Reagan had a powerful effect on the Washington political universe. Government funding for interest groups unquestionably was reduced, especially for those groups of professionals in the nonprofit sector working in social welfare fields that were heavily dependent upon support from sympathetic government agencies. Very few groups, however, were put completely out of operation, because new sources of support were discovered by enterprising group leaders who successfully turned to business firms, unions, churches, and to their members for increased financial aid. While Reagan was able to contribute to the disruption of previously quiescent subgovernmental politics, he was not successful at turning back the changes in the interest-group community that had brought forceful new advocates into many policy arenas. Most groups that Reagan attacked ultimately could adjust their bases of financial support, and many had never become dependent upon government grants and contracts in the first place.

The stubborn resistance of interest groups to the determined efforts of the Reagan administration to curtail their influence illustrates several underlying trends that shaped American political institutions in the 1980s. The president and the leaders of interest groups were both responding to the same pressures that were leading away from the politics of regional, religious, and ethnic blocs toward the new politics of the postindustrial middle class, carried out through the mass media and dominated by provocative ideological themes. As the ideological content of the national political debate intensifies and the attentive public grows, many different elements of the country's diverse population feel that their interests are threatened and are prompted to join associations pledged to protect them. These associations fill the mails with dire warnings of environmental disaster, the triumph of secular humanism, or the incineration of civilization in a nuclear war.

As the circle of participants in the dialogue over public policy grows and the political system becomes increasingly polarized along ideological lines, each individual interest group will be under pressure to encourage the fortunes of the political party that affords it the best access to government. Pressures will increase for all interest groups of liberal persuasion to form loose alliances during elections to work for the victory of the political party that best represents their views. For most citizen groups there will be no other path to influence. Groups that have developed close, cooperative relationships within subgovernments increasingly will be pressed to take sides in the partisan struggle. As ideological polarization pushes interest groups into large contending camps, political parties emerge as the only agencies logically capable of exercising leadership and providing coordination. The enhanced prominence of the programmatic goals of the parties, however, will pose new threats to more and more elements of the population, thus stimulating the continued expansion of the system of interest groups.

The same broad social forces are determining the future of both the political parties and the interest-group system in America. The Reagan administration's efforts to reshape the rules under which the representative system is governed are harbingers of a new form of ideological politics in America. If these trends continue, both political parties and interest groups will alter their behavior, and those who control our governing institutions will be confronted with many severe tests of leadership.

# CHAPTER 9

# The Litigation Strategies of Interest Groups

*Kim Lane Scheppele and Jack L. Walker, Jr.*

## Interest Groups in the Courts

One day in the late fall of 1969, Justice Hugo Black was working in his chambers at the Supreme Court when an old friend stopped by to visit. Thomas G. ("Tommy the Cork") Corcoran had been a strong supporter of the New Deal along with Black, but Corcoran had since gone into private law practice in Washington where he was known as an important lobbyist. Black assumed Corcoran was coming by to discuss his daughter, a former law clerk of Black's. Instead, Corcoran brought up a case that the court had decided against the El Paso Natural Gas Company the term before. The case was before the Court again on a petition for rehearing. Corcoran had come to lobby his old friend to vote for his client. As Woodward and Armstrong in their book, *The Brethren*, described it:

> Black was shocked. No one came to the Supreme Court to lobby, even to "put in a good word" for a petitioner. The mere mention of a pending case at a cocktail party was forbidden. Out-of-court contacts with Justices about cases were unethical . . . . Black cut his old friend off quickly. *No.* He shooed Corcoran out of his office. (Woodward and Armstrong 1981, 89)

Undaunted, Corcoran then made an appointment to see Justice William Brennan. As soon as Corcoran made the purpose of his visit clear, Brennan refused to discuss the case and asked Corcoran to leave. Brennan had already decided to vote in favor of the rehearing, but he was afraid that doing so after being approached in this way would create the appearance of impropriety. After discussing the matter with Black, Brennan decided to recuse himself. But Black had already decided before the Corcoran visit to vote against the rehearing petition. He did not withdraw from the case, since the direction of his vote meant that no one could accuse him of having been influenced in his friend's favor. When the matter finally came up for a vote, the petition was denied. Had Brennan stayed in for the vote, however, the petition would probably have been accepted. As it turned out, the actions of this particular lobbyist, in combination with the traditions of the Court, produced the opposite of the outcome he sought. The Court might well have come out in Corcoran's favor had he not intervened in this unseemly manner.

Clearly, many of the strategies and tactics available for lobbying Congress, administrative agencies, and the executive branch are not available for lobbying the courts. This does not mean, however, that courts are free from the influence of organized interests. Though they may have an ivory tower reputation, courts have become important to interest groups in their quests for favorable policy. Groups file lawsuits to safeguard the interests of their members, promote test cases or class action suits to secure judicial favor for a particular principle, defend against formal charges rather than settle out of court, and file amicus briefs to provide new information to courts hearing disputes between others. These are all strategies that ensure that courts will hear interest groups' points of view, though they by no means assure that the interests of the groups will prevail. Attempting to exercise influence in the courts is a very different matter from attempting to exercise influence in other political arenas.

Some groups are quite well known for their strategic use of the courts. The NAACP, for example, was able to engage in a deliberate, carefully crafted, and enormously successful campaign in the courts to undermine the legal validity of restrictive covenants in housing. They did this through the strategic promotion of test cases until they succeeded in getting the Supreme Court to strike down the provisions (Vose 1959). The ACLU has been involved in many legal battles on many different issues, using litigation as one of its key methods of influencing national policy. Many groups on both sides of the abortion conflict, including the National Abortion Rights Action League, the ACLU Reproductive Rights Project, the National Right to Life Committee, and others, have tried to influence the Supreme Court by filing amicus briefs every time the Court agrees to hear an abortion case, culminating in a record 78 briefs filed by different groups and coalitions of groups for the Court's consideration in *Webster v. Reproductive Health Services* (1989). Clearly, the courts are an important battleground for interest groups. But the battles are fought in public—in case filings and legal briefs—rather than behind the scenes in private lobbying.

Political scientists studying the courts have devoted substantial effort to working out the influence of interest groups on the judiciary and on the outcomes of legal disputes. Some studies have examined particular interest groups or clusters of interest groups and the strategies they have used to influence the courts (Vose 1959; Manwaring 1962; Handler 1978; O'Connor

1980; Olson 1984; Epstein 1985). From these detailed studies, it is clear that many specific groups find the use of the courts crucial to achieving their broader policy goals and that the courts have often supported them in their efforts. Other studies have examined particular courts and the interest groups that have appeared in these forums (Hakman 1966; Casper 1972; O'Connor and Epstein 1981; Olson 1990). Here, too, it is clear that interest groups play a large role in sponsoring litigation and filing amicus briefs to promote their interests. Still other studies have examined a particular policy issue and traced the various groups that have gotten involved in that policy debate (Birkby and Murphy 1964; Barker 1967; Cortner 1968; Sorauf 1976; Olson 1984; O'Neill 1985; Kobylka 1987). And finally, another group of studies has considered litigation strategies over a wide range of different groups to see what seems to lead some groups but not others to try to influence policy-making through the courts (Schlozman and Tierney 1986; Caldeira and Wright 1988, 1989, 1990; Bruer 1986 and 1988). Though the studies vary in focus and methodology, their cumulative force indicates that a thorough understanding of the legal process is impossible without considering the substantial and varied role of interest groups.

But when will groups use the courts for policy purposes? And how do they tailor their strategies once they decide to use the courts? Existing studies are not at all agreed on what leads groups to turn to the courts. Several different explanations, drawn from these radically different sorts of investigations, compete to account for why some groups rather than others use the courts to promote their policy agendas. Most of the theories have been developed in the context of detailed knowledge of particular case studies, which, no matter how illuminating and interesting as case studies, do not address the broader question of what makes interest groups use the courts in general. This problem of generalizable knowledge is particularly troubling in light of the fact that 51 of the 60 papers published on interest-group litigation between Clement Vose's study of the NAACP in 1959 and Lee Epstein's study of conservative interest groups in 1985 reported on the activities of liberal groups (Epstein 1985, 7) and most of those examined what we have been calling citizen groups. As we have seen throughout this book, citizen groups represent a minority of the groups in the interest-group universe. Any general theory developed in the context of such a skewed sample is likely to be misleading. The organized interests that are not citizen groups have not been very well represented in the interest-group litigation literature. Though this is changing as researchers begin to focus on broader samples of interest groups (see, particularly, Schlozman and Tierney 1986; Caldeira and Wright 1988, 1989, 1990; Bruer 1986 and 1988), we do not yet know whether the theories that have been discussed in the case study literature apply to the broad range of interest groups operating in the courts.

**Explanations of Interest-Group Litigation**

As the literature on interest-group litigation has grown, a number of different explanations have been developed to account for why some groups use the courts more than others. These explanations focus on the extent to which the group in question is politically disadvantaged in the electoral process, the extent to which the group can frame its interests in terms of rights, and the demographic characteristics of the organization itself. Though individual studies tend to focus on one of these features to the exclusion of others, we will argue that they should be thought of together in any broader study of interest-group litigation. In addition, we will argue that interest groups are more likely to use the courts when groups' goals and characteristics allow them to exploit the special advantages of courts as a setting for policy-making. Institutional compatibility of the courts with some groups rather than others may account for why some groups litigate and some groups do not. We will look at each of these explanations in turn.

*Political Disadvantage.* The political disadvantage theory argues that groups are likely to seek remedies in the courts when they are not likely to succeed in the electoral process (Olson 1990). Growing originally out of studies of the NAACP, whose litigation drive has been the subject of much research (Vose 1959; Cortner 1968; Kluger 1977), the political disadvantage theory has been supported by some case studies (Manwaring 1962; Sorauf 1976; O'Connor 1980) and refuted by others (Epstein 1985; Olson 1984 and 1990). If the political disadvantage theory is correct, we would expect groups that represent those on the political "outs" to use courts quite extensively and those who have access to the political process to use the courts less often. Outsiders should use the courts more often than insiders.

*Rights Claims.* Some researchers have seen the increase in collective rights consciousness in the last several decades as central to interest-group litigation (see Olson 1984, 5–7). Groups that see themselves in terms of uncompromising rights will find themselves in the courts more often than those who see themselves as having interests that can be bargained over in the political process. In fact, the presentation of a claim on government as a rights claim helps to mobilize constituencies who might otherwise remain unmoved (Scheingold 1974). Court victories tend to be complete for one side or the other, but they also tend to be long-drawn-out battles. So, the rights explosion theory goes, groups that see themselves as having rights to promote and who are willing to hang in there for the long haul will use the courts more than those who do not frame their policy goals in such terms. Citizen groups, which tend to be organized around rights rather than merely around interests, will tend to litigate more than other sorts of groups, if this view is correct.

*Organizational Characteristics.* Researchers have looked at a number of different characteristics of interest groups as shaping their litigation patterns.

Karen O'Connor, reviewing the literature making these claims, found that the characteristics of an interest group that had been found to be positively related to its propensity to use litigation in pursuit of its policy goals were longevity, full-time staff and attorneys, sharp issue focus, financial resources, use of technical data, ability to generate publicity, close coordination between national headquarters and local affiliates, coordination with other interest groups, and ability to persuade the Justice Department or Solicitor General to enter on its side of the case (O'Connor 1980, 17–28). While this is a large array of factors to take into account, there are two main dimensions represented in this list. The first is, broadly speaking, organizational resources, including financial capacity, dedicated staff, and advanced age of the organization. The second is the ability to form coalitions and win others over to the interest group's side. Large organizational resources and elaborate organizational networks lead groups to use the courts.

*Institutional Compatibility.* When interest groups consider using the courts to press their views, they immediately come up against a variety of barriers. In contrast with the relatively open avenues of access to other sources of governmental authority, courts operate behind walls of procedural rules that groups must get over before they can present their views. Not all interest groups will find these walls worth scaling, and many will not be able to—it is important to note that interest groups' use of courts may depend more on the requirements of litigation and on the special limitations and capacities of courts than on the group's specific agenda. Getting standing in court requires suing someone in particular for a specific, demonstrable harm, and a group is more likely to be successful if its opponents are clear and conflict is intense. A group is also more likely to be successful if its fortunes vary a great deal with changes in the political climate, for then it can demonstrate concrete losses. A group is more likely to prevail in a lawsuit if it is suing under favorable legislation that the group lobbied to pass, and so, on this view, we would expect government insiders to be found in court. A group is also more likely to be successful if it is working in a policy area where the courts have clear jurisdiction. Foreign policy and national security are issues that courts tend to avoid, while economic growth and human services are issues that do tend to be resolved by courts. The match between an organization's agenda and the rules courts use to screen cases will make some organizations more likely than others to use the courts.

## Developing a Model of Interest-Group Litigation

Taking these different explanations together, we can see that a variety of factors might be important in an interest group's decision to use the courts. In this section, we explore the measureable components of each explanation in more depth.

*Organizational Resources.* Using the courts is expensive. It also requires substantial control over the group's strategy to be in the hands of lawyers. And courts are very time consuming to use, both at any moment a case is active and over the years it takes cases to run the gauntlet of appeal. Organizations need the resources of money, ability to turn control of policy over to lawyers, and a long time-horizon to use the courts. These are crucial resources any organization must have to find the courts attractive as a place to achieve policy goals.

Expenses mount because at least one, and often many, lawyers are needed to argue cases in court. Even to file a case and then settle out of court calls for the advice of lawyers, and employing lawyers, whether on staff or on a piecemeal basis for particular cases, means that the interest group needs large organizational resources unless it has a lot of volunteered legal assistance. Submitting amicus curiae briefs is much cheaper. Interest groups may file amicus briefs with the courts with fewer resources and less specialized legal expertise. Even so, one estimate puts the average cost of an amicus brief at $8,000 per filing, with actual reported costs ranging from $500 to $50,000 for one brief (Caldeira and Wright 1990). Amicus briefs are certainly cheaper than full-blown litigation, but their cost is far from negligible. We would expect that the greater the organization's financial resources, the more likely it is to engage in both litigation and filing amicus briefs, though we would expect the influence of resources to be weaker on the latter than on the former.

How might we measure financial resources? The obvious measure is organizational budget. But, as we have seen in chapters 5 and 6, many of our respondents left the budget question unanswered. For those who did answer the budget question, estimates of budget correlated highly with staff size ($r = .9$). Instead of relying on budget estimates and losing part of our sample, then, we have chosen to use staff size as the best proxy measure of group resources. Since the impact of each additional staff member is likely to decrease with the total size of staff, we have used log of staff size as a measure of financial resources here, following the usage in chapters 5 and 6.

Not all dollars are alike when it comes to organizational resources, though. As we noted in chapter 5, groups vary in the dominant source of their revenue. Some groups get most of their funds from members or a diffuse range of sources. Others are kept going by a few wealthy patrons, particularly foundations, corporations, and large gifts from other interested private parties.[1] Whether groups turn to litigation will depend not only on how many

---

1. Our patron variable reflects the percentage of an organization's budget that comes from (*a*) gifts or bequests beyond normal dues, (*b*) foundation grants, (*c*) gifts or grants from corporations or businesses, (*d*) interest from cash balances or endowments, (*e*) funds from other organizations or associations, and (*f*) funds from churches.

resources a group has, but also on where those resources come from. As Handler (1978) and Olson (1984) have argued, groups that use litigation typically cede substantial control over the cases to lawyers, and this is much easier to do with a diverse resource base where no single contributor pays enough to feel entitled to call the shots. Ligitation is likely to be less attractive to patrons than other forms of political activity because litigation uses a lot of resources in a few campaigns and litigation also uses experts who can second-guess the patrons in devising strategy. When those who pay for the activities of a group are more dispersed, the concentration of decision making in a few people with expertise cannot easily be challenged by a large and diffuse membership. We would expect that the more an organization's resources come from a few patrons, the less likely the group is to use litigation.

Litigation may also be unattractive to patrons because it runs the risk of disqualifying the interest group from a special kind of tax exemption. If it qualifies under 26 USCA 501(c)(3), one part of the U.S. Code devoted to tax matters, a group carries tax-exempt status and its contributors are allowed to deduct their contributions on their own personal tax forms. Although there are a number of other ways for groups to be tax-exempt, only 501(c)(3) comes with this special benefit for contributors. Since a number of foundations (Ford and Carnegie among them) cannot give money to organizations that fail to achieve the 501(c)(3) exemption (Berry 1977, 48), many groups find it important to keep their activities within the limits that the IRS allows for such groups. Section 501(c)(3) includes a specific prohibition on lobbying Congress, but groups with that designation are allowed to approach administrative agencies and to litigate. There are a number of strings attached to litigation strategies of these groups, however. According to IRS guidelines, any litigation a 501(c)(3) organization engages in must be "in representation of a broad public interest rather than a private interest" and the organization must not receive either fees for its services or court-awarded judgments that exceed half the organization's operating costs in the preceding five years (Revenue Procedure 71–39, C.B. 575 [1971–72]). These rules might be interpreted as requiring a 501(c)(3) group to bring litigation that would otherwise not be provided in the "traditional marketplace for legal services" (Chisolm 1987, 214).

If a group believes it cannot meet these restrictions, then it may still be eligible for tax-exempt status under some other section of 501(c). The main benefit the group loses is the ability to offer its donors the option of deducting contributions to the group on the donors' tax forms. Even among groups explicitly devoted to furthering the public interest, however, 501(c)(3) status is not the only tax game in town. A recent interview with an IRS official found that "27 of 167 tax-exempt organizations engaging in public interest litigation were exempt under 501(c)(4) rather than section 501(c)(3)" (Simon 1989, 1099, n. 177). Organizing under some section other than 501(c)(3) may have the effect of reducing the range of possible patrons, but it may still preserve the group's tax-exempt status. We would expect the extent of patronage to vary strongly with the type of litigation done, but not as strongly with whether litigation is done.[2]

Finally, in the organizational resource category, the longevity of the organization is a consideration. Litigation is a long-term process, and the current age of an organization is one measure (however imperfect) of the ability of an organization to hang in for the long time it takes to press cases. Given the long time-horizon of lawsuits, we would expect that the longer a group has been around, the more it will be willing to take the long view necessary to think of generating policy success through lawsuits. Of course, the newness of a group does not preclude its being founded with a long time-horizon at the start, but we believe this to be less likely. We would therefore expect age of the organization to have a positive, but weak, effect on use of the courts.

*The Structure of Conflict.* Lawsuits are fights. More particularly, they are fights between two or more parties arranged around a bipolar split. Courts generally cannot handle policy questions that do not have this structure, because the "case or controversy" rule limits court intervention to real disputes between opposing parties.[3] The U.S. Constitution restricts the jurisdiction of courts to these structured contests and has been interpreted not to allow courts to handle issues on which a group would simply like a ruling or on which the law could lend some moral support to a particular point of view without settling an actual controversy.

Having a structured conflict alone is not enough to be able to gain entry to the courts. The opponent cannot just be a person or group that the organization objects to on principle, or a person or group who opposes the organization's interests or stands in the way of its policy goals. To bring someone else into court, plaintiffs have to have *standing* and they have to demonstrate sufficient *nexus* between the defendants' actions and the plaintiffs' injuries. That is, plaintiffs have to have legally recognizable claims that generally, though not always, require that they demonstrate that (*a*) defendants have

---

2. Some groups have gotten the best of both worlds by organizing themselves as 501(c)(4) organizations to lobby Congress, with 501(c)(3) litigating arms. As Shaiko (1991) notes, the percentage of public interest groups organized in such a fashion increased from 11 percent in 1972 to 22 percent in 1985. Unfortunately, though we know that 93 percent of the organizations in our sample have some form of tax exemption, we do not know under which IRS rule they have achieved this status. Thus, we are not in a position to determine whether groups organized in such a fashion litigate differently from those organized solely under one heading or the other.

3. This rule is stated too strongly. Courts have been finding ingenious ways around the bipolar splits that are typical of litigation in structuring some public interest lawsuits. But these are still the exception rather than the rule. See Chayes 1976 for a sympathetic discussion of these developments, and see Horowitz 1977, especially chap. 2, for a criticism of this practice and a discussion of the special structure of litigation.

done identifiable and significant damage to the plaintiffs, (*b*) were it not for the defendants' actions, the damage would not have occurred, and (*c*) the court has within its power the ability to provide relief for the injury that has occurred. Standing and nexus rules have liberalized in some areas of doctrine in the last several decades, particularly in the environmental area where statutes have explicitly incorporated private rights of action. This allows plaintiffs working in those areas to bring lawsuits alleging quite limited amounts of harm. But this is the exception rather than the rule, and the tendency of courts has been to limit standing and expand the requirement that defendants' actions be directly responsible for the plaintiffs' injuries in order to allow litigation to proceed.

In addition, there are complicated rules regulating when an organization can bring suit on behalf of its members, rules that vary with the statute under which the suit is being brought. In the most general formulation, an organization has standing to bring suit on behalf of its members when (*a*) the members of the organization would have standing to sue in their own right, (*b*) the interests alleged are relevant to the organization's purpose, and (*c*) the participation of the members of the group is not necessary either to assert the claim or to request relief (*Hunt v. Washington Apple Advertising Commission*, 1977).

Unfortunately, we would need data about the precise statute under which a group plans to litigate to determine the effect of these considerations on interest-group litigation. But we can say something about the very large differences between litigation and other forms of advocacy. Even if courts were inclined to hear a case filed by a particular group under a particular statute, not all sorts of opposition of interests would be likely to lead to litigation in the first place. Conflict with *recurring* opponents is more likely to generate lawsuits than conflict with others who might be allies on other issues. We asked groups directly whether they repeatedly faced the same opponents to measure the extent to which conflicts a group faced were transient or recurring.

We would also expect *intensity* of conflicts to increase the likelihood of bringing lawsuits, since the high costs and high stakes of lawsuits only make them worthwhile where the parties are deeply engaged in the conflict. Lawsuits are often the choice of last resort for contesting parties because, once two sides are engaged in legal combat, it becomes very difficult to make up or cooperate in future ventures.[4] We asked groups whether they worked in areas

---

4. Stewart Macaulay first made the case that the use of formal law undermines future cooperation (1963), although some more recent evidence suggests that corporations, in New York at least, experienced a spurt of litigiousness in the 1970s that suggests that this pattern may no longer hold. For the new work on this subject, see Galanter and Rogers 1988, and Nelson 1988. It is not clear whether the current pattern among corporations, where suing rather than negotiating is the preferred method of settling disputes, applies to interest groups interested in policy formation.

marked by intense conflict, frequent conflict, or lack of consensus, and scores on the three questions were added together to form an index.

If a group is engaged in a policy arena with shifting coalitions on different issues among a variety of groups (where its opponent on one issue is its ally on the next), then litigation will not be a very attractive option. We would expect groups in policy arenas with active, structured conflict to be more involved in litigation than those groups that operate in more fluid or less contentious areas.

*Political Sensitivity.* Winning in court gives a more permanent victory to groups that persist in working through the courts than does political success by other means. The rule of stare decisis and the general reluctance of courts to overrule themselves mean that victories at law are very valuable to an interest group once they have been achieved. If a group has been buffeted about by the winds of political change and stands to be blown around in the future by changes in administrations, then having precedent on its side can be an enormously stabilizing force. If interest groups, like other organizations, want to buffer themselves from uncertainty (Thompson 1967), then a judicial strategy will look very attractive, indeed, because it makes the environment as predictable as possible. We can expect that those groups that are more politically sensitive will seek out the courts to achieve and consolidate victories, at least as long as they believe the courts will issue favorable rulings. Since legal doctrine, especially on constitutional subjects, changes more slowly than the political scene, groups that stand to gain or lose a great deal with changes in political fortunes can be expected to prefer judicial solutions to all others, especially when a new, unfavorable administration has not yet had time to consolidate its influence in the courts. So, we would expect to find politically sensitive groups in courts more than other groups. Political sensitivity here identifies those groups that report substantial changes in their environment when there is a change from a Democratic to a Republican administration as well as those who report substantial changes when an administration shifts from Republican to Democratic. The *direction* of the shift does not matter in the way we have measured this effect; the *extent* of the shift does.

*Strategies of Influence: Insiders and Outsiders.* Courts are institutions in which it arguably does not help to be an insider. Federal judges are relatively insulated from political pressure after they are appointed, and even state judges are often remarkably protected from the push and shove of ordinary interest-group politics. The federal judges with whom national organizations generally deal do not have to appeal to constituencies, nor do they stand to gain personally from the outcomes of specific cases. Judges and jurors are disqualified if they know the litigants personally or even if they have some personal interest in the litigants' area of dispute. This means that one does not gain from having inside contacts with the judicial establishment, the way one might gain by knowing members of Congress or policymakers in federal agencies. In fact, as the story about Justices Black and Brennan revealed, inside contacts may even hurt.

There is an important qualification to this generalization, however. If a group has succeeded in getting a statute passed in Congress or a special rule adopted by an agency, litigation may be more likely to result in victory for the group because the courts will be interpreting the statute or rule that the interest group got enacted (in the first place) by virtue of having inside contacts in Congress or the relevant agency. As Susan Olson points out (1990), new statutes create new bases for bringing suits by those who have pressed to get the statute enacted in the first place. Judicial victories are, then, more likely because cases are being brought under favorable rules. But even here, courts may consider other interests too, interests that are protected under competing legal rules, so victory is not necessarily guaranteed even in these cases. It would make sense that a group involved in pressing for change using inside strategies (working with agencies or members of Congress to get favorable rules enacted) would also press for change through litigation, if those inside strategies were at all successful. After all, what inside pressure often tries to achieve is a change in the law.

Being an outsider to the political process, and using strategies like getting attention through the media or engaging in public demonstrations, will not guarantee success in the courts either, though sometimes waves of doctrinal change follow on the growth of social movements (Vose 1959; Handler 1978). But one might expect that an interest group that uses outside strategies will also be likely to use that one point of policy leverage where being an insider does not help and being an outsider does not hurt: the courts. Outside litigants may find courts receptive in a variety of areas where the political process may be closed to them, for one does not have to demonstrate the size of one's constituency or what one can do for the policymaker if one has the law on one's side. The strength of one's case in law, rather than the strength of one's backers in politics, makes or breaks the outcome in court. A creative group can make good legal arguments even in cases arising under the hostile statutes that a group's opposition has succeeded in getting passed by Congress. By drawing on provisions of other laws or by arguing that the statute should be interpreted in a way favoring the groups that initially opposed it, a group can still prevail even when the law looks unpromising at the start.[5]

For our purposes, we can measure inside status by strongly affirmative

---

5. Though the point was made about another place and another time, there is an important lesson to be learned from E. P. Thompson's argument (1975) that even statutes as skewed against outsiders as the Black Act of 1723 in England could be used successfully by those without political power to defend themselves. The rule of law, which requires written rules applied equally to all, actually does serve to constrain the untrammeled exercise of discretion and privilege and so qualifies law, in Thompson's view, as an "unqualified human good," whether one has political influence or not.

responses to questions indicating that the group in question works with agencies, with members of Congress or their staffs, or with groups of experts in a particular field. Those groups considered outsiders reported that their main strategies included influencing public opinion through mass media and publicity and organizing or carrying out public demonstrations and protests.

We can see, then, why there may be pressures for groups with inside influence to use the courts to consolidate their gains and for groups without such influence, the outsiders, to use the courts as a way of getting a first shot at being heard by policymakers. The inside groups would use courts after they have achieved victories in other spheres while the outside groups would go to the courts first.

*The Substance of Policy.* Just as the propensity of groups to engage in legal action is affected by their political environments and their organizational and financial structures, the types of policy areas in which groups are active also should shape their approaches to litigation. Groups interested in social welfare policies or domestic economic issues operate in policy areas where existing statues make legal rights and legal remedies more clear and specific harms more evident. Though there are elaborate legal rules limiting when a group can bring suit on the claims of individuals, statutes in the social welfare and domestic economic areas often provide explicit legal remedies for unfavorable government action. Groups working in issue areas like foreign policy or national security, however, are likely to encounter the political question doctrine, which courts use to kick contentious foreign policy questions back to the elected branches of government. We would expect, therefore, that most of litigation arising from the group system would be stimulated by associations operating in domestic policy areas concerning social welfare, economic development, the regulation of business activity, or labor-management relations, and that groups with an emphasis on foreign policy or international security issues would be unlikely to find the courts helpful.

*The Universe of Interest Groups.* The distinctive organizational character of interest groups also prompts some to pursue their goals through litigation, while others concentrate on contacts with executive agencies, lobbying Congress, mounting campaigns in the mass media, or even staging public protests in the streets.

Profit sector groups, including trade associations, professional societies whose members operate on a fee-for-service basis, and other groups that represent commercial constituencies, are very involved in policy matters protecting their members from adverse regulation. Profit sector groups would use the courts for two reasons: (1) they have achieved success with agencies or with Congress and are using the courts to enforce the favorable regulations they have gotten, or (2) they are in court to protect their members' interests when their members are drawn into litigation by others.

Nonprofit sector groups, including government agencies at the state and local level, colleges and universities, hospitals and salaried professionals operating in public health agencies, educational institutions, and other nonprofit or governmental settings, would be far less likely to use the courts to achieve policy goals because they often represent constituencies that have no natural enemies. Conflict exists in general terms about the size of the federal budget that would go to further the causes these groups champion, but there are few organizations that directly challenge groups representing children, the elderly, or the mentally ill. Lacking organized opponents, it is more difficult for their groups to pursue their policy goals through the courts. Groups in the nonprofit sector also are patronized by government agencies and private foundations that encourage them to avoid open hostilities and the full-scale confrontations that are inherent in most lawsuits. Many groups in the nonprofit sector also are composed of professionals who naturally avoid the appearance of partisanship or intense controversy for fear of compromising their professional status and, thus, avoid adversarial court room battles. For all these reasons, we would expect nonprofit sector groups to litigate less than other groups.

Mixed groups, operating in both the profit and nonprofit realms, generally have members with different organizational styles, historical traditions, patterns of intergroup relations, and financial structures, and they typically find it difficult to arrive at a consensus on public policy questions. The group's leadership is presented with difficult organizational and political problems that often restrain it from any aggressive efforts to wield political influence. As a result, we would not expect these mixed groups to be active in using the courts.

Trade unions, on the other hand, have strong reasons to use the courts.[6] Because unions are governed by an elaborate regulatory apparatus that relies heavily on court interpretation and because the relationship between unions and management is largely contractual, leading any breach into at least arbitration and often litigation, we would expect to see unions using the courts extensively to achieve their policy goals.

Citizen groups such as the Sierra Club, Common Cause, or the American Civil Liberties Union generally have as their broad purpose to create or to protect some broader public good rather than the more concrete and narrow interests of their individual members. Insofar as many of these claims are rights based, we would expect these groups to find courts helpful as staging grounds when they pursue their policy agendas. In addition, because many of

---

6. Unions are different from our other groups in that they are not necessarily voluntary organizations, since workers are often required to join, or at least pay union dues, if they accept a job in a unionized workplace.

these groups are part of larger social movements that have succeeded in getting favorable legislation passed, or at least in getting private rights of action embedded in statutes as a spur to governmental enforcement, we might also expect to see these groups using the courts extensively. But there is a feature of these groups that limits their use of the courts. Because groups of this sort often have serious financial problems, they must often rely on financial grants from foundations, wealthy individuals, or other patrons. As we have seen in our earlier discussion of tax exemption, this dependence on foundations and others who may want or need tax write-offs for their own contributions may place a limit on the kinds of litigation that a group may bring. In addition, grants from patrons are often awarded in exchange for particular commitments about political advocacy or action that may lead such groups into the courts in pursuit of their goals, but, of course, some patrons may virtually prohibit the use of litigation as a strategy of influence because it might put the tax status of the group in doubt.

## Hypotheses

If our general arguments about the way interest groups might use the courts are correct, and our description of the interest-group universe is accurate, we would expect to find the following.

1. Interest groups with more organizational resources relevant to litigation requirements, including larger staffs, more diffuse financial support, and a longer time-horizon, are more likely to use the courts than those interest groups who have fewer of these resources.
2. Those groups that are engaged in structured and intense conflict with regular opponents are more likely to be in court than those groups that operate in a consensual policy environment or that have partially but not completely conflicting interests with other groups in their policy arena.
3. Groups whose fortunes are politically sensitive will attempt to buffer themselves from these changes by achieving the longer lasting victories that courts provide.
4. Active groups of all sorts will be more likely to press their demands in court than those groups that are less active. This includes those groups who are active as political insiders and have achieved success with agencies or with Congress so that they can litigate under favorable rules, as well as political outsiders who may be politically disadvantaged and have not achieved success elsewhere. Both sets of activists will be drawn to litigate for different reasons.
5. Groups are more likely to engage in litigation if they are interested in

policies that involve transfer payments to individuals, regulation of commercial transactions among individuals or businesses, and contracting for services among business firms, individuals, and government agencies. Groups operating in areas such as foreign policy or national security, where access to courts is blocked by the political question doctrine, will be less likely to use the courts.

6. The type of constituency being represented by an interest group (and therefore the organizational and financial structure it adopts) will influence that group's use of the courts. We would expect to see profit sector groups, unions, and citizen groups using the courts in greater numbers than the nonprofit or mixed groups, each for distinctive institutional reasons.

## Who Uses the Courts? A Preliminary Analysis

Most groups confine themselves to lobbying Congress or administrative agencies, to the production of pamphlets and reports, or to the conduct of seminars and conferences meant to explain the needs of their members (see chap. 5). Still, fully 55.7 percent of the interest groups that responded to our 1985 survey reported that they used the courts for some reason, and only 9.7 percent of those groups filed amicus briefs and did nothing else.[7] Even so, litigation remains one of the least popular forms of advocacy pursued by interest groups. The only forms of interest-group activity engaged in less frequently than litigation are electioneering (33 percent) and public protests (18 percent).

In table 9-1, we indicate the bivariate relationships between the use of the courts and each of the influences that we have discussed. The dependent variable here taps the organization's "yes or no" response to the question: "Does this association engage in litigation or any other legal activities?" The generalizations we have proposed about the use of the courts seem to be confirmed. However, since the table summarizes bivariate relationships, we refer to it only as a useful point of departure, not for hypothesis testing. In the next section, we present a multivariate examination.

Organizational resources, measured here by the natural log of staff size, are strongly related to a group's propensity to use the courts. The table runs smoothly from a below average 34.4 percent of the groups in the lowest quartile of resources saying they engage in legal actions, to an impressive 82.2 percent of those in the highest quartile. Litigation requires expertise, time, and money, and these results make it appear that the more of these

---

7. These results are similar to the proportion of groups initiating federal lawsuits reported in Bruer 1988.

**TABLE 9-1. Groups Using Courts to Achieve Policy Goals**

| Variable | N | Percentage |
|---|---|---|
| Organizational resources | | |
| Log of staff size (R1) | | |
| Low | 93 | 34.4 |
| Lower middle | 411 | 46.5 |
| Upper middle | 228 | 64.9 |
| High | 146 | 82.2 |
| Age of the group (R2) | | |
| Less than 10 years | 197 | 49.7 |
| At least 10 years | 686 | 58.2 |
| Budget from patrons (R3) | | |
| 0–4 percent | 310 | 60.7 |
| 5–34 percent | 402 | 56.8 |
| 35–100 percent | 147 | 45.2 |
| Structure of conflict | | |
| Intensity of disputes (C1) | | |
| Low | 605 | 51.2 |
| High | 271 | 66.1 |
| Faces same opponents (C2) | | |
| No | 332 | 38.9 |
| Yes | 547 | 66.9 |
| Political sensitivity | | |
| Change in fortunes with partisan shifts (S1) | | |
| None | 382 | 42.2 |
| Little | 169 | 60.0 |
| Moderate amount | 172 | 68.6 |
| A great deal | 151 | 71.5 |
| Strategy of influence | | |
| Inside Strategies (I1) | | |
| Low use | 192 | 20.8 |
| Moderate use | 398 | 61.6 |
| High use | 284 | 73.3 |
| Outside Strategies (I2) | | |
| Low use | 488 | 44.0 |
| Moderate use | 322 | 67.4 |
| High use | 40 | 87.5 |
| Substance of policy | | |
| Human services (P1) | | |
| Emphasized | 129 | 70.5 |
| Not emphasized | 730 | 54.5 |
| Economic Growth (P2) | | |
| Emphasized | 70 | 80.0 |
| Not emphasized | 730 | 54.9 |
| National Security (P3) | | |
| Emphasized | 48 | 33.3 |
| Not emphasized | 812 | 58.6 |

**TABLE 9-1**—*Continued*

| Variable | N | Percentage |
|---|---|---|
| Group type | | |
| Profit (*T*1) | 326 | 66.2 |
| Mixed (*T*2) | 50 | 30.0 |
| Nonprofit (*T*3) | 281 | 46.3 |
| Citizen (*T*4) | 206 | 51.9 |
| Unions (*T*5) | 29 | 100.0 |

*Source:* 1985 Survey.

resources, at a group's command, the more likely it is to pursue its goals through the courts.[8] A group's institutional commitment to long-term goals is a second organizational resource, which we indicate here by age. Older groups are more likely than younger groups to use the courts. Further, as we expected, groups that are heavily supported by a few large patrons are less likely to use the courts than groups that are wholly dependent on membership dues or other diffuse sources of support.

In the structure of conflict measures, groups engaged in policy areas characterized by intense disputes are more likely to use the legal process than groups that operate in calmer waters. Also important, as we suspected given the structural constraints imposed by the court system, is the structure of the conflict in which groups are involved. Table 9-1 shows that groups that face the same opponents over and over again in dispute after dispute are nearly twice as likely to employ the courts as are groups that face different opponents or those that seldom face any direct opposition at all.

Table 9-1 also demonstrates that as groups become more active, in pursuing either an insider strategy of lobbying and consensus building or an outsider strategy of publicity and protest, they are more likely to enter the courts in pursuit of their policy goals. Among the most highly active groups pursuing an outside strategy, 87.5 percent report using the courts to advance their cause.

---

8. This finding tends to confirm earlier research (see, for example, O'Connor 1980; Epstein 1985; Schlozman and Tierney 1986, 376–78). Bruer (1988), however, finds no independent effect of budget size, and he concludes that "the absolute budget size does not influence the propensity of [groups] to initiate either federal or state litigation." We think Bruer's findings differ from ours for two reasons. First, his conclusion is vulnerable to a type 2 error of inference. If we take a "budget impact" as our null hypothesis, we have no way of knowing, from Bruer's results, that we can reject this hypothesis. Second, his sample (unlike ours) includes public interest law firms who litigate a great deal on shoestring budgets and are, therefore, not representative of the large universe of interest groups.

Similarly, groups that operate in policy areas that are sensitive to changes in the outcomes of national elections also are more likely to resort to litigation as a strategy of influence. Groups in our sample that reported that the party shift in the White House and Senate in 1980 greatly affected their fortunes (no matter whether their influence increased or decreased as a result of these changes) were more likely to turn to the courts than were groups whose fortunes were somehow insulated from the outcome of partisan conflict. The propensity to use the courts increases monotonically from only 42.2 percent of the groups who report no change in their fortunes as a result of the Republican victories in 1980 to 71.5 percent of those who reported that the change in partisan control made a great deal of difference to their operations.

We can see in table 9-1 that the courts are not the appropriate forum for the resolution of disputes in all policy areas. In table 9-1, groups reporting great interest in the delivery of human services (education, housing and urban policy, health and other human services), and those generally concerned with economic development (transportation policy, energy and natural resources) were much more likely to engage in litigation than those groups that expressed little interest in these policy areas, which should come as no surprise. Groups that expressed interest in defense, national security, and foreign policy, however, were much less likely than those who did not concern themselves with those subjects to enter the court system in pursuit of their policy goals.

The last entries in table 9-1 show that there are large differences among the types of interest groups in the degree to which they pursue their goals through the courts. All the trade unions that responded to our survey reported that they employed the courts in their efforts to wield influence, followed by the trade associations and other groups representing the profit sector of the economy, where 66.2 percent report using the courts. All the other types of groups, however, report below average use of legal means to pursue their goals, and this is most clearly true of the so-called mixed groups, caught between the great divide of the profit and nonprofit sectors, where only 30.0 percent report any efforts to use the courts to advance their interests. Groups that have difficulty dealing with controversy among their own members are usually not suited for the use of legal maneuvers in pursuing their goals. Nonprofits use the courts more than mixed groups and less than citizen groups. Given the focus on citizen groups in the interest-group litigation literature, however, the biggest surprise is that substantially fewer citizen groups report using the courts than profit groups.

## Multivariate Models of Litigation Use and Strategies

We have seen how each of the factors described in table 9-1 is associated with the propensity to litigate, but how do all these variables interact? Politically sensitive groups may litigate more because they tend to have the same opponents on every issue. Profit sector groups may litigate more because they are richer, or because they are more likely to have organized opposition. Citizen groups may litigate as much as they do, despite being short of resources, because they operate in contentious policy environments. To untangle interrelationships among the independent variables, we report the results of four multiple regressions below. The explanatory variables have been constructed to be as continuous as possible, and they are scaled to range from zero to one to aid in interpreting the estimated coefficients.

Following the notation developed in table 9-1, we estimate coefficients for the model:

$$L_t = B_1 R_1 + B_2 R_2 + B_3 R_3 + B_4 C_1 + B_5 C_2 + B_6 S_1 + B_7 I_1 +$$

$$B_8 I_2 + B_9 P_1 + B_{10} P_2 + B_{11} P_3 + B_{12} T_1 + B_{13} T_2 +$$

$$B_{14} T_3 + B_{15} T_4 + B_{16} T_5 + U.[9]$$

The subscript $t$ takes on a different value for each of four regressions. The first regression estimates the emphasis on litigation as a strategy for policy influence. This is followed by three models reflecting the choice of specific litigation strategies: (1) filing amicus curiae briefs, (2) filing suits on behalf of group members, and (3) filing class action lawsuits.

Table 9-2 reports the results of a multivariate regression analysis of the importance of litigation for interest groups. Respondents were asked to assess the importance of legal assistance as a benefit to group members. Answers ranged along a six-point scale from "not engaged in" to "one of the most important benefits or activities." The variable then captures both the propensity to engage in litigation and the intensity of preference for this activity. The six possible responses were scaled from 0 to 100. For the full sample of groups, the mean response was 28.8.

The pattern of relationships in table 9-2 presents a vivid picture of the broad connections between interest groups and the court system. Almost all the relationships that appeared in table 9-1 are still present, even after the effects of the other independent variables are controlled.

The clearest explanatory factors associated with the importance of litigation to a group include: (1) the resources at the command of a group, (2) the degree to which the group's fortunes were affected by the shift to Republican

---

9. The model is specified without a constant term so that we can generate intercept terms for the five group type dummy variables. Suppressing the constant term does not affect the estimates of any of the other coefficients.

**TABLE 9-2. Determinants of the Importance of Litigation to Groups**

| Variable | b (S.E.) |
|---|---|
| Organizational resources | |
| Log of staff size (R1) | 21.03*** |
| | (5.07) |
| Age of group (R2) | 0.08* |
| | (0.04) |
| Support from patrons (R3) | −12.23*** |
| | (4.86) |
| Structure of conflict | |
| Intensity of disputes (C1) | 7.03* |
| | (3.48) |
| Faces same opponents (C2) | 11.21** |
| | (3.40) |
| Political sensitivity | |
| Change of fortunes with | 8.44** |
| partisan shifts (S1) | (3.40) |
| Strategy of influence | |
| Inside strategies (I1) | 11.83** |
| | (4.79) |
| Outside strategies (I2) | 29.76*** |
| | (5.42) |
| Substance of policy | |
| Human services (P1) | −0.12 |
| | (4.54) |
| Economic growth (P2) | 4.29 |
| | (4.99) |
| National security (P3) | −12.99** |
| | (5.64) |
| Group type intercepts | |
| Profit (T1) | 0.70 |
| Mixed (T2) | −15.48 |
| Nonprofit (T3) | −6.59 |
| Citizen (T4) | −4.10 |
| Unions (T5) | 8.46 |
| N = 774     SE = 26.98     $R^2$ = .32 | |

*Note:* Table entries are unstandardized regression coefficients; standard error estimates are in parentheses.
$*p < .05.$     $**p < .01.$     $***p < .001.$

control of the Senate and the presidency in 1980, no matter whether they were hurt or helped by the shift, (3) the degree to which groups are generally active in seeking political influence, no matter whether they follow an inside or an outside strategy, and (4) both the intensity and, more important, the structure of the policy conflict in which the group is engaged—especially the degree to which the group faces the same opponents over and over again. We also find a somewhat weaker, but statistically significant, positive relationship between the age of a group and its propensity to litigate. These data clearly illustrate that it is the better endowed, active, older groups facing a highly structured, contentious policy environment that are the most likely to turn to the courts to achieve their policy goals.

In addition, the larger the proportion of a group's budget that is supplied by private patrons (mainly foundations or individual philanthropists), the less important litigation is to a group. Our analysis strongly suggests that patrons of this kind encourage interest groups to pursue other paths to influence, outside the courts, perhaps because they are worried about the tax consequences or because they do not want to have to cede control over strategy and tactics to lawyers or, in some cases, because they do not wish to become embroiled in the kind of focused, structured controversies that arise out of litigation. There also is more evidence in table 9-2 that the courts are not readily available to deal with disputes in all policy areas. As we saw in table 9-1, groups interested mainly in national security issues are highly unlikely to engage in litigation of any form, showing how effective the political question doctrine is at keeping foreign policy questions out of the courts. Neither of the other two issue areas spotlighted makes any particular difference, however.

Table 9-2 also displays the intercepts associated with the dummy variables that represent the five group types. The numbers appearing in each cell of this section of the table are the intercept points for these variables, and they represent the degree to which each type of group engages or does not engage in the activity under scrutiny, after all of the other variables and all the other group types have been taken into account. The group type intercepts reflect the patterns we found in table 9-1. Unions are the most litigious, even after controlling for other strong influences. Groups whose members work in the profit sector of the economy are the second most litigious, with an intercept term of .70. Citizen groups are somewhat less likely to engage in litigation than one would expect, given their other characteristics, and it is this result that is most surprising. Given all the attention paid to these groups in the political science literature, one would expect citizen groups to be among the heaviest litigators. But once all the other factors are controlled, citizen groups are less likely to turn to the courts than are unions or profit sector groups. Nonprofit sector groups are even less likely to use the courts, and for the groups whose memberships are mixed between the profit and nonprofit sectors, the $-15.48$ intercept indicates that they are much less likely to engage in litigation than one might expect, given their organizational and financial characteristics and the political environments in which they operate. It is likely that other unmeasured variables, such as the professional training and experience of their staffs or the specific concerns of their principal patrons, must be at work preventing mixed, nonprofit sector, and citizen groups from engaging in litigation as much as we would expect them to, given the results of our linear model.

## Choosing a Legal Strategy

We have identified several factors related to the initial decisions of groups to emphasize litigation as part of their strategy of influence. When we turn from the importance of legal action to the question of what approach groups adopt after deciding to enter the courts, the relationships begin to change, revealing a fascinating pattern of interest-group involvement in different forms of legal action. In this part of the analysis, we look only at that 55.7 percent of the original sample who answered "yes" to the question about whether their group engaged in legal action of any sort, referring to these groups as litigators.

Litigators choose among the three possible means of legal action at very different rates. While 90.7 percent of litigators use amicus briefs, 69.1 percent file suits on behalf of the business and professional interests of the group's members, and only 50.4 percent file class action suits that affect more than just their members. Overwhelmingly, those who submit amicus briefs also use the courts more directly, since a mere 9.7 percent of litigators only filed amicus briefs and did nothing else.

Higher values of a dependent variable indicate that a particular type of court-related activity is an increasingly good description of the group's activity. Among the litigators, the mean score for filing amicus curiae briefs is 64.7 out of a possible 100. Likewise, the mean score for filing suits on behalf of members is 47.5, and the mean score for filing class action lawsuits is 30.6.

In the multivariate analysis shown in table 9-3, both the results and nonresults are striking. We will discuss each of the models in turn.

*Filing Amicus Briefs.* The most striking relationship in this model relates the impact of support from private patrons on the choice of legal strategy. Though the receipt of private patronage clearly reduces the tendency of groups to enter the legal process in the first place, heavily patronized groups are much more likely to file amicus briefs than nonpatronized groups, once they enter the legal arena. This finding lends further support to the view that private patrons have broad policy interests that can be advanced by amicus briefs, which put a group on record without plunging it into direct confrontations with clearly defined opponents. In addition, amicus briefs are more likely to appear as the sort of educational activity that 501(c)(3) organizations can engage in without losing their special tax status. Filing amicus briefs can also be done without such heavy reliance on the expertise (and therefore control) of lawyers. The strong negative association of patronage with member-oriented lawsuits also supports the explanation that powerful patrons seek to avoid all-out litigation or that member-oriented lawsuits are less likely

TABLE 9-3.   Determinants of the Choice of Litigation

| Variable | Amicus Briefs | Suits for Members | Class Actions |
|---|---|---|---|
| Organizational resources | | | |
| Log of staff size (*R*1) | 9.38 | 13.78 | −2.60 |
| | (9.00) | (10.33) | (9.87) |
| Age of group (*R*2) | 0.12* | −0.06 | 0.00 |
| | (0.06) | (0.07) | (0.07) |
| Support from patrons (*R*3) | 33.86*** | −33.67** | 0.41 |
| | (10.67) | (11.50) | (11.50) |
| Structure of conflict | | | |
| Intensity of disputes (*C*1) | 9.65 | 12.47* | 15.53** |
| | (5.77) | (6.50) | (6.36) |
| Faces same opponents (*C*2) | 0.13 | 4.84 | −4.54 |
| | (5.85) | (6.61) | (6.41) |
| Political sensitivity | | | |
| Change of fortunes with | 13.57* | 6.97 | 3.89 |
| partisan shifts (*S*1) | (5.83) | (6.62) | (6.43) |
| Strategy of influence | | | |
| Inside strategies (*I*1) | 10.26 | 35.42*** | 12.62 |
| | (9.74) | (11.07) | (10.64) |
| Outside strategies (*I*2) | 14.91 | 8.97 | 37.26*** |
| | (9.68) | (10.99) | (10.63) |
| Substance of policy | | | |
| Human services (*P*1) | 14.25* | −17.20* | 16.31* |
| | (7.50) | (8.71) | (8.20) |
| Economic growth (*P*2) | −4.63 | −0.03 | −3.06 |
| | (7.94) | (9.11) | (8.65) |
| National security (*P*3) | −15.35 | 9.92 | 2.33 |
| | (9.99) | (11.47) | (11.07) |
| Group type intercepts | | | |
| Profit (*T*1) | 35.67 | 23.49 | −8.13 |
| Mixed (*T*2) | 18.13 | −1.36 | −5.79 |
| Nonprofit (*T*3) | 28.78 | 1.67 | −3.49 |
| Citizen (*T*4) | 18.74 | −16.04 | 13.51 |
| Unions (*T*5) | 3.23 | 40.35 | −5.27 |
| *N* | 341 | 340 | 340 |
| SE | 30.27 | 34.48 | 33.21 |
| $R^2$ | .16 | .33 | .25 |

*Note:* Table entries are unstandardized regression coefficients; standard error estimates are in parentheses.
*$p < .05$.     **$p < .01$.     ***$p < .001$.

to be associated with the 501(c)(3) tax status that many patrons need to contribute to an interest group.

Beyond the strong relationship with private patrons, our analysis of the factors affecting the filing of amicus briefs yields three more discernible relationships. Groups are more likely to file amicus briefs: (1) the more their fortunes were changed by the shift in the partisan balance as a result of the 1980 election; (2) the more deeply they are concerned with policies in the area of human service delivery (the center of the Reagan revolution in the early 1980s); and (3) the older they are. All the other factors that affected the initial decision to litigate disappear or are weakened below standard levels of statistical significance, except for group type.

The group type intercepts demonstrate how much organizational style influences the actions of groups. The intercept for groups in the profit sector is 35.67, indicating that those groups are the most likely to say that filing amicus briefs is a good description of their legal activities. But all of the other groups, with the strong exception of unions, also report that they file amicus briefs. Once we examine only litigators, all types of groups, except unions, engage in a good deal of amicus activity.

*Choosing Member Suits or Class Actions.* The litigation patterns reflected in table 9-3 are much clearer when we examine whether groups tend toward initiating member-related suits or class action suits. To begin with, the intensity of conflict, which mattered only slightly in causing parties to enter the court, matters a great deal more in choice of strategy. Groups that tend strongly toward the choice of member suits and those that tend toward the choice of class action suits were both more likely than other groups to report that they had intense conflict in their policy area. So, intensity of conflict affects the degree to which groups rely on the courts for achieving policy goals, and it also seems to push groups toward a stronger emphasis upon either filing member suits or filing class action suits, whichever type fits their tactical needs.

The policy emphasis of a group also seems to be influential in prompting it toward the choice of a legal strategy. Though we see no association among litigators between policy area and litigation strategy for those groups focusing on national security or economic policy, we do find that concern with the delivery of human services strongly pushes groups away from suits oriented toward the interests of the group members and toward class action suits that will benefit clients.

The strongest influence on the choice of either a member-oriented or class action strategy, however, is the group's fundamental political strategy—the approach it takes to all aspects of political action. Groups that adopt the classic inside stance, in which lobbying and consensus building among policy leaders and elected representatives are paramount, are much more likely than other groups to employ the courts narrowly to advance the business and professional interests of their members. Member suits can take advantage of existing favorable rules lobbied for by the interest group to benefit those whom the group serves. Conversely, associations emphasizing the classic outside strategies of mobilizing interests through protest and the manipulation of the mass media tend to choose class action suits as their preferred vehicle of legal influence. This shows such groups are more likely to use the courts to fight for broad policy goals rather than just for the interests of their members. Class action suits are not only devices for compensating classes of people, they are also ways of creating policy through court action. The pattern of intercept terms dealing with the choice between member and class action suits reinforces this explanation. It is easy to see that profit sector groups and trade unions, the ultimate insiders in contemporary American politics, are much more likely to file member suits if they decide to use the courts, while the citizen groups, the ultimate outsiders, are much more likely to file class action suits. All the group type variables except the one representing citizen groups have negative intercepts on the class action regression, while both the profit groups and the trade unions have large, positive intercept terms in the regression on the propensity to file member suits. Citizen groups are much less likely to file member suits (with a $-16.04$ intercept term) but are much more likely to be engaged in class action suits (with a strongly positive 13.51 intercept term). These findings indicate that once interest groups choose a distinctive organizational style built around an inside or outside strategy, their approach to the court system follows closely.

## Discussion

We have provided a broad overview of the activities of interest groups in the courts. Two sets of variables are powerful in accounting for interest groups' use of the courts in the first place. The first is a set of threshold rules governing when groups can make use of the courts.[10] Organizations must possess substantial resources in order to make use of the courts and they need to be willing to fight their battles over the long haul to make protracted court effort worthwhile. A group's resources, the degree to which its funding is derived from certain types of patrons, and its longevity are all positively related to the use of the courts. In addition, organizations need to engage in structured, recurring, and intense conflict with the same opponents before they have someone against whom they can litigate. Groups operating in areas with shifting and loose coalitions are not prime candidates for litigation. Groups whose political fortunes change drastically with changes in administration also find themselves in court, because court victories are more protected from the winds of political change.

Other influences on interest groups' use of the courts include the struc-

---

10. The concept of a *threshold rule* is developed in Scheppele 1988 and describes the rules that courts use to govern access to legal remedies.

tures and strategies of the organizations themselves. Groups that are active with both inside and outside strategies of policy influence use the courts more than those who are active on neither dimension. Policy area matters too, with national security–oriented groups particularly unlikely to use the courts. And, perhaps most important, the set of interests a group represents, whether of trade associations, trade unions, nonprofit organizations, or citizen groups, influences whether interest groups litigate. Trade associations and unions are far more likely to litigate than other groups, though citizen groups run a distant third.

Though we have not done a direct test here of competing explanations of interest-group litigation, we can draw some conclusions about the general applicability of these approaches following this analysis. First, the political disadvantage theory has received some limited support here. Outsider groups do use the courts to try to achieve their policy aims through class actions suits, but focusing on this group alone leaves out the larger and potentially more powerful set of profit groups that uses the courts in greater numbers to press the particular claims of their members. The political disadvantage theory does not seem to be wrong, but it captures only a fraction of the interest-group litigation activity.

The rights claims view also has only partial support here. If we consider citizen groups and class action suits as places where rights claims are promoted, we reach much the same conclusion as we did for the political disadvantage theory. The groups most likely to use the courts are the wealthy and established groups that seek court favor for conservative purposes, not the citizen groups who use class action suits to advance their more liberal policy goals. The groups that are in the courts most often are those profit sector groups and unions who are protecting their members' professional or business interests and not the cause-oriented groups pressing for the expansion of civil liberties or for the expansion of governmental benefits to outsiders. The rights-claiming groups do act in ways that the case studies reveal, but rights claims are not the largest part of the picture of interest-group litigation.

We have also found some support for the traditional set of organizational characteristics. Age of the organization, the presence of a full-time (preferably large) staff, the resources available to the group, and the networks the group finds itself in (having the same opponents, for example) do matter, but they matter for reasons that have not been explored in depth in the existing literature. In order for groups to be able to use the courts, they have to have not only the internal characteristics that push them in that direction, but also the external characteristics that make courts see them as appropriate litigators. The set of characteristics that we have identified as important predictors of litigation activity by groups can all be justified in terms of the match between the characteristics of the interest group and the special requirements of courts.

This leads us to see that the institutional compatibility of groups and courts matters a great deal. Not all groups will be able to make use of courts because court rules will exclude them, and not all those who might benefit from a court forum will find it worthwhile to pursue this complicated and expensive strategy. To understand the larger patterns of interest-group litigation, then, we need to consider both sets of factors and how they work together.

In terms of the specific strategy selected, almost all groups that say they use the courts in some way file amicus briefs. But amicus briefs, however common, are not where most of the serious action is in interest groups' use of the court. Almost all of those filing amicus briefs use other legal strategies as well, devoting far more of their resources to actual litigation. While the filing of amicus briefs has gotten a great deal of attention in the literature, our research shows that amicus briefs are a relatively small piece of a much larger picture. Interest groups are engaged in litigation in far more institutionally committed ways than just filing amicus briefs.

Our findings suggest a reorientation of research in political science on interest groups and the courts. There has been an emphasis on class action suits and the use of the courts by citizen groups all out of proportion to their actual frequency or importance in the big picture of interest groups in the courts, as evidenced by the popularity of the political disadvantage and rights explosion explanations. But while some interest groups use the courts to bypass electoral politics and to make rights claims that cannot be made elsewhere, these uses are not the most frequent activities that find interest groups in the courts. Political scientists have taken far less notice of member-oriented suits and the use of the courts by trade associations and unions than those activities deserve. The political disadvantage and rights claims views take the focus off the actual location of much of the activity.

Even though litigation remains one of the least frequently used strategies employed by interest groups, the court system still represents a significant path to influence for many voluntary associations. Much of the litigation flowing into the court system is generated as part of a general strategy of political action by organized interests, but the courts are not for everyone. Our analysis shows that courts have their own rigorous institutional capacities and limitations that open doors for some groups, while closing them firmly to others.

CHAPTER 10

# The Three Modes of Political Mobilization

The American political system is one of the most permeable in the world, yet not all social groups are equally represented before government. One example of inactivity that is especially puzzling is the lack of political organization among the unemployed—a large group that obviously is suffering distress. Members of Congress often call for action to end unemployment, and several pieces of legislation meant to deal with the problem have been passed during recent sessions of Congress, yet no organization is operating in Washington claiming to directly represent those who are out of work. Trade union leaders attempt to speak for them but usually oppose measures like the graduated minimum wage, subsidized employment of teenagers, or any other proposal that might possibly impose costs upon their membership or diminish their control over entry into the skilled trades.

Recent studies of unemployment conducted by Schlozman and Verba, however, clearly show that the unemployed are suffering an extraordinary amount of personal distress, and that most of them believe that the government should take measures either to create new jobs or help them find work (Schlozman and Verba 1979). Almost all of those surveyed felt that the government was not doing enough to alleviate their distress. The unemployed are not as politically aware as employed workers; they are dispersed, typically uneducated, and not well equipped for political activity; but they believe that their government should intervene in the economy in their behalf, and that they have a right to such aid. These same surveys also uncovered virtually no evidence of any organizational activity on behalf of the unemployed. Most of those who lost their jobs immediately dropped out of their unions, leaving themselves isolated and politically impotent.

There is no way to prove that the unemployed in America *ought* to be better organized for political advocacy than they are, but research has shown that their feelings, attitudes, and beliefs make them ripe for political action. Since so many new political organizations representing other distressed groups—such as African-Americans, Hispanics, native Americans, the handicapped, children, and the mentally ill—have been organized during the past 20 years, the question arises once again. Why is there no organization to directly represent the unemployed? To state the problem broadly, why, within the same political system, do levels of organization differ for what would seem to be analogous social groups?

The preceding chapters have developed several ideas that may help answer this and other practical questions about whether a particular social or economic group will become organized and be represented before government. Without entirely discounting the importance of the great differences in the capacity of citizens to understand questions of public policy or in the skill with which they utilize the political resources at their disposal, I have argued that the differential rates of political mobilization among social groups within any population are mainly a product of the structure of opportunities presented to each citizen by the legal, political, and organizational environment. Members of different social groups face entirely different sets of opportunities and obstacles to political activity. The actions of groups representing them depend not so much upon their constituents' level of education or their annual income, their values, or the intensity of their feelings, as upon the organizational, legal, financial, and institutional environment in which they find themselves. Political action is seldom a spontaneous outburst growing out of frustration, anxiety, or personal strain. In predicting whether the unemployed will organize for political action, it is useful to know whether they feel exploited or whether they believe that they have a right to relief from the government. However, it is much more important to understand the political scope allowed by the tax code to nonprofit agencies working in their behalf, whether foundations exist that will take an interest in their cause, how willing government agencies are to sponsor political advocacy in their favor, or, even more important, the likely political or financial sanctions that would be applied against any individual or organization that took up their cause.

To put my central point more precisely, the amount of political action engaged in as a result of individual distress in the American political system at any time is determined mainly by political and administrative policies toward political activity, the presence and accessibility of willing patrons of political action, and the patterns of conflict and social cleavage in the society. If groups do not materialize representing the unemployed, this does not automatically mean that people who are out of work are essentially satisfied with the prevailing distribution of goods or status. It also is not necessarily an indication that they are too cynical or alienated to take part in the democratic process. Although citizens are not likely to become involved in politics if they feel no distress at all or have no desires that could be fulfilled through public policy, institutional and organizational variables are more important as determinants of political mobilization than the attitudes, feelings of political efficacy, or the political beliefs of individual citizens. Political action is largely the result of the differential impact of the rules of the political game on citizens.

Although the particular rules, political cleavages, and institutional configurations confronting specific constituencies vary enormously from one to another, the preceding chapters have demonstrated the close connections among a group's constituency, political context, sources of financial support, and political strategy. These interrelationships suggest that there is a small number of general modes of mobilizing and representing political interests in the American system. If that is true—and I believe it is—then it is possible to predict whether a group such as the unemployed will be vigorously represented in American politics by determining whether it could possibly fit into one of these representative modes.

**Three Classic Modes of Political Mobilization**

There are essentially three main formulas for success in organizing political groups that have been used in our political system. These three schemes form the basis for the three central methods of political mobilization in America.

The first, and most familiar, organizational formula is to base an association upon a tightly knit commercial or occupational community in the profit sector whose members share a concern for protecting or advancing their economic interests. Such a group usually can be supported with membership dues and patronage in various forms from business firms operating in the area. The most familiar and numerous political organizations in American politics are classic economic interest groups of this type, such as the American Petroleum Institute, the National Association of Automobile Manufacturers, or the Mortgage Bankers Association. The second formula for organizational maintenance is also rooted in occupational communities and capitalizes upon the possibilities for strong institutional support, but entrepreneurs following this strategy operate in the nonprofit or governmental realm and often make strong appeals to the professional needs and obligations of their potential members. Groups of this kind, such as the National Association of State Alcohol and Drug Abuse Directors or the Association of American Medical Colleges, often are instigated, supported, and encouraged by permanent agencies of government. These groups began appearing in Washington in the latter part of the nineteenth century and have increased in number in recent years, stimulated by the rapid growth of government since the late 1960s.

The third type of successful organizational formula taps the enthusiasm and energy of social movements. Groups such as the Wilderness Society, Common Cause, Citizens for Clean Air, and the Women's International League for Peace and Freedom are based on the commitment of individuals attracted by a cause, along with a package of financial contributions and other forms of patronage from foundations, wealthy individuals, churches, and other institutions that operate mostly in the nonprofit realm. In order to illustrate how these three organizational formulas are used in the real world of

TABLE 10-1. **Composition and Revenue Sources of Three Policy Communities in 1980**

| | Community | | |
| --- | --- | --- | --- |
| | Farmers | Handicapped | Women |
| Group type[a] | | | |
| Profit | 82 | 3 | 8 |
| Mixed | 10 | 3 | 8 |
| Nonprofit | 4 | 57 | 14 |
| Citizen | 4 | 37 | 70 |
| Total | 100 | 100 | 100 |
| N | 52 | 35 | 50 |
| Revenue source[b] | | | |
| Dues | 75 | 44 | 39 |
| Government patron | 7 | 11 | 9 |
| Private patron | 3 | 18 | 26 |
| Other | 15 | 27 | 26 |
| Total | 100 | 100 | 100 |
| N | 40 | 33 | 40 |

*Source:* 1980 Survey.

[a]Each entry is the percentage of interest groups in the policy community of each membership type.

[b]Each entry is the mean percentage of total revenues from a specific source.

interest groups as the basis for the mobilization of large segments of the population, three sets of interest groups operating at the national level in 1980 are examined in table 10-1. First, there are the groups that claim to represent farmers, a classic economic policy community; second are groups representing the handicapped, a policy community dominated by public sector professionals who act as advocates for their disadvantaged clients, with support and encouragement from many institutional patrons, including the government; and third are groups making up the women's movement, a community of interest groups that emerged from one of the most important social movements of recent years.

The data in table 10-1 show that each of the three policy communities was dominated by a different type of group. The table shows that most groups with an interest in agricultural issues in 1980, not surprisingly, had members who came from occupations in the profit sector. Most of the groups in this field actually were built around the cultivation of specific crops or were restricted to certain areas of the country. A small number of groups were built around public sector professions, such as feedgrain inspectors or agricultural educators and, in recent years, a few citizen groups were organized in this area, usually attempting to represent consumers or seeking to raise environmental issues. The citizen groups increased in number during the 1970s and interjected new issues and an unfamiliar source of conflict into this once settled, predictable policy community.

Presenting a sharp contrast to those in agriculture, most organizations that expressed an interest in the problems of the handicapped in 1980 were made up of public sector professionals working in nonprofit agencies engaged in delivering services to handicapped people. There were a few trade associations made up of firms that manufactured products or equipment used by the handicapped, and there were a number of citizen groups operating in this field, often begun by the parents of handicapped children or by social service professionals concerned in general about the social status of handicapped persons.

Among the groups engaged in 1980 in the debate over women's issues, citizen groups predominated. There were a small number of women's groups made up of professionals in the profit sector, but even these groups were principally concerned with the general status of women in society. Since there were few social service programs targeted specifically for women in 1980, there were not many social service specialties that could serve as the foundation for interest groups in the nonprofit area.

We can also see that the funding patterns for the groups in these three policy communities fit neatly with the types of groups that predominated in each area. Financial support for political activities in the agricultural area was available from large firms that manufacture farm implements, chemicals, and feeds, and in dues from the individual farmers who could expect to receive important individual benefits if their advocates were successful in the legislative process. Groups representing the handicapped had the most diversified sources of income. They received less than half of their support from membership dues but were much more likely than the farm groups to receive grants from private foundations, wealthy individuals, and government agencies. Women's groups were the least dependent on member dues, and the most likely to receive money from patrons outside the government.

Since many of the members of the occupationally based groups in the agricultural and handicapped areas were business firms or social agencies rather than individuals, table 10-1 does not accurately portray the amount of patronage received from institutions. Even where a group is made up entirely of individuals, their participation often has been encouraged and subsidized by their employers, who believe that these activities add to the knowledge and professional standing of their employees.

These data illustrate the importance of financial support from institutions and other patrons of political action, but patrons cannot operate in the political realm with impunity. They must be careful not to put their own operations in jeopardy by supporting causes or taking actions that might invite some form of political retaliation. The extent to which patrons support political causes

**TABLE 10-2.   Amount of Political Conflict within Three Policy Communities**

| Policy Community | N | Level of Reported Conflict[a] |
|---|---|---|
| Farmers | 45 | .31 |
| Handicapped | 26 | −.69 |
| Women | 28 | .31 |

*Source:* 1980 Survey.

[a]Entries represent standard deviations from the sample mean.

depends, to a large degree, on the amount of conflict existing in the area and on the likelihood that important political leaders would come to their defense if they came under attack for becoming involved in controversial questions of public policy. Patrons do not automatically withdraw once conflict begins, but they are likely to continue their activities only so long as they feel that they can muster the necessary political support to protect their interests.

This sensitivity to conflict is illustrated in table 10-2, where we summarize the answers of groups in the three communities to questions about whether there were any organized opponents to their political activities in 1980. The entries in table 10-2 show the number of standard deviations between the mean for the groups in the cells of the table and the mean for the entire sample of national interest groups in the 1980 survey. A positive number in the table indicates that groups report more organized conflict in the area than average, and a negative number means that less conflict is reported than average.

These data reveal an uneven pattern of conflict that helps to explain the types of patronage these groups depend on. Both the women's groups and the agricultural groups were more likely than average to report the existence of organized opponents working against their interests. Both areas stand in sharp contrast to the handicapped groups, which seldom reported the existence of any organized opposition. Many political leaders strenuously opposed the Equal Rights Amendment or called for an end to agricultural subsidies. Some also complained about the size and cost of the welfare state and called for a general reduction in government spending, but no prudent politician in 1980 would have openly attacked programs for the handicapped. In highly consensual policy areas dealing with the handicapped, the aged, children, or other obviously vulnerable groups, government agencies could risk providing financial aid for their constituents, but they were bound to be much more cautious in the conflictual atmosphere surrounding policies toward women or agriculture (Nelson 1984).

The varying configurations of conflict and the demands of organizational maintenance determine the relationships between government agencies and interest groups. Advocates for the handicapped were able to make strong financial and political alliances with normally cautious administrative agencies of government in 1980 because they were almost never directly confronted by interests intent on reducing benefits or terminating programs designed for their clients. The Department of Agriculture had a close, supportive relationship with most of the largest interest groups that represented its constituency, because those groups were closely allied with the committees and subcommittees in Congress that exercised control over the department's affairs. Women's groups, on the other hand, were not closely allied with any large bureau or agency because there were few programs in place (at the time) that delivered social services directly to women. Lacking close ties with government, most of the women's groups engaged in highly controversial efforts to change established social customs and public policies.

The situation facing the women's movement might have been entirely different if Richard Nixon had not vetoed the Comprehensive Child Development Act that was designed to create a national system of day care centers in 1972. Such a large national program, employing many social service professionals, would have been an important source of leadership and patronage for political action—important enough, perhaps, to have produced a different type of women's movement in the 1980s with much closer ties to government. It was organizational and strategic considerations of this kind, shaped by history and the development of public policy, that determined for each of the three policy communities the characteristic relationships with agencies of government that they experienced in 1980. These relationships are illustrated by the data presented in table 10-3.

In order to produce an index of cooperation between government agencies and interest groups, answers to three questions concerning relations with government agencies were combined to create the same measure used in chapter 7. A group receiving the very highest score on this index reported that a member of its staff served on an advisory committee for a government agency, that the group had a high level of interaction with government agencies, and that agencies consulted with the group prior to making policy decisions. Groups with the lowest possible score had no advisory committee memberships, little interaction, and were not consulted prior to policymaking. Scores were combined to produce two categories, high and low cooperation. Placement on this index, reported in table 10-3, reveals that groups representing the handicapped, which were predominantly composed of public sector professionals and nonprofit social service agencies, reported the closest relationships with government agencies, followed closely by the groups representing farmers. Women's groups, not surprisingly, were clearly the least well connected on average, with only 42 percent reporting high

**TABLE 10-3.   Degree of Conflict with Bureaucratic Agencies within Three Policy Communities**

| Index of Bureaucratic Cooperation | Policy Community | | |
|---|---|---|---|
| | Farmers | Handicapped | Women |
| High | 84 | 90 | 42 |
| Low | 16 | 10 | 58 |
| N | 52 | 35 | 50 |

*Source:* 1980 Survey.

*Note:* Each entry is the percentage of interest groups placing high or low on the index of bureaucratic cooperation. This index is an additive combination of answers to three questions: "Does the Executive Director or any member of the permanent staff currently hold a position on an official government advisory committee or commission? [Yes or No]"; "How frequent is the interaction of this association's staff and officers with agencies of the national government? [Frequenct, Infrequent, or No Interaction]"; "Is this association regularly consulted by government agencies when they are considering new legislation or changes in policy? [Yes or No]."

scores on government interaction. In fact, almost one-third of the women's groups reported no contact of any kind with agencies of the federal government.

As argued in chapter 6, groups that experience little conflict and enjoy close, cooperative relationships with government agencies are unlikely to spend much time trying to influence public opinion. Programs designed to serve them are usually in place, and their access to government policymakers is one of their most important sources of strength. These advantages lead them to work within the established legislative process to exploit their favored role in the system. The opposite might be expected of groups that are not readily accepted within the inner circles of government, whose financial support comes largely from sponsors that expect strenuous advocacy for controversial causes in exchange for their patronage. Such groups might be expected to adopt an outside strategy, one directed toward changing the fundamental political environment as a first step toward achieving their goals. The choice of political strategies by any interest group, in other words, reflects the financial, organizational, and political realities it faces.

In order to illustrate the sharp differences in the tactics employed by the groups representing farmers, the handicapped, and women in 1980, an index of inside strategies was created, based on the degree to which groups engaged in lobbying Congress, administrative agencies, and the judiciary. A contrasting index of outside strategies was also created, based upon whether groups made appeals to the public through the mass media, staged large informational conferences open to the public, provided speakers at conventions and other events, and engaged in protest demonstrations. The dramatic differences

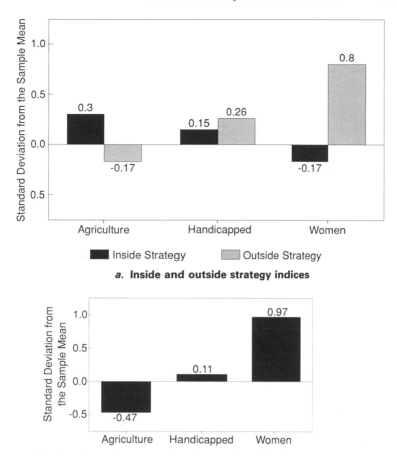

*a.* **Inside and outside strategy indices**

*b.* **Index of outside strategies minus index of inside strategy**

**Fig 10-1. Balance between inside and outside strategies. (Data from 1980 Survey.)**

between these three policy communities is illustrated in figure 10-1, where the use of inside and outside strategies and the balance between them are portrayed.

If groups emphasized a strategy more than the interest-group sample as a whole, their scores will be above the line in figure 10-1, but if their emphasis on inside or outside strategies was less than the sample, their scores will fall below the line. The graph shows clearly that the agricultural groups were trying to exploit their connections to policymakers in 1980 by heavy reliance on lobbying with few efforts to mold public opinion, while the women's groups were mainly trying to expand the scope of the conflict through appeals to the public and acts of protest, rather than concentrating on conventional means of policy-making through the established procedures of the legislative or other institutional processes. The groups representing the handicapped enjoyed close relationships with policymakers but also engaged in efforts to educate the public about the special problems of their members, thus employing almost an even balance of tactics. Figure 10-1 summarizes these different strategic approaches by displaying a single index measuring a group's reliance on outside over inside strategies. The dominant political strategies in each of these communities of groups could hardly be more different.

## Summary and Conclusion

Political mobilization is seldom spontaneous. Before any large element of the population can become a part of the American political process, organizations must be formed, advocates must be trained, and the material resources needed to gain the attention of national policymakers must be gathered. The key to successful political mobilization is seldom an upsurge of intense feelings of discontent within the disadvantaged group—many important political movements in America were long underway before there was any indication of widespread discontent among those in whose behalf the efforts were being made. The essential prerequisites for successful political mobilization are mainly organizational, and many are subject to manipulation through public policy.

The Reagan administration, for example, in its campaign to "defund the left," proposed a change in the rules covering government contractors that would prevent any group receiving federal funds from using the space or equipment paid for with these funds in any form of political advocacy. This would have required many organizations in Washington to rent separate facilities and equip them with separate telephones, furniture, and office machines if they wanted to make presentations to Congress or the bureaucracy on behalf of their members or clients. Even though this rule was not enacted in such an extreme form, it illustrates how dependent the modern advocacy system has become on the rules governing contracting and consulting with the federal government, on the tax laws that govern the political behavior of business firms and nonprofit corporations, and on a series of other rules and common practices that regulate the interactions among advocates, their patrons, elected policymakers and their staffs the court system, the federal bureaucracy, and the electoral system.

As I argued in preceding chapters, most citizen groups that emerged from social movements in the past have simply faded away once the intense enthusiasms of their followers began to cool, or when a string of policy defeats or compromises caused marginal supporters to lose hope. In the

1980s, however, many of the citizen groups born during the 1960s and 1970s were still in business, with help from their individual and institutional patrons, even though public interest in their causes had declined. These groups now promote concern for their issues and stand ready to exercise leadership whenever there is a new burst of public enthusiasm.

Political mobilization led by social service professionals, government agencies, and other patrons from the nonprofit sector has been successful mainly in areas of low controversy. It cannot be used whenever the level of controversy rises, because the policy professionals and bureaucrats who take the lead in this process cannot count on support from the political leadership to protect their agencies against hostile critics. If a single majority party with a clearly articulated ideology were firmly in control of the entire governmental system for a prolonged period—as was the Social Democratic Party of Sweden for more than four decades after the 1930s—bureaucratic leaders might enter more willingly into potentially explosive policy areas. In the decentralized American political system, however, where control of the presidency and each house of Congress often is not in the hands of the same political party, public officials must exercise caution. The Administration on Aging may work openly to organize the elderly—sometimes going as far as paying to transport their clients to state legislatures to lobby their elected representatives in favor of programs for the aged—but government agencies working in less consensual areas must be careful not to make themselves vulnerable to attacks from antagonists who do not approve of their programs or missions (Pratt 1976; Hayes 1981; Chubb 1983; Nelson 1984).

Our analysis takes us full circle, returning to the problem of representation for the unemployed. One of the principal reasons there is no organization dedicated exclusively to advancing the welfare of the unemployed is that their cause is inherently controversial, and there are no readily accessible patrons prepared to subsidize political entrepreneurs who might wish to organize them. There are no agencies of the government or private foundations that feel politically capable of organizing bus loads of the unemployed for marches on their state capitals—much less Washington. Nor is there any professional community whose institutional roles and norms clearly and exclusively ally them with the needs of the unemployed. Marches on Washington by Coxey's Army of the unemployed in 1894 or the Bonus Army of unemployed veterans in 1932 were met with hostility, and eventually the marchers were dispersed by force. Without the appropriate political, organizational, and financial prerequisites, a group called the National Association of the Unemployed is unlikely ever to appear.

The reason why some of the most deprived elements of American society are either ignored or represented in the legislative process only by small, nonmember organizations is not that they are essentially satisfied with their status and have no interest in political activity; it is because there is no institutional foundation from which a successful effort at mobilization can be launched. Political mobilization of those at the bottom of the social order is exceedingly difficult because there are few patrons able or willing to risk the danger to their own political well-being that might arise from heavy political conflict over redistributive social programs. Elected officials, of course, are free to take the lead in promoting legislation designed to aid disadvantaged groups without prompting from any outside force, but they know that once conflict begins over their proposals, there will be few organizations in place that can mobilize expressions of support, supply information and ideas, or raise the financial resources needed to combat the program's critics. The uneven pattern of political mobilization resulting from these forces is reflected in our bewildering array of narrowly focused social welfare programs, each dealing with some purpose upon which consensus among the political leadership has been achieved. The American system provides veterans of World War II with a wide range of services, including a comprehensive system of socialized medicine in government-owned hospitals with government-paid physicians, while providing little assistance at all for black teenagers, almost half of whom are unemployed (Steiner 1971).

This book began by asking why certain groups were represented in Washington by political organizations while others were not, even though they seemed equally in need of representation. The explanation I have offered does not allow us to predict exactly which groups will be mobilized and which will not, but it does lead to the conclusion that only certain types of discontent are likely to gain expression. Political entrepreneurs are required to initiate the process of mobilization, but a successful set of political organizations representing a constituency will not come into being, no matter how clever or energetic the leaders of the movement may be, unless institutions can be identified that will serve as sponsors or patrons for their efforts. The behavior of potential patrons is largely determined by the degree of conflict or consensus revolving around the policies being proposed by the political movement. Some proposals and some groups are simply outside the prevailing consensus among elected representatives and the attentive public. It is doubtful that any political organization could be maintained over a long time providing exclusive representation for such groups. The array of political advocates existing at any moment in our political system does not accurately mirror the pattern of discontents felt by the citizenry; it is a much better reflection of both the prevailing consensus over the legitimate scope of public policy existing among those active in politics and the institutions in the society that are available as patrons of political action.

# Epilogue: Unfinished Research Agenda

*Joel D. Aberbach and Frank R. Baumgartner*

As Jack Walker wrote in a haunting phrase in the Introduction of this book, he knew that if he were ever to finish this manuscript in his lifetime, he would have to draw some clear boundaries and make some difficult choices about what not to do. Therefore, many important topics related to interest groups and political mobilization in America are not covered here. As two of the group of friends and collaborators who put these chapters together from Jack's chapter drafts and papers, we point to some of the questions that Jack did not have time to address. This effort makes painfully clear the scope of the discipline's loss with Jack's death, but we hope that others will be inspired to study some of these questions in the future, carrying on Jack's work in the scholarly tradition of building on the ideas and findings of those who have blazed trails before us.

Jack's unfinished research agenda is essentially of three types: questions that could not be adequately addressed with the research design and data collection that Jack eventually decided on for this project, but which he recognized to be important areas of research anyway; questions that could be discussed with the existing data but were not fully exploited in these pages, either because of Jack's untimely death or because of the limitations of space available in any single book; and questions that are posed by the findings of this book and even discussed in detail but where more work could profitably be undertaken. Since Jack had an unusually fertile mind, the research reported in the book points to a great number of potential areas for further refinement of our understanding of interest representation and mobilization.

Some important areas of investigation related to interest groups and political mobilization were excluded because of the nature of the surveys that form the basis for the book. Law firms, private businesses, and governmental agencies play important roles in the lobbying system. Any complete discussion of interest groups and political mobilization should include a discussion of them. However, as Jack discussed in chapter 1, he had to draw the line for his survey somewhere, so he made the choice to study only membership organizations operating at the national level. How nonmember organizations differ from those groups discussed in this book is an obvious question.

Jack's death came at a time in this project when the vast bulk of the book was either completed or mapped out so well that putting the final touches on it was not difficult. Still, there are many points at which Jack might have gone further: the discussion of the relations between interest groups and political parties, the analysis of groups' use of the courts, the discussion of membership benefits, and changes within groups during the first five years of the Reagan administration. In short, even the existing data sets could not be fully mined for their richness in one book. Luckily, there is nothing to stop those who have read this book from using the data set to investigate those avenues for further research to which this book points. Jack would have liked nothing more than to see his book used in a graduate seminar in conjunction with the data set, where students and researchers might carry his analysis a step further in those areas where the limitations of time and space forced him to stop short of what he might have done.

The third area to which this book points is probably the most interesting, but also the most difficult to describe. Jack was an imaginative thinker, and his thoughts naturally led him into many new areas of research that could not have been foreseen when he devised his surveys. Most prominent, here, is probably his insight into the important role of philanthropies, the government, and other patrons of political action. Jack's data clearly show that these were important influences on the creation and maintenance of large numbers of groups. But we know little about the motivations or the hopes of the patrons themselves. If many groups are not dependent on membership dues, as Jack's research indicates, then we need a more complete understanding of the large institutions, government agencies, foundations, and affluent individuals that provide the lifeblood of many organizations, and whose efforts have dramatically altered the nature of representation through the group system in America.

Researchers have often noted the importance of institutions and large organizations in structuring political life. Jack's finding that many organizations relied on what he called member patrons—single members providing, by themselves, a large proportion of the organization's entire annual revenue—was one of the few ways in which he agreed with Mancur Olson. Olson wrote of the likelihood of the exploitation of the strong by the weak, and Jack indeed found that many organizations seemed to have dues structures that fit that bill. But in what direction does the exploitation really run?

Enormous private benefits often accrue to the largest members of industrial groups when public policies are changed, to take one example. Legitimacy in arguing for changes in public policies, however, often requires large memberships, and the willingness to make the goods public, not only selective. If large organizations know that the only way to achieve public policies likely to lead to enormous private gain is through the mobilization of others who might share their interests, then who is exploiting whom, and in which direction does the by-product theory of group political action run? The large may induce the small to join in order to increase the likelihood that the large will be influential in government, just as the small may join a group when they realize their memberships are heavily subsidized, and may even demand greater and greater services or lower and lower dues. So exploitation may be a two-way street, at a minimum.

In addition, where Olson viewed political activities as a by-product of the formation of groups motivated by other reasons, Jack's data point to the possibility (and it remains only a possibility at this time) that it is not political activity that is the by-product of the group, but rather the group itself may be the by-product of the political activities of the largest member or members. After realizing that they can be more successful in their political activities if they speak as the leader of a group rather than only as a private organization, large agencies, corporations, and organizations move to mobilize others who might join them, becoming member patrons along the way, and allowing themselves to be "exploited" by agreeing to carry the largest burden of membership dues. So Jack's work calls for a greater investigation of the exploitation of the strong by the weak, and of the by-product theory of political activities.

Jack's study of interest groups covers only a part of the broader question of influence and representation within policy networks. Clearly, membership organizations are an important component of these networks, but so are government agencies, private and university researchers, and others. Another area of research to which this book points, therefore, is the way in which the internal characteristics of policy networks determine public policies. What are the consequences of conflict and consensus within such networks? What policy areas come to be dominated by leaders able to maintain their independence from broader political forces, and what areas tend constantly to be dragged into public and political controversies? How do ideas come to be accepted across whole communities, and how do policy communities exert their influence on the broader political system?

Jack was able to discuss some of these questions through the comparison of a small number of issue areas, but his research points to the importance of understanding these networks more completely. These questions could be addressed in a longitudinal fashion, comparing one or more areas over long periods of time and noting how their characteristics have changed. They could be addressed through a comparative approach across countries. Or they could be addressed through a cross-sectional study of a variety of policy communities in the United States. Each of these approaches would involve some new findings complementary to those presented in this book, and perhaps better able to link the group system with the representation of ideas within policy communities and with the policy outputs that those communities collectively create.

Jack's concern with the representation of the disadvantaged rose from a desire to understand the nature of democracy. The discussion in the final chapter about the potential to mobilize the unemployed makes it clear that his conclusion about the representation of interests in America is not falsely reassuring. Many social groups are well represented, and the group system, even as it grows unwieldy and causes presidents and others to complain that the system cannot be controlled, represents more groups now than it did only decades ago. So Jack was impressed by the ability of groups to overcome the obstacles to mobilization, and noted that they did so in increasing numbers every year.

Where others saw a breakdown in consensus and yearned for the days when government decisions were less likely to be the subject of street protests and where legislators operated in an environment of much greater freedom of action, Jack rejoiced in the obvious increase in citizen mobilization and interest in public affairs. The reason governing seemed easier in earlier decades, he often argued, was that tens of millions of Americans were shut out of the political process because of their skin color, their poor education, or their lack of an advocacy group to look after their interests. Jack did not pine for an elitist past, as he sometimes thought others did. However, he also fully understood that the interest-group system is not, and probably will never be, a perfect mirror of American society. One obvious question that Jack's work leaves unanswered is the potential for different social groups to organize and to become players in the interest-group system, which is so important to political representation in Washington and elsewhere.

Jack's work was characterized by a desire to address questions going to the heart of the democratic process through systematic empirical investigation. Starting with a concern for how the disadvantaged find representation through the party and the group systems in the United States, Jack went a long way toward answering key questions in this area. There remain, of course, many unanswered questions. We hope this book will inspire others to think about and address them.

# Appendixes

# APPENDIX A

## Description of the Data Sets

The bulk of the statistical analysis reported in this book is based on two general surveys of interest groups active at the national level in Washington, D.C., conducted by mail at the Institute of Public Policy Studies of the University of Michigan. Some groups were contacted only in 1980, others only in 1985, and a number were contacted in both waves, creating two cross-sectional surveys and a panel data set. Questionnaires were mailed to the executive secretaries or other officers who bore the principal responsibility for managing the associations (see appendixes B and C for the texts of the two questionnaires).

Most of the groups in the two surveys were drawn from the *Washington Information Directory*, (Congressional Quarterly 1979 and 1984). All groups in the directory that were open to membership were included in the sample. Mailing for the first survey began with a small, test sample of groups in the area of aging, mailed in 1978. The remaining questionnaires were mailed between June 29, 1979, and August 4, 1981, with the bulk of the responses coming in 1980; this is referred to throughout the book as the 1980 study. In addition to the groups included in the general directory, the 1980 study was supplemented with extensive efforts to identify every organization representing various constituencies (women, African-Americans, Hispanics, and the handicapped), and policy communities (aging, antipoverty, housing, pharmaceuticals, and urban mass transportation). This was done in order to counteract any possible bias in the general directory, and to get more complete views of a few individual policy communities. In each of the categories where searches were conducted, a number of groups were found that did not appear in the *Washington Information Directory*. These supplementary groups were discovered by consulting other general directories, such as the *Encyclopedia of Associations*, from listings in the *New York Times Index*, from lists of witnesses at congressional hearings in the relevant committees, from Washington, D.C., telephone books, from other specialized organizational directories, and from lists of active organizations provided by group leaders during personal interviews. In almost every case, however, the groups identified through these searches were found to be very small (usually without a professional staff), or to be headquartered outside of Washington and seldom to

**TABLE A-1. Summary of 1980 and 1985 Surveys and Panel Data Set**

| Type of Group | 1980 | | | 1985 | | | |
| --- | --- | --- | --- | --- | --- | --- | --- |
| | Total Contacted | Total Responses | Response Rate | Total Contacted | Total Responses | Response Rate | Number in Panel |
| Associations in CQ directory | 902 | 558 | 61.8% | 1,501 | 828 | 55.2% | 385 |
| Associations not in CQ directory | 424 | 176 | 41.5 | 135 | 64 | 47.4 | 63 |
| Total | 1,326 | 734 | 55.4 | 1,636 | 892 | 54.5 | 448 |

engage in efforts to influence national policy. In some cases, it was unclear whether the groups existed at all outside of a file drawer in the office of some Washington law firm.

This effort to identify each group in several policy areas reassured us that the *Washington Information Directory* included a relatively complete set of all the major groups active at the national level. In the 1985 data set, therefore, we sampled all groups in the directory, and all those that had been contacted in 1980, but we made no supplementary effort to identify additional groups. A revised and expanded questionnaire was mailed in five subsets to a total of 1,636 groups, beginning on December 4, 1984. The bulk of these questionnaires were returned during the 1985 calendar year. Table A-1 summarizes the survey efforts.

The summaries of the data sets displayed in table A-1 show that the 1980 survey included 1,326 organizations from all sources of which 734, or 55.4 percent, responded. For the 902 groups identified only from the *Washington Information Directory,* however, 558 responded, a rate of 61.8 percent. The highest response rates were obtained from larger groups rather than smaller, and from groups in the nonprofit sector rather than the profit sector, but the differences in response rates were generally small.

The 1985 survey was sent to the 1,501 membership associations listed in the *Directory* and to 135 additional associations that had responded to the 1980 survey, were still active as of December, 1984, and for which current addresses could be found. The 1985 data set includes 892 respondents, 54.5 percent of the 1,636 organizations that were contacted. Considering only the 1,501 groups listed in the 1984–85 *Washington Information Directory,* a total of 828 responses were received, yielding a response rate among that group of 55.2 percent.

There is one exception to the generally uniform response rates found for different types of groups. Unions showed a particularly low response rate (29 responses out of 94 questionnaires mailed, for a response rate of only 30.9 percent, about half of that for the rest of the sample in 1985). Most analysis reported in the book differentiates by group type and excludes the union responses. For nonunion organizations in 1985, response rates may be adjusted to 863 of 1,542, or 56.0 percent.

A portion of this data set can be regarded as a panel since it includes responses to both the 1980 and the 1985 surveys. This panel includes 448 groups, of which 385 were identified in the *Directory,* and 63 came from the supplementary sources.

## APPENDIX B

# The 1980 Questionnaire

This appendix lists the questions from the 1980 questionnaire. Scales and answer blanks have been omitted.

1. What is the official name of this association?
2. In what year was it founded?
3. Some associations are composed of representatives of organizations, while other associations are made up only of individuals. Still other associations have a membership that includes a mixture of individuals and organizational representatives. To which membership category does your association belong?
   1. Membership composed of organizational representatives.
   2. Membership is a mixture of individuals and organizational representatives.
   3. Membership made up of individuals.
4. How important is the occupation or profession of an individual for membership in this association?
   1. *Very Important.* Association membership is dependent on membership in certain occupations or professions.
   2. *Important.* Most association members belong to certain occupations or professions but this is not a requirement for membership.
   3. *Not Important.* Membership in this association has nothing to do with an individual's occupation or profession.
5. How important is the organizational affiliation of an individual for membership in this association?
   1. *Very Important.* Association membership is dependent on membership in certain types of organizations or agencies.
   2. *Important.* Most association members belong to certain organizations or agencies but this is not a requirement for membership.
   3. *Not Important.* Membership in this association has nothing to do with an individual's being involved in certain organizations or agencies.
6. Was this association the product of a merger of older groups or associations? [If yes:] What groups took part in the merger and in what years were they founded?
7. Did this association originally grow out of or split off from a parent group? [If yes:] What were these parent associations and in what years were they founded?
8. What is the total membership of this association? [Indicate number of individuals and of organizations.]
9. How large was the membership five years ago?
   0. Association was not in existence five years ago.

      1. Larger than current size.

      2. Approximately same size as today.

      3. Smaller than current size.

10. Which of the following statements is the most accurate description of this organization?

    a. Members join or participate in this association mainly because they are *providers* of certain services or products or because they administer certain governmental programs.

    b. Members join or participate in this association mainly because they are *consumers* of certain services or products or because they are citizens strongly affected by certain governmental policies or services.

    c. This association includes some members who are providers and others who are consumers of certain services, programs, or products.

    d. Membership in this association is not related to specific programs, services, or products.

11. Do any of the following types of people belong to this association or its constituent organizations?

    a. Elected officials. If yes, circle percentage of total membership: 1–25%, 26–75%, 76–100%.

    b. Civil servants. If yes, circle percentage of total membership: 1–25%, 26–75%, 76–100%.

    c. Employees of governmental nonprofit agencies such as universities, hospitals, or prisons. If yes, circle percentage of total membership: 1–25%, 26–75%, 76–100%.

    d. Employees of private, nonprofit agencies such as universities, hospitals, religious bodies, or social agencies. If yes, circle percentage of total membership: 1–25%, 26–75%, 76–100%.

    e. Employees of profit-making institutions or business firms. If yes, circle percentage of total membership: 1–25%, 26–75%, 76–100%.

    f. Self-employed professionals. If yes, circle percentage of total membership: 1–25%, 26–75%, 76–100%.

12. Does the association employ an executive director (or any other permanent staff member)? [If yes:]

    a. Is the executive director a full-time employee?

    b. In what year did the association first employ an executive director?

    c. Besides the executive director, are there any other part-time or full-time staff members? [If yes:]

        *a.* How many full-time equivalent persons are employed?

        *b.* How large was the association's staff five years ago?

           0. Association not in existence five years ago.

           1. Larger than current size.

           2. Approximately same size as today.

           3. Smaller than currently.

    d. Has the executive director or any member of the permanent staff held any of the following positions:

        *a.* Elected Government Office

     *b.* Appointed Government Office

     *c.* Government Civil Service

     *d.* Legislative Staff Aide

     *e.* Staff Positions in other Associations

    e. Does the executive director or any member of the permanent staff currently hold a position on an official government advisory committee or commission?

13. What are the principal benefits received by members of this association? [Indicate level of importance: 1 = important; 2 = not important; 3 = not provided.]

    a. Informative Publications

    b. In-Service Training

    c. Conferences and Meetings

    d. Low-Cost Insurance

    e. Advocacy for Important Policies

    f. Contacts with Professional Colleagues

    g. Organized Tours or Trips

    h. Discounts on Consumer Goods

    i. Representation of Members' Opinions before Government Agencies

    j. Opportunity for Participation in Public Affairs

    k. Friendship with Other Members

    l. Coordination of the Activities of Voluntary Organizations in This Field

    m. Other (Please specify)

14. Does the association have a permanent headquarters?

15. Has the association's headquarters ever been in another city? [If yes:] What was the last city and the year in which the move to the present location took place?

16. Does this association have local offices, chapters, headquarters, or other such organized bodies below the level of the central staff and headquarters?

17. In their initial stages most associations receive financial grants or other forms of assistance that help them get established. Did this association receive assistance from any of the following sources in the beginning of its history? If yes, please identify source.

    a. Private Foundation Grants

    b. Other Associations

    c. Government Agencies

    d. Private Agencies

    e. Private Individuals (no identification required)

    f. Other (Please specify source)

    Check here if no forms of assistance were received.

18. Once established most associations receive financial support for their administrative and program costs from many different sources. Please indicate whether the following financial sources are used by this association and circle the percentage of the association's total financial support provided by each source during the last fiscal year.

    a. Membership dues. If yes, circle percentage of total financial support: 1–10%, 11–30%, 31–70%, 71–100%.

    b. Publication sales. If yes, circle percentage of total financial support: 1–10%, 11–30%, 31–70%, 71–100%.

    c. Conference fees. If yes, circle percentage of total financial support: 1–10%, 11–30%, 31–70%, 71–100%.

    d. Commissions from insurance sales. If yes, circle percentage of total financial support: 1–10%, 11–30%, 31–70%, 71–100%.

    e. Fees from individuals for staff services. If yes, circle percentage of total financial support: 1–10%, 11–30%, 31–70%, 71–100%.

    f. Grants or contracts from government agencies. If yes, circle percentage of total financial support: 1–10%, 11–30%, 31–70%, 71–100%.

    g. Fees for services to private firms. If yes, circle percentage of total financial support: 1–10%, 11–30%, 31–70%, 71–100%.

    h. Royalties and honoraria. If yes, circle percentage of total financial support: 1–10%, 11–30%, 31–70%, 71–100%.

    i. Individual gifts. If yes, circle percentage of total financial support: 1–10%, 11–30%, 31–70%, 71–100%.

    j. Foundation grants. If yes, circle percentage of total financial support: 1–10%, 11–30%, 31–70%, 71–100%.

    k. Interest from cash balances or endowments. If yes, circle percentage of total financial support: 1–10%, 11–30%, 31–70%, 71–100%.

    l. Loans. If yes, circle percentage of total financial support: 1–10%, 11–30%, 31–70%, 71–100%.

    m. Funds from other associations. If yes, circle percentage of total financial support: 1–10%, 11–30%, 31–70%, 71–100%.

    n. Other (please specify).

19. What was the total revenue for this association from all sources during the last fiscal year?

20. Are there associations or groups with whom your association consults, communicates, or cooperates? If yes, please specify the two most important groups.

21. Are there associations or groups with similar purposes or goals with whom your association competes for new members, funds, contracts, or other resources? If yes, please specify the two most important groups.

22. Are there associations or groups with whom this association finds itself in disagreement or opposition? If yes, please specify the two most important groups.

23. Some associations interact principally with the government in Washington. Others interact mainly at the state and local levels, while still other groups deal with the government at all levels. How frequent is the interaction of this association's staff and officers with each of the following levels of government? [Indicate level of interaction: 1 = frequent; 2 = infrequent; 3 = no interaction.]

    a. National Government

    b. State Government

    c. Local Government

24. Are there agencies of the federal government with which this association communicates, consults, or interacts? If yes, please specify the two most important agencies.

25. Is this association regularly consulted by government agencies when they are considering new legislation or changes in policy?

26. How did the change in 1976 from Republican to Democratic control of the Presi-

dency affect the amount of cooperation and consultation between this association and federal agencies?

1. Important increase in cooperation.
2. Moderate increase in cooperation.
3. No change in the relationship.
4. Moderate decrease in cooperation.
5. Important decrease in cooperation.
0. This association had no contact with federal agencies at that time.

27. In general, do the policy positions of this association tend to call for (check one):
    a. Much more government provision of social services?
    b. Some additional government provision of social services?
    c. Present level of services?
    d. Less government provision of social services?
    e. Much less government provision of social services?

28. In general, do the policy positions of this association tend to call for (check one):
    a. Much more government regulation of business and industry?
    b. Some additional government regulation of business and industry?
    c. Present level of regulation?
    d. Less government regulation of business and industry?
    e. Much less government regulation of business and industry?

29. Are there Committees or Subcommittees of the U.S. Congress with which this association communicates, consults, or interacts? If yes, please specify the two most important committees or subcommittees.

30. What is the relative importance of each of the following activities in the work of this association? [Indicate importance: 1 = very important; 2 = important; 3 = not very important; 4 = association does not engage in this activity.]
    a. Organizing conferences and meetings for specialists in this field
    b. Organizing conferences and meetings for interested laymen, citizens, or other nonspecialists in this field
    c. Publishing newsletters, magazines, journals, monographs, or books
    d. Providing information for the membership on job opportunities in this field
    e. Conducting in-service training for specialists in this field
    f. Collecting and diffusing information about administrative techniques, new equipment, products, or practices in the field
    g. Working for the passage of needed legislation at the local, state, or national level
    h. Working to improve the administration of government programs being conducted in this field
    i. Working to insure the election of political leaders sympathetic to the goals of this association
    j. Engaging in litigation of class action lawsuits or the preparation of amicus curiae briefs
    k. Conducting or organizing research into the problems of this field
    l. Developing and conducting demonstration projects in this field
    m. Developing publicity for the association or drawing the attention of the mass media to important developments in this field

n. Organizing or carrying out public demonstrations or protests
o. Conducting solicitation campaigns or contacting potential donors in a search for private contributions to the association
p. Serving as consultants or advisers to operating agencies of the federal, state, or local government
q. Making efforts through mailings, personal contacts, or other means to increase the membership of the association
r. Applying for grants or contracts from government agencies, private foundations, or business firms
s. Answering questions or handling requests for service or aid from the membership of the association
t. Providing speakers or other program materials for events sponsored by local chapters or by other associations
u. Doing staff work or general organizational activity for other associations in this field
v. Administering service programs on contract with government agencies
w. Other (Please describe)
31. Are there any topics or subjects not treated in this questionnaire that you feel are important for understanding associations like this one? Are there any comments you would like to make about this study? Please give us any reactions you may have.
32. Approximately how many minutes were required to complete this questionnaire?

Thank you very much for your cooperation.

## APPENDIX C

# The 1985 Questionnaire

This appendix lists the questions from the 1985 questionnaire. Scales and answer blanks have been omitted.

1. If the name of the association printed above is incorrect, please make the appropriate corrections.
2. In what year was this association founded?
3. Some associations are composed of organizations or representatives of organizations, such as companies, institutions, or associations, while other associations are made up only of individuals representing themselves. Still other associations have a membership that includes a mixture of organizations or organizational representatives and individuals. Which membership category best describes this association?
   1. Membership is composed of organizations or organizational representatives.
   2. Membership is a mixture of organizations or organizational representatives and individuals.
   3. Membership is composed of individuals.
4. What is the total membership of this association? [Indicate number of organizations or organizational representatives and of individuals.]
5. How large is the membership of this association compared to five (5) years ago? Please indicate the approximate amount of change by marking the appropriate position on the scale provided.
6. Listed below are a number of statements that could describe the membership of an association. Some of these statements may be good descriptions of the association. Think of them as being rated "5" on a scale that goes from 1 to 5. Other statements may be poor descriptions of the association. They would be rated a "1" on the scale. For each statement, please indicate your best estimate of whether it is a good or poor description of this association, or something in between.
   a. Association membership is dependent on being a member of certain occupations or professions
   b. Any individual or organization may belong to this association
   c. Members of this association are affiliated with a single profit-making industry or occupation
   d. Membership in this association is necessary for members to practice their occupations or professions
   e. Membership in this association has nothing to do with a member's occupation or other organizational affiliation

    f. Members of this association tend to have similar occupational or organizational affiliations
7. Associations may be comprised of many different kinds of members. For each of the following categories of members, please indicate your best estimate of the percentage that each category contributes to the total membership of this association.
    a. Elected officials
    b. Civil servants
    c. Employees of governmental or private nonprofit agencies, such as universities, hospitals, or prisons
    d. Employees of profit-making institutions or business firms
    e. Self-employed professionals or others who own and operate their own business
    f. Retirees or other currently nonemployed individuals
8. How many full-time equivalent persons are employed on the staff, including those financed by grants or contracts administered by this association?
    8a. How large is the association's staff compared to five (5) years ago? Please indicate the approximate amount of change by marking the appropriate position on the scale provided.
    8b. Has the executive director or any other member of the permanent staff held any of the following positions?
        b1. Elected government office
        b2. Appointed government office
        b3. Government civil service
        b4. Legislative staff aide
        b5. Staff positions in other associations
9. There may be a variety of benefits or activities that attract members to join an association. Some of these factors may be the most important ones for attracting the association's membership. Other factors are of the least importance. Still others may be not provided at all by the association. For each of the following factors, please indicate on the scale provided your best estimate of the importance of that factor for attracting members to this association.
    a. Publications or other informational services
    b. Training, education, or technical assistance
    c. Conferences and meetings
    d. Low-cost insurance
    e. Advocacy of important values, ideas, or policies
    f. Communication with professional peers or colleagues
    g. Organized tours or trips
    h. Collective bargaining
    i. Research
    j. Discounts on consumer goods
    k. Legal assistance
    l. Licensing, accreditation, or codes development
    m. Representation of members' opinions before government agencies or legislative bodies
    n. Opportunity for participation in public affairs

o. Friendship with other members

p. Coordination of activities of organizations in this field

q. Other (Please specify)

10. Does this association have state or local offices, chapters, headquarters, or other such organized bodies below the level of the central staff and headquarters? [If yes:]

    10a. Do the state or local organizations of this association have their own memberships, with those members paying dues that go directly to the state or local units?

    10b. Do the state or local organizations of this association generally employ their own professional staffs?

11. In their initial stages, associations often receive financial grants or other forms of assistance that help them to get established. Did this association receive assistance from any of the following sources in the beginning of its history? If "YES," please identify the sources.

a. Private foundation grants

b. Trade unions

c. Churches

d. Other associations

e. Corporations or business firms

f. Government agencies

g. Large contributions from a few individuals (No identification required)

h. Small contributions from many individuals (No identification required)

i. Other (Please specify source)

12. Once established, associations may receive financial support for their administrative and program costs from many different sources. For each of the following financial sources, please indicate your best estimate of the percentage that each source contributed to this association's total financial support during the last fiscal year. IN THOSE ESTIMATES, PLEASE INCLUDE FUNDS THAT FINANCE PROGRAMS OR SERVICES PROVIDED BY THE ASSOCIATION FOR NON-MEMBERS. [Respondents could mark on a scale from "None" to "100%."]

a. Membership dues

b. Revenues beyond dues payments from publications sales or advertising

c. Conventions, conferences, or exhibitions

d. Sale of merchandise

e. Commissions from insurance sales

f. Grants or contracts from government agencies

g. Gifts or grants from corporations or business firms

h. Royalties or honoraria

i. Gifts or bequests beyond normal dues from individuals

j. Foundation grants

k. Rent

l. Interest from cash balances or endowments

m. Loans

n. Funds from other associations or organizations

o. Funds from churches

p. Funds from trade unions

q. Fundraising events, such as dinners, dances, parties, or theatrical events

r. Other (Please specify)

13. For some associations, all members pay the same amount of dues. Other associations use a sliding scale, with some members paying higher dues than others. Which of the following statements best describes the dues structure of this association?

    1. All members pay the same amount of dues.

        13a. How much do members pay in dues?

    2. Dues are paid on a sliding scale, with some members paying more than other members.

        13b. What is the highest amount of dues paid by a member?

        13c. Approximately what percentage of the members pay within 10% of the highest amount of dues?

        13d. What is the lowest amount of dues paid by a member?

        13e. Approximately what percentage of the members pay within 10% of the lowest amount of dues?

14. In the last five years, has this association provided programs or services on contract from agencies of the federal government? [If yes:]

        14a. Since 1980, have these federal government contracts become a more significant or less significant part of the activities and finances of this association, or have they remained of the same significance?

        1. More significant part of the activities and finances.

        2. Same significance.

        3. Less significant part of the activities and finances.

15. What was the total revenue for this association from all financial sources including grants and contracts, during the last fiscal year?

16. Which of the following statements concerning competition with other organizations in your field best describes this association?

    1. This association experiences little competition for members or resources from other associations in this field.

    2. This association competes for members or resources only from time to time with other associations in this field.

    3. This association engages in continuous competition for members or resources with other associations in this field.

17. Listed below are a number of statements that might describe your association. Some of these statements may be a good description of the association, while others may be a poor description. For each statement, please indicate your best estimate of whether it is a good or poor description of this association, or something in between. [Respondents could mark on a scale from "1. Poor Description" to "5. Good Description."]

    a. This association works in a policy area marked by intense conflict or disagreement over fundamental policy goals

    b. This association works in a policy area marked by consensus on the appropriate means for achieving policy objectives

    c. This association works in a policy area where conflict erupts very often

d. This association repeatedly faces the same opponents on each of the policy issues of interest to it
e. Some important elected officials oppose the policy aims of this association
f. Some organized groups oppose the policy aims of this association
g. Some important government agencies oppose the policy aims of this association
h. This association perceives an important difference between the two major political parties on those issues most relevant to its goals

18. When formulating positions on governmental affairs, some associations may consult with a variety of individuals or organizations. For each group listed below, please indicate whether this association always consults, often consults, sometimes consults, or seldom or never consults with them when considering public affairs.
a. Individual experts in the policy area
b. Other organizations active in the policy area
c. Members of this association
d. Members of Congress or their staffs
e. Directors of government agencies or their staffs
f. Presidential or White House staff
g. Foundations that provide funds for this association
h. Other nongovernmental agencies that provide funds for this association
i. Members of the press or media
j. Political party leaders or others in party organizations
k. Others (Please specify)

19. Associations differ, when engaging in public affairs, in the degree to which they coordinate their activities with other associations. Which of the following three statements best describes this association?
1. This association normally operates alone when engaging in public affairs.
2. This association operates alone some of the time but sometimes joins ad hoc coalitions with other organizations.
3. This association normally coordinates its public affairs activities with other organizations that share its goals.

20. Is this association regularly consulted by government agencies when they are considering new legislation or changes in policy?

21. How many different cabinet departments and independent agencies of the federal government did this association communicate, consult, or interact with during the past year?
21a. For the federal agency with which this association communicates, consults, or interacts the most, does this association interact with it frequently, occasionally, seldom, or almost never?
21b. When there is interaction between this association and administrative agencies of the federal government, how would you characterize the relationship? Is it normally cooperative, occasionally cooperative, seldom cooperative, or almost never cooperative?

22. How many subcommittees of the Congress did this association communicate, consult, or interact with during the past year?
22a. For the subcommittee of the Congress with which this association communi-

cates, consults, or interacts the most, does this association interact with it frequently, occasionally, seldom, or almost never?

22b. When there is interaction between this association and subcommittees of the Congress, how would you characterize the relationship? Is it normally cooperative, occasionally cooperative, seldom cooperative, or almost never cooperative?

23. Listed below are a number of individuals and offices within the Executive Office of the President with which an association may interact. For each of those offices, please indicate whether this association communicates, consults, or interacts with them frequently, occasionally, seldom, or almost never.
   a. Office of Public Liaison (OPL)
   b. Other Presidential Assistants in the White House Office
   c. Office of Management and Budget (OMB)
   d. Any other office or agency within in the Executive Office of the President (EOP)

24. When there is interaction between this association and offices or agencies within the Executive Office of the President, how would you characterize the relationship? Is it normally cooperative, occasionally cooperative, seldom cooperative, almost never cooperative, or is there no interaction?

25. Does this association have tax-exempt status under the federal Internal Revenue Code?

26. How did the change in 1981 from Democratic to Republican control of the Presidency affect the amount of cooperation and consultation between this association and federal agencies?
   0. This association had no contact with federal agencies at that time.
   1. Important increase in cooperation.
   2. Moderate increase in cooperation.
   3. No change in the relationship.
   4. Moderate decrease in cooperation.
   5. Important decrease in cooperation.

27. How did the change in 1981 from Democratic to Republican control of the United States Senate affect the amount of consultation and cooperation between this association and the Congress?
   0. This association had no contact with the Congress at that time.
   1. Important increase in cooperation.
   2. Moderate increase in cooperation.
   3. No change in the relationship.
   4. Moderate decrease in cooperation.
   5. Important decrease in cooperation.

28. Many associations have an interest in the level of federal government involvement in various areas of public policy. For each of the following policy areas, please indicate whether this association is very interested, somewhat interested, or not very interested in the level of federal government involvement.
   a. Agriculture
   b. Civil rights and civil liberties
   c. Education
   d. Housing and urban policy

e. Transportation

f. Health and other human services

g. Energy and natural resources

h. Management of the economy

i. Changes in government, including federal personnel policy, administrative organization, and elections

j. Defense, national security, and foreign policy

29. For each of the following policy areas, please indicate which statement reflects most accurately the policy of this association concerning expenditures or the provision of services by the federal government: There should be much more provision of federal services, somewhat more, the present level, somewhat less, much less, or this association has no position on that issue.

a. Agriculture

b. Civil rights and civil liberties

c. Education

d. Housing and urban policy

e. Transportation

f. Health and other human services

g. Energy and natural resources

h. Management of the economy

i. Changes in government, including federal personnel policy, administrative organization, and elections

j. Defense, national security, and foreign policy

30. For each of the following policy areas, please indicate which statement most accurately reflects the policy of this association concerning the level of federal regulation: There should be much more federal regulation, somewhat more, the present level, somewhat less, much less, or this association has no position on that issue.

a. Agriculture

b. Civil rights and civil liberties

c. Education

d. Housing and urban policy

e. Transportation

f. Health and other human services

g. Energy and natural resources

h. Management of the economy

i. Changes in government, including federal personnel policy, administrative organization, and elections

31. Associations may engage in a variety of activities in order to achieve their public policy goals. Some of these activities may be the most important ones conducted by the association. Others may be the least important. Still others may be not engaged in at all. For each of the following activities, please indicate on the scale provided your best estimate of the importance of that activity for this association. [Respondents could mark on a scale from "1. One of Least Important" to "5. One of Most Important" or could check "Not Engaged In."]

a. Working with government agencies in policy formulation and implementation

b. Working with members of Congress or their staffs on the formulation or implementation of legislation

    c. Pursuing issues through litigation in the courts

    d. Seeking to influence public opinion through the mass media and publicity

    e. Working to aid the election of political leaders

    f. Organizing or carrying out public demonstrations or protests

    g. Working to develop a policy consensus among experts in the field

    h. Other approaches to achieving public policy goals (Please specify)

32. Associations may engage in a variety of activities concerned with securing financial support or other resources for the association. Using the same technique as in the last question, please rate the importance of each of the following activities for this association. [Respondents could mark on a scale from "1. One of Least Important" to "5. One of Most Important" or could check "Not Engaged In."]

    a. Conducting solicitation campaigns, contacting potential donors, or sponsoring fundraising events in a search for private donors to this association

    b. Making efforts through mailings, personal contacts, or other means to increase the membership of this association

    c. Applying for grants or contracts from government agencies, private foundations, or business firms

    d. Administering service programs on contract with government agencies

    e. Other approaches for obtaining resources (Please specify)

33. Does this association engage in litigation or any other legal activities?

34. Listed below are a number of statements that could describe the kinds of litigation in which an association may be involved. For each statement, please indicate your best estimate of whether it is a good or poor description of this association's legal activities. [Respondents could mark on a scale from "1. Poor Description" to "5. Good Description" or could check "Not Engaged In."]

    a. Litigation is employed by this association to defend its members against the actions of government agencies, or otherwise to reduce the scope of government authority.

    b. Litigation is employed by this association to encourage stronger governmental action on behalf of its members, or otherwise to extend the scope of government authority.

    c. This association normally files suits that bear directly upon the business or professional activities of its members.

    d. This association normally files class action suits or test cases directed at problems affecting both its members and the interests of citizens who are not members of this association.

    e. This association normally files amicus curiae (friends of the court) briefs that support suits brought by other organizations or associations.

35. Are there any topics or subjects not treated in this questionnaire that you feel are important for understanding associations like this one? Are there any comments that you would like to make about this study? Please give us any reactions you may have.

36. Roughly how many minutes were required to complete this questionnaire?

Thank you very much for your cooperation!

# Bibliography

Aberbach, Joel D., and Jack L. Walker, Jr. 1970a. The Attitudes of Blacks and Whites toward City Services: Implications for Public Policy. In *Financing the Metropolis: Public Policy in Urban Economics*, ed. John P. Crecine. Beverly Hills: Sage.

Aberbach, Joel D., and Jack L. Walker, Jr. 1970b. The Meanings of Black Power: A Comparison of White and Black Interpretations of a Political Slogan. *American Political Science Review* 64:367–88.

Aberbach, Joel D., and Jack L. Walker, Jr. 1970c. Political Trust and Racial Ideology. *American Political Science Review* 64:1199–1219.

Aberbach, Joel D., and Jack L. Walker, Jr. 1973. *Race in the City: Political Trust and Public Policy in the New Urban System*. Boston: Little, Brown.

Adelson, Alan. 1972. *SDS*. New York: Scribner's.

Aldrich, Howard, and Udo H. Staber. 1984. The Creation and Persistence of Business Interest Associations: An Ecological Approach. University of North Carolina, Chapel Hill, Department of Sociology. Photocopy.

Aldrich, Howard, and Udo II. Staber. 1986. How American Business Organized Itself in the 20th Century. University of North Carolina, Chapel Hill, Department of Sociology. Photocopy.

Arnold, Peri E. 1982. "Herbert Hoover and the Positive State." In *Public Values and Private Power in American Politics*, ed. J. David Greenstone. Chicago: University of Chicago Press.

Arnold, R. Douglas. 1979. *Congress and the Bureaucracy*. New Haven: Yale University Press.

Austen-Smith, David, and William H. Riker. 1987. Asymetric Information and the Coherence of Legislation. *American Political Science Review* 81:897–918.

Axelrod, Robert. 1984. *The Evolution of Cooperation*. New York: Basic Books.

Babcock, Charles R. 1982. Policies on Education Grants Become an Issue. *Washington Post*, August 14.

Bach, Stanley, and Steven S. Smith. 1988. *Managing Uncertainty in the House of Representatives: Adaption and Innovation in Special Rules*. Washington, DC: Brookings Institution.

Bachrach, Peter, and Morton Baratz. 1962. The Two Faces of Power. *American Political Science Review* 56:947–52.

Baker v. Carr. 1962. 369 U.S. 186.

Barbrook, Alec, and Christine Bolt. 1980. *Power and Protest in American Life*. New York: St. Martin's Press.

222      Bibliography

Barker, Lucius. 1967. Third Parties in Litigation: A Systematic View of the Judicial Function. *Journal of Politics* 24:41–69.

Barringer, Felicity. 1983. OMB Releases Proposed Restrictions on Lobbying by Contractors, Grantees. *Washington Post*, November 3, Sec. A.

Baskin, Mark A. 1989. The Evolution of Policy Communities in Socialist Yugoslavia: The Case of Worker Migration Abroad. *Governance* 2:67–85.

Baumgartner, Frank R. 1989a. *Conflict and Rhetoric in French Policymaking*. Pittsburgh: University of Pittsburgh Press.

Baumgartner, Frank R. 1989b. Independent and Politicized Policy Communities: Education and Nuclear Energy in France and the United States. *Governance* 2:42–66.

Baumgartner, Frank R., and Jack L. Walker, Jr. 1988. Survey Research and Membership in Voluntary Associations. *American Journal of Political Science* 32:908–28.

Baumgartner, Frank R., and Jack L. Walker, Jr. 1989. Educational Policy Making and the Interest Group Structure in France and the United States. *Comparative Politics* 21:273–88.

Baumgartner, Frank R., and Jack L. Walker, Jr. 1990. Response to Smith's "Trends in Voluntary Group Membership: Comments on Baumgartner and Walker": Measurement Validity and the Continuity of Results in Survey Research. *American Journal of Political Science* 34:662–70.

Berry, Jeffrey M. 1977. *Lobbying for the People*. Princeton: Princeton University Press.

Berry, Jeffrey M. 1989a. *The Interest Group Society* 2d ed. Glenview, IL: Scott, Foresman.

Berry, Jeffrey M. 1989b. "Subgovernments, Issue Networks, and Political Conflict." In *Remaking American Politics*, ed. Richard Harris and Sidney Milkis. Boulder, CO: Westview Press.

Bibby, John F., Thomas E. Mann, and Norman J. Ornstein. 1980. *Vital Statistics on Congress, 1980*. Washington, DC: American Enterprise Institute.

Birkby, Robert, and Walter Murphy. 1964. Interest Group Conflict in the Judicial Arena: The First Amendment and Group Access to the Courts. *Texas Law Review* 42:1018–48.

Blumenthal, Sidney. 1986. *The Rise of the Counter-Establishment: From Conservative Ideology to Political Power*. New York: Times Books.

Boles, Janet K. 1979. *The Politics of the Equal Rights Amendment*. New York: Longman.

Bosso, Christopher J. 1987. *Pesticides and Politics: The Life Cycle of a Public Issue*. Pittsburgh: University of Pittsburgh Press.

Brint, Steven. 1984. "New Class" and Cumulative Trend Explanations of the Liberal Political Attitudes of Professionals. *American Journal of Sociology* 90:30–71.

Broder, David S. 1980. *Changing of the Guard: Power and Leadership in America*. New York: Simon and Schuster.

Browne, William P. 1977. Organizational Maintenance: The Internal Operation of Interest Groups. *Public Administration Review* 37:48–57.

Browne, William P. 1988. *Private Interests, Public Policy, and American Agriculture*. Lawrence, KS: University Press of Kansas.

Browne, William P. 1990. Organized Interests and Their Issue Niches: A Search for Pluralism in a Policy Domain. *Journal of Politics* 52:477–509.

Bruce-Briggs, William, ed. 1981. *The New Class?* New Brunswick, NJ: Transaction Books.

Bruer, Patrick J. 1986. The Environment of Interest Group Litigation. Presented at the annual meeting of the Law and Society Association, Chicago.

Bruer, Patrick J. 1988. Washington Interest Group Organizations and Modes of Legal Advocacy. Presented at the annual meeting of the American Political Science Association, Washington, DC.

Bureh, Deborah M., Karin E. Koek, and Annette Novallo, eds. 1989. *Encyclopedia of Associations: 1990.* 24th ed. Detroit: Gale Research.

Burns, James MacGregor. 1963. *The Deadlock of Democracy.* Englewood Cliffs, NJ: Prentice-Hall.

Cain, Bruce E., John Ferejohn, and Morris P. Fiorina. 1987. *The Personal Vote: Constituency Service and Electoral Independence.* Cambridge, MA: Harvard University Press.

Caldeira, Gregory A., and John R. Wright. 1988. Organized Interests and Agenda Setting in the U.S. Supreme Court. *American Political Science Review* 82:1109–27.

Caldeira, Gregory A., and John R. Wright. 1989. Parties, Direct Representatives, and Agenda Setting in the Supreme Court. Presented at the annual meeting of the Midwest Political Science Association, Chicago.

Caldeira, Gregory A., and John R. Wright. 1990. Amicus Curiae Before the Court: Who Participates, When, and How Much? *Journal of Politics* 52:782–806.

Califano, Joseph A., Jr. 1981. *Governing America: An Insider's Report From the White House.* New York: Simon and Schuster.

Cameron, David. 1974. Toward a Theory of Political Mobilization. *Journal of Politics* 36:138–71.

Campbell, John Creighton. 1989. Bureaucratic Primacy: Japanese Policy Communities in an American Perspective. *Governance* 2:5–23.

Campbell, John Creighton, with Mark A. Baskin, Frank R. Baumgartner, and Nina P. Halpern. 1989. Afterword on Policy Communities: A Framework for Comparative Research. *Governance* 2:86–94.

Cantor, Joseph E. 1982. *Political Action Committees: Their Evolution and Growth and Their Implication for the Political System.* Washington, DC: Congressional Research Service.

Carden, Maren Lockwood. 1974. *The New Feminist Movement.* New York: Sage.

Carson, Clayborne. 1981. *In Struggle: SNCC and the Black Awakening of the 1960s.* Cambridge, MA: Harvard University Press.

Carter, Jimmy. 1981. President Jimmy Carter's Farewell Address. *Congressional Quarterly Weekly Report* no. 39, January 17.

Casper, Jonathan. 1972. *Lawyers Before the Warren Court.* Urbana: University of Illinois Press.

Cater, Douglass. 1964. *Power in Washington.* New York: Vintage Books.

Chambers, William Nisbet, and Walter Dean Burnham, eds. 1972. *The American Party Systems: Stages of Development.* New York: Praeger.

Chayes, Abraham. 1976. The Function of the Judge in Public Interest Litigation. *Harvard Law Review* 89:1281–1316.

Chisolm, Laure B. 1987. Exempt Organization Advocacy: Matching the Rules to the Rationales. *Indiana Law Journal* 63:201–99.

Chubb, John E. 1983. *Interest Groups and the Bureaucracy*. Stanford, CA: Stanford University Press.

Cigler, Allan. 1989. Interest Groups: A Subfield in Search of an Identity. Presented at the annual meeting of the Midwest Political Science Association, Chicago.

Cigler, Allan J., and Burdett A. Loomis, eds. 1986. *Interest Group Politics*. 2d ed. Washington, DC: Congressional Quarterly.

Clark, Peter B., and James Q. Wilson. 1961. Incentive Systems: A Theory of Organizations. *Administrative Science Quarterly* 6:129–66.

Close, Arthur C., Gregory L. Bologna, and Curtis W. McCormick, eds. 1989. *Washington Representatives: 1989*. Washington, DC: Columbia Books.

Commager, Henry Steele, ed. 1973. *Documents of American History*. New York: Appleton, Century, Crofts.

Commission on Foundations and Private Philanthropy. 1970. *Foundations, Private Giving and Public Policy*. Chicago: University of Chicago Press.

Committee on Political Parties. 1950. Toward a More Responsible Two-Party System. *American Political Science Review* 44: supplement.

Common Cause. 1989. *Annual Report*. Washington, DC: Common Cause.

Common Cause. 1990. *Common Cause 1991 Budget*. Washington, DC: Common Cause.

Congressional Quarterly. 1979. *Washington Information Directory 1980–81*. Washington, DC: Congressional Quarterly.

Congressional Quarterly. 1984. *Washington Information Directory 1984–85*. Washington, DC: Congressional Quarterly.

Cortner, Richard C. 1968. Strategies and Tactics of Litigants in Constitutional Cases. *Journal of Public Law* 17:287–307.

Crenson, Matthew A. 1971. *The Unpolitics of Air Pollution*. Baltimore, MD: Johns Hopkins University Press.

Crenson, Matthew A. 1983. *Neighborhood Politics*. Cambridge, MA: Harvard University Press.

Cronin, Thomas E. 1980. *The State of the Presidency*. 2d ed. Boston: Little, Brown.

Crotty, William J., and Gary C. Jacobson. 1980. *American Parties in Decline*. Boston: Little, Brown.

Cutler, Lloyd N. 1980. To Form a Government. *Foreign Affairs* 59 (Fall): 126–43.

Dahl, Robert A. 1961. *Who Governs?* New Haven: Yale University Press.

Dahl, Robert A. 1982. *Dilemmas of Pluralist Democracy: Autonomy vs. Control*. New Haven: Yale University Press.

Dahl, Robert. 1985. *A Preface to Economic Democracy*. Berkeley: University of California Press.

Davidson, Roger H. 1988. The New Centralization on Capitol Hill. *Review of Politics* 50:345–64.

Dodd, Lawrence C., and Bruce I. Oppenheimer. 1977. *Congress Reconsidered*. New York: Praeger Publishers.

Dodd, Lawrence C., and Bruce I. Oppenheimer. 1985. "The House in Transition." In *Congress Reconsidered,* ed. Lawrence C. Dodd and Bruce I. Oppenheimer. 3d ed. Washington, DC: Congressional Quarterly.

Dodd, Lawrence C., and Richard L. Schott. 1979. *Congress and the Administrative State.* New York: Wiley.

Downs, Anthony. 1972. Up and Down with Ecology—The Issue Attention Cycle. *Public Interest* 28:38–50.

Drew, Elizabeth. 1983. *Politics and Money: The New Road to Corruption.* New York: Macmillan.

Edelman, Murray. 1964. *The Symbolic Uses of Politics.* Urbana: University of Illinois Press.

Edelman, Murray. 1971. *Politics as Symbolic Action: Mass Arousal and Quiescence.* Chicago: Markham.

Edelman, Murray. 1988. *Constructing the Political Spectacle.* Chicago: University of Chicago Press.

Elkin, Stephen L. 1982. Markets and Politics in Liberal Democracy. *Ethics* 92:720–32.

Elster, Jon. 1989. *The Cement of Society: A Study of Social Order.* New York: Cambridge University Press.

EDF. 1990. *1990–91 Annual Report.* New York: Environmental Defense Fund.

Epstein, Lee. 1985. *Conservatives in Court.* Knoxville: University of Tennessee Press.

Fenno, Richard F., Jr. 1973. *Congressmen in Committees.* Boston: Little, Brown.

Fenno, Richard F., Jr. 1978. *Home Style.* Boston: Little, Brown.

Fiorina, Morris P. 1974. *Representatives, Roll Calls, and Constituencies.* Lexington, MA: D.C. Heath.

Fiorina, Morris P. 1989. *Congress: Keystone of the Washington Establishment.* 2d ed. New Haven: Yale University Press.

Fiorina, Morris P., and Roger G. Noll. 1979. Majority Rule Models and Legislative Elections. *Journal of Politics* 41: 1081–1104.

First National Bank of Boston v. Bellotti. 1978. 435 U.S. 765.

Fox, Stephen. 1981. *John Muir and His Legacy: The American Conservation Movement.* Boston: Little, Brown.

Freeman, J. Leiper. 1965. *The Political Process: Executive Bureau–Legislative Committee Relations.* Rev. ed. New York: Random House.

Freeman, Jo. 1973. "Origins of the Women's Liberation Movement." In *Changing Women in a Changing Society,* ed. Joan Huber. Chicago: University of Chicago Press.

Freeman, Jo. 1975. *The Politics of Women's Liberation.* New York: David McKay.

Fritschler, A. Lee. 1983. *Smoking and Politics.* 3d ed. Englewood Cliffs, NJ: Prentice-Hall.

Frohlich, N., and J. Oppenheimer. 1970. I Get by With a Little Help From My Friends. *World Politics* 23:104–20.

Gable, R. W. 1953. N.A.M.: Influential Lobby or Kiss of Death? *Journal of Politics* 15:254–73.

Gais, Thomas L. 1983. On the Scope and Bias of Interest Group Involvement in Elections. Presented at the annual meeting of the American Political Science Association, Chicago.

Gais, Thomas L., Mark A. Peterson, and Jack L. Walker, Jr. 1984. Interest Groups, Iron Triangles, and Representative Institutions in American National Government. *British Journal of Political Science* 14:161–85.

Gais, Thomas L., and Jack L. Walker, Jr. 1983. Pathways to Influence in American Politics: Factors Affecting the Choice of Tactics by Interest Groups. Presented at the annual meeting of the Midwest Political Science Association, Chicago.

Galanter, Marc, and Joel Rogers. 1988. The Rebirth of Contract Litigation. Presented at the annual meeting of the Law and Society Association, Vail, CO.

Gallup. 1980. *The Gallup Opinion Index*. Report no. 182 (October-November). Princeton, NJ: American Institute of Public Opinion.

Gamson, William. 1975. *The Strategy of Social Protest*. Homewood, IL: Dorsey Press.

Garson, G. David. 1978. *Group Theories of Politics*. Beverly Hills, CA: Sage.

Gaventa, John. 1980. *Power and Powerlessness: Quiescence and Rebellion in an Appalachian Valley*. Urbana: University of Illinois Press.

Gelb, Joyce, and Marian Lief Palley. 1982. *Women and Public Policies*. Princeton: Princeton University Press.

Gibson, James L., Cornelius P. Cotter, John F. Bibby, and Robert J. Huckshorn. 1983. Assessing Party Organizational Strength. *American Journal of Political Science* 27:193–222.

Gilligan, Thomas, and Keith Krehbiel. 1987. Collective Decision Making and Standing Committees: An Informational Rationale for Restrictive Amendment Procedures. *Journal of Law, Economics, and Organization* 3:287–335.

Ginsberg, Benjamin, and Martin Shefter. 1988. "The Presidency and the Organization of Interests." In *The Presidency and the Political System*, ed. Michael Nelson. 2d ed. Washington, DC: Congressional Quarterly.

Goldstone, Jack A. 1980. The Weakness of Organizations: A New Look at Gamson's *The Strategy of Social Protest*. *American Journal of Sociology* 84:1017–42.

Goulden, Joseph C. 1971. *The Money Givers*. New York: Random House.

Greenberg, George D., Jeffrey A. Miller, Lawrence B. Mohr, and Bruce C. Vladeck. 1977. Developing Public Policy Theory: Perspectives from Empirical Research. *American Political Science Review* 71:1532–43.

Greenstein, Fred I., and Nelson W. Polsby, eds. *Handbook of Political Science*. Vol. 4. Reading, MA: Addison-Wesley.

Greenstone, J. David, ed. 1982. *Public Values and Private Power in American Politics*. Chicago: University of Chicago Press.

Greider, William. 1981. *The Education of David Stockman and Other Americans*. New York: E. P. Dutton.

Griffith, Ernest S. 1939. *The Impasse of Democracy*. New York: Harrison-Milton Books.

Guinther, John. 1976. *Moralists and Managers: Public Interest Movements in America*. New York: Anchor Books.

Hakman, Nathan. 1966. Lobbying the Supreme Court: An Appraisal of "Political Science Folklore." *Fordham Law Review* 35:15–50.

Hall, Richard L., and Frank W. Wayman. 1990. Buying Time: Moneyed Interests and the Mobilization of Bias in Congressional Committees. *American Political Science Review* 84:797–820.

Halpern, Nina P. 1989. Policy Communities in a Leninist State: The Case of the Chinese Economic Policy Community. *Governance* 2:23–41.

Handler, Joel. 1978. *Social Movements and the Legal System*. New York: Academic Press.

Hannan, Michael T., and John Freeman. 1978. The Population Ecology of Organizations. *American Journal of Sociology* 82:924–64.

Hansen, John Mark. 1985. The Political Economy of Group Membership. *American Political Science Review* 79:79–96.

Hardin, Charles M. 1974. *Presidential Power and Accountability: Toward a New Constitution*. Chicago: University of Chicago Press.

Hardin, Russell. 1982. *Collective Action*. Baltimore, MD: Johns Hopkins University Press.

Harmel, Robert, and Kenneth Janda. 1982. *Parties and Their Environments: Limits to Reform?* New York: Longman.

Hayes, Michael T. 1981. *Lobbyists and Legislators*. New Brunswick, NJ: Rutgers University Press.

Hays, Samuel P. 1957. *The Response to Industrialism: 1885–1914*. Chicago: University of Chicago Press.

Hays, Samuel P. 1969. *Conservation and the Gospel of Efficiency: The Progressive Conservation Movement: 1890–1920*. New York: Atheneum.

Hays, Samuel P. 1981. "Politics and Society: Beyond the Political Party." In *The Evolution of the American Electoral Systems*, ed. Paul Klepper. Boston: Greenwood Press.

Heclo, Hugh. 1978. "Issue Networks and the Executive Establishment." In *The New American Political System*, ed. Anthony King. Washington, DC: American Enterprise Institute.

Heinz, John P., Edward O. Laumann, Robert H. Salisbury, and Robert L. Nelson. 1990. Inner Circles or Hollow Cores? Elite Networks in National Policy Systems. *Journal of Politics* 52:356–90.

Herring, E. Pendleton. 1929. *Group Representation before Congress*. Washington, DC: Brookings Institution.

Hess, Stephen. 1967. *Organizing the Presidency*. Washington, DC: Brookings Institution.

Horowitz, Donald. 1977. *Courts and Social Policy*. Washington, DC: Brookings Institution.

Hrebrenar, Ronald J., and Ruth K. Scott. 1982. *Interest Group Politics in America*. Englewood Cliffs, NJ: Prentice-Hall.

Hunt v. Washington Apple Advertising Commission. 1977. 432 U.S. 333.

Hunter, Floyd. 1953. *Community Power Structure*. Chapel Hill: University of North Carolina Press.

Huntington, Samuel P. 1973. The Democratic Distemper. *Public Interest* 14:9–38.

Huntington, Samuel P. 1981. *American Politics: The Promise of Disharmony*. Cambridge, MA: Harvard University Press.

James, Dorothy Buckton. 1969. *The Contemporary Presidency*. New York: Pegasus.

Janda, Kenneth. 1983. *Vox Pop: The Newsletter of Political Organizations and Parties*. Evanston, IL: Northwestern University.

Jenkins, J. Craig. 1985. *The Politics of Insurgency*. New York: Columbia University Press.

Jenkins, J. Craig, and Charles Perrow. 1977. Insurgency of the Powerless: Farm Workers Movements, 1946–1972. *American Sociological Review* 42:248–68.

Johnson, Paul Edward. 1987. Foresight and Myopia in Organizational Membership. *Journal of Politics* 49:679–703.

Johnson, Terrence J. 1972. *Professions and Power*. London: Macmillan.

Kariel, Henry. 1961. *The Decline of American Pluralism*. Stanford, CA: Stanford University Press.

Karl, Barry D., and Stanley N. Katz. 1987. Foundations and Ruling Class Elites. *Daedalus* 116:1–40.

Keller, Bill. 1981. Special Interest Lobbyists Cultivate the Grass Roots to Influence Capitol Hill. *Congressional Quarterly Weekly Report* (September 12): 1740–41.

Kernell, Samuel. 1986. *Going Public: New Strategies of Presidential Leadership*. Washington, DC: Congressional Quarterly.

Kinder, Donald R. 1983. "Diversity and Complexity in American Public Opinion." In *Political Science: The State of the Discipline,* ed. Ada W. Finifter. Washington, DC: American Political Science Association.

King, Anthony. 1975. Overload: Problems of Governing in the 1970s. *Political Studies* 23:162–74.

King, Anthony. 1978. "The American Polity in the Late 1970s: Building Coalitions in the Sand." In *The New American Political System*, ed. Anthony King. Washington, DC: American Enterprise Institute.

King, David C., and Jack L. Walker, Jr. 1989. The Provision of Benefits by American Interest Groups. Presented at the annual meeting of the Midwest Political Science Association, Chicago.

King, Lauriston R. 1975. *The Washington Lobbyists for Higher Education*. Lexington, MA: Lexington Books.

Kingdon, John W. 1984. *Agendas, Alternatives, and Public Policies*. Boston: Little, Brown.

Kirkpatrick, Jeanne J. 1978. *Dismantling the Parties: Reflections on Party Reform and Party Decomposition*. Washington, DC: American Enterprise Institute.

Klepper, Paul, ed. 1981. *The Evolution of American Electoral Systems*. Boston: Greenwood Press.

Kluger, Richard. 1977. *Simple Justice*. New York: Random House.

Knoke, David. 1988. Incentives in Collective Action Organizations. *American Sociological Review* 53:311–29.

Knoke, David. 1990. *Organizing for Collective Action: The Political Economies of Associations*. Hawthorne, NY: Aldine de Gruyter.

Knoke, David, and Edward Laumann. 1982. "The Social Organization of National Policy Domains." In *Social Structure and Network Analysis*, ed. Peter V. Marsden and Nan Lin. Beverly Hills: Sage.

Kobylka, Joseph F. 1987. A Court-Created Context for Group Litigation: Libertarian Groups and Obscenity. *Journal of Politics* 49:1061–78.

Kumar, Martha Joynt, and Michael Baruch Grossman. 1984. "The Presidency and Interest Groups." In *The Presidency and the Political System*, ed. Michael Nelson. Washington, DC: Congressional Quarterly.

Ladd, C. Everett, Jr. 1977. "Reform" Is Wrecking the U.S. Party System. *Fortune*, November.

Lammers, William W. 1979. *Presidential Politics: Patterns and Prospects*. New York: Harper and Row.

Larson, Gary O. 1983. *The Reluctant Patron: The United States Government and the Arts*. Philadelphia: University of Pennsylvania Press.

Larson, Magali Sarfatti. 1977. *The Rise of Professionalism*. Berkeley: University of California Press.

Laumann, Edward O., David Knoke, and Yong-hak Kim. 1985. An Organizational Approach to State Policy Formation: A Comparative Study of Energy and Health Domains. *American Sociological Review* 50:1–19.

Leibman, Robert C., and Robert Wuthnow, eds. 1983. *The New Christian Right: Mobilization and Legitimation*. Hawthorne NY: Aldine Publishing Co.

Light, Paul C. 1982. *The President's Agenda: Domestic Policy Choice from Kennedy to Carter*. Baltimore, MD: Johns Hopkins University Press.

Lindblom, Charles E. 1977. *Politics and Markets*. New York: Basic Books.

Lippmann, Walter. [1914]. 1961. *Drift and Mastery*. Englewood Cliffs, NJ: Prentice-Hall.

Lowi, Theodore J. 1964. American Business, Public Policy, Case Studies, and Political Theory. *World Politics* 16:677–715.

Lowi, Theodore J. 1969. *The End of Liberalism*. New York: Norton.

Lowi, Theodore J. 1972. Four Systems of Policy, Politics, and Choice. *Public Administration Review* 32:298–310.

Lowi, Theodore J. 1985. *The Personal President: Power Invested, Promise Unfulfilled*. Ithaca, NY: Cornell University Press.

Maass, Arthur. 1951. *Muddy Waters: Army Engineers and the Nation's Rivers*. Cambridge, MA: Harvard University Press.

Maass, Arthur. 1983. *Congress and the Common Good*. New York: Basic Books.

McAdam, Doug. 1982. *Political Process and the Development of Black Insurgency: 1930–1970*. Chicago: University of Chicago Press.

McCarthy, John D., and Mayer N. Zald. 1978. Resource Mobilization and Social Movements: A Partial Theory. *American Journal of Sociology* 82:1212–41.

McCarthy, Kathleen D. 1987. From Cold War to Cultural Development: The International Cultural Activities of the Ford Foundation, 1950–1980. *Daedalus* 116:93–118.

Macaulay, Stewart. 1963. Non-Contractual Relations in Business: A Preliminary Study. *American Sociological Review* 28:55–67.

McConnell, Grant. 1966. *Private Power and American Democracy*. New York: Alfred A. Knopf.

McCubbins, Mathew D., and Terry Sullivan, eds. 1987. *Congress: Structure and Policy*. New York: Cambridge University Press.

McDonald, Terrance J., and Sally K. Ward, eds. 1984. *The Politics of Urban Fiscal Policy*. Beverly Hills, CA: Sage.

McFarland, Andrew S. 1976. *Public Interest Lobbies*. Washington, DC: American Enterprise Institute.

McFarland, Andrew S. 1984. *Common Cause: Lobbying in the Public Interest*. Chatham, NJ: Chatham House.

McFarland, Andrew S. 1987. Interest Groups and Theories of Power in America. *British Journal of Political Science* 17:129–47.

McFarland, Andrew S. 1989. Interest Groups and Political Time. Presented at the annual meetings of the American Political Science Association, Atlanta.

McGerr, Michael E. 1986. *The Decline of Popular Politics: The American North, 1865–1928*. New York: Oxford University Press.

McIntosh, Wayne. 1986. Amicus Curiae in the Courts of Appeals. Presented at the annual meeting of the Law and Society Association. Chicago.

McKean, Dayton David. 1949. *Party and Pressure Politics*. Boston: Houghton Mifflin.

Mackenzie, A. 1981. When Auditors Turn Editor: The IRS and the Nonprofit Press. *Columbia Journalism Review* 20:29–34.

McQuaid, Kim. 1982. *Big Business and Presidential Power*. New York: William Morrow.

Mansbridge, Jane J., ed. 1990. *Beyond Self-Interest*. Chicago: University of Chicago Press.

Manwaring, David. 1962. *Render Unto Caesar: The Flag Salute Controversy*. Chicago: University of Chicago Press.

Margolis, Howard. 1984. *Selfishness, Altruism, and Rationality: A Theory of Social Choice*. Reprint. Chicago: University of Chicago Press.

Margolis, Howard. 1990. "Dual Utilities and Rational Choice." In *Beyond Self-Interest*, ed. Jane J. Mansbridge. Chicago: University of Chicago Press.

Marris, Peter, and Martin Rein. 1973. *Dilemmas of Social Reform* 2d ed. Chicago: Aldine de Gruyter.

Marwell, Gerald, and Ruth E. Ames. 1979. Experiments on the Provision of Public Goods: Resources, Interest, Group Size, and the Free Rider Problem. *American Journal of Sociology* 84:1335–60.

Melnick, Shep. 1983. *Regulation and the Courts: The Case of the Clean Air Act*. Washington, DC: Brookings Institution.

Meyer, Cord. 1980. *Facing Reality*. New York: Harper and Row.

Miles, Robert H. 1982. *Coffin Nails and Corporate Strategies*. Englewood Cliffs, NJ: Prentice-Hall.

Mills, C. Wright. 1956. *The Power Elite*. New York: Oxford University Press.

Mitchell, Robert Cameron. 1979. "National Environmental Lobbies and the Apparent Illogic of Collective Action." In *Collective Decision Making: Applications from Public Choice Theory*, ed. Clifford S. Russell. Baltimore, MD: Johns Hopkins University Press.

Moe, Terry M. 1980. *The Organization of Interests: Incentives and the Internal Dynamics of Political Interest Groups*. Chicago: University of Chicago Press.

Moe, Terry M. 1981. Toward a Broader View of Interest Groups. *Journal of Politics* 43:531–43.

Morris, Aldon D. 1984. *The Origins of the Civil Rights Movement*. New York: Free Press.

Mosher, Frederick C. 1968. *Democracy and the Public Service*. New York: Oxford University Press.

Mosher, Frederick C. 1980. The Changing Responsibilities and Tactics of the Federal Government. *Public Administration Review* 40:541–48.

Mueller, John E. 1973. *Wars, Presidents and Public Opinion*. New York: Wiley.

Nadel, Mark V. 1971. *The Politics of Consumer Protection*. Indianapolis, IN: Bobbs-Merrill.

National Society of Professional Engineers v. United States. 1978. 435 U.S. 679.

Nelson, Barbara J. 1984. *Making an Issue of Child Abuse*. Chicago: University of Chicago Press.

Nelson, William. 1988. Business Litigation and the Elite Bar in New York City. Presented at the annual meeting of the Law and Society Association, Vail.

Neustadt, Richard E. 1980. *Presidential Power: The Politics of Leadership from FDR to Carter*. New York: Macmillan.

Newfield, Jack A. 1966. *Prophetic Minority*. New York: Signet Books.

Nielsen, Waldemar A. 1972. *The Big Foundations*. New York: Columbia University Press.

Nordlinger, Eric A. 1981. *On the Autonomy of the Democratic State*. Cambridge, MA: Harvard University Press.

Oberschall, A. 1973. *Social Conflict and Social Movements*. Englewood Cliffs, NJ: Prentice-Hall.

O'Connor, Karen. 1980. *Women's Organizations' Use of the Courts*. Lexington, MA: Lexington Books.

O'Connor, Karen, and Lee Epstein. 1981. Amicus Curiae Participation in U.S. Supreme Court Litigation. *Law and Society Review* 16:311–20.

Olson, Mancur, Jr. 1965. *The Logic of Collective Action*. Cambridge, MA: Harvard University Press.

Olson, Susan. 1984. *Clients and Lawyers: Securing the Rights of Disabled Persons*. Westport, CT: Greenwood Press.

Olson, Susan. 1990. Interest Group Litigation in Federal District Court: Beyond the Political Disadvantage Theory. *Journal of Politics* 52:854–82.

O'Neill, Timothy. 1985. *Bakke and the Politics of Equality: Friends and Foes in the Classroom of Litigation*. Middletown, CT: Wesleyan University Press.

Ornstein, Norman J., and Shirley Elder. 1978. *Interest Groups, Lobbying and Policymaking*. Washington, DC: Congressional Quarterly.

O'Rourke, Timothy G. 1980. *The Impact of Reapportionment*. New Brunswick, NJ: Transaction Books.

Pavalko, Ronald M. 1971. *Sociology of Occupations and Professions*. Itasca, IL: Peacock.

Peterson, Bill. 1981. Coalition Pushes Block Grants to "Defund the Left." *Washington Post*, July 2.

Peterson, Mark A. 1990a. *Legislating Together: The White House and Capitol Hill from Eisenhower to Reagan*. Cambridge, MA: Harvard University Press.

Peterson, Mark A. 1990b. Interest Groups and the Presidency: Style of White House Public Liaison. Unpublished paper.

Peterson, Mark A. n.d. "Interest Mobilization and the Presidency." In *The Transformation of Interest Group Politics*, ed. Mark P. Petracca. Boulder, CO: Westview Press.

Peterson, Mark A., and Jack L. Walker, Jr. 1986. "Interest Group Responses to Partisan Change: The Impact of the Reagan Administration upon the National Interest Group System." In *Interest Group Politics*, ed. Alan J. Cigler and Burdett A. Loomis, 2d ed. Washington, DC: Congressional Quarterly.

Peterson, Mark A., and Jack L. Walker, Jr. 1990. "The Presidency and the Nominating System." In *The Presidency and the Political System*, ed. Michael Nelson, 3d ed. Washington, DC: Congressional Quarterly.

Pfeffer, J., and G. R. Salancik. 1978. *The External Control of Organizations*. New York: Harper and Row.

Pifer, Alan. 1987. Philanthropy, Voluntarism, and Changing Times. *Daedalus* 116:119–32.

Pika, Joseph A. 1982. Dealing with the People Divided: The White House Office of Public Liaison. Presented at the annual meeting of the Midwest Political Science Association.

Pika, Joseph A. 1983. "Interest Groups and the Executive: Presidential Intervention." In *Interest Group Politics*, ed. Allan J. Cigler and Burdett A. Loomis. Washington, DC: Congressional Quarterly.

Polsby, Nelson W. 1963. *Community Power and Political Theory*. New Haven: Yale University Press.

Pomper, Gerald M., ed. 1980. *Party Renewal in America*. New York: Praeger.

Pratt, Henry J. 1976. *The Gray Lobby*. Chicago: University of Chicago Press.

Reynolds v. Sims. 1964. 377 U.S. 533.

Richman, Timothy. 1982. Can the U.S. Chamber Learn to Think Small? *Inc.* 4:81–86.

Ripley, Randall B., and Grace A. Franklin. 1980. *Congress, the Bureaucracy, and Public Policy*. Rev. ed. Homewood, IL: Dorsey Press.

Robyn, Dorothy. 1987. *Braking the Special Interests: Trucking Deregulation and the Politics of Policy Reform*. Chicago: University of Chicago Press.

Rose, Richard, and Guy Peters. 1978. *Can Government Go Bankrupt?* New York: Basic Books.

Ross, Robert L. 1970. Relations Among National Interest Groups. *Journal of Politics* 32:96–114.

Rothenberg, Lawrence S. 1988. Organizational Maintenance and the Retention Decision in Groups. *American Political Science Review*. 82:1129–52.

Rudder, Catherine E. 1977. "Committee Reform and the Revenue Process." In *Congress Reconsidered*, ed. Lawrence C. Dodd and Bruce I. Oppenheimer. New York: Praeger.

Russell, Clifford S., ed. 1979. *Collective Decision Making: Applications from Public Choice Theory*. Baltimore, MD: Johns Hopkins University Press.

Sabato, Larry J. 1984. *PAC Power: Inside the World of Political Action Committees*. New York: Norton.

Salisbury, Robert H. 1969. An Exchange Theory of Interest Groups. *Midwest Journal of Political Science* 13:1–32.

Salisbury, Robert H. 1975. "Interest Groups." In *Handbook of Political Science*, ed. Fred I. Greenstein and Nelson W. Polsby. Vol. 4. Reading, MA: Addison-Wesley.

Salisbury, Robert H. 1984. Interest Representation: The Dominance of Institutions. *American Political Science Review* 78:64–76.

Salisbury, Robert H., John P. Heinz, Edward O. Laumann, and Robert L. Nelson. 1987. Who Works with Whom? Interest Group Alliances and Opposition. *American Political Science Review* 81:1217–34.

Schattschneider, E. E. 1942. *Party Government*. New York: Holt, Rinehart and Winston.

Schattschneider, E. E. 1948. *The Struggle for Party Government*. College Park: University of Maryland Press.

Schattschneider, E. E. 1960. *The Semi-Sovereign People*. New York: Holt, Rinehart and Winston.

Scheingold, Stuart. 1974. *The Politics of Rights*. New Haven: Yale University Press.

Scheppele, Kim Lane. 1988. *Legal Secrets: Equality and Efficiency in the Common Law*. Chicago: University of Chicago Press.

Scheppele, Kim Lane, and Jack L. Walker, Jr. 1986. Interest Groups and Litigation Strategies. Presented at the annual meeting of the Midwest Political Science Association, Chicago.

Schick, Allen. 1980. *Congress and Money: Budgeting, Spending, and Taxing*. Washington, DC: Urban Institute.

Schlesinger, Joseph A. 1985. The New American Political Party. *American Political Science Review* 79:1152–69.

Schlozman, Kay Lehman. 1984. What Accent the Heavenly Chorus? Political Equality and the American Pressure System. *Journal of Politics* 46:1006–32.

Schlozman, Kay Lehman, and John T. Tierney. 1983. More of the Same: Washington Pressure Group Activity in a Decade of Change. *Journal of Politics* 45:351–77.

Schlozman, Kay Lehman, and John T. Tierney. 1986. *Organized Interests and American Democracy*. New York: Harper and Row.

Schlozman, Kay Lehman, and Sidney Verba. 1979. *Injury to Insult: Unemployment, Class, and Political Response*. Cambridge, MA: Harvard University Press.

Schmitter, Philippe C., and Donald Brand. 1982. Organizing Capitalists in the United States: The Advantages and Disadvantages of Exceptionalism. University of Chicago. Mimeo.

Seaberry, J. 1982. The Mailed Fist: Nonprofit Groups Hit by Postage Jump. *Washington Post*, January 7.

Seidman, Harold. 1980. *Politics, Position, and Power: The Dynamics of Federal Organization*. 3d ed. New York: Oxford University Press.

Shabecoff, Philip. 1979. Big Business on the Offensive. *New York Times Magazine*, December 9, 134–46.

Shaiko, Ronald G. 1991. "More Bang for the Buck: The New Era of Full-Service Public Interest Associations." In *Interest Group Politics*, ed. Allan J. Cigler and Burdett A. Loomis. 3d ed. Washington, DC: Congressional Quarterly.

Silk, Leonard, and Mark Silk. 1980. *The American Establishment*. New York: Basic Books.

Simon, Roy D., Jr. 1989. Fee Sharing Between Lawyers and Public Interest Groups. *Yale Law Journal* 98:1069–1133.

Sinclair, Barbara. 1983. *Majority Leadership in the U.S. House*. Baltimore, MD: Johns Hopkins University Press.

Skowronek, Stephen. 1982. *Building a New American State*. Cambridge: Cambridge University Press.

Smith, Steven S. 1989. *Call to Order: Floor Politics in the House and Senate*. Washington, DC: Brookings Institution.

Sorauf, Frank J. 1976. *The Wall of Separation: The Constitutional Politics of Church and State*. Princeton, NJ: Princeton University Press.

Staber, Udo H., and Howard Aldrich. 1985. Government Regulation and the Expansion of Trade Associations: An Exploration of Some Ecological Propositions. College of Business Administration, Pennsylvania State University. Photocopy.

Stanfield, R. 1981. Defunding the Left. *National Journal,* August 1, 1374–78.

Steiner, Gilbert Y. 1971. *The State of Welfare*. Washington, DC: Brookings Institution.

Sundquist, James L. 1968. *Politics and Policy: The Eisenhower, Kennedy, and Johnson Years*. Washington, DC: Brookings Institution.

Sutton, Francis X. 1987. The Ford Foundation: The Early Years. *Daedalus* 116:41–92.

Thompson, E. P. 1975. *Whigs and Hunters*. New York: Pantheon.

Thompson, James D. 1967. *Organizations in Action*. New York: McGraw-Hill.

Tropman, John E., Milan Dluhy, and Roger Lind, eds. 1981. *New Strategic Perspectives on Social Policy*. New York: Pergamon Press.

Truman, David B. 1951. *The Governmental Process: Political Interests and Public Opinion*. New York: Alfred A. Knopf.

Truman, David B. 1971. *The Governmental Process*. 2d ed. New York: Alfred A. Knopf.

Tulis, Jeffrey K. 1987. *The Rhetorical Presidency*. Princeton, NJ: Princeton University Press.

Useem, Bert, and Mayer N. Zald. 1982. From Pressure Group to Social Movement: Organizational Dilemmas of the Effort to Promote Nuclear Power. *Social Problems* 30:144–156.

Verba, Sidney, Norman H. Nie, and Jae-on Kim. 1978. *Participation and Political Equality*. Cambridge, MA: Harvard University Press.

Vogel, David. 1989. *Fluctuating Fortunes: The Political Power of Business in America*. New York: Basic Books.

Vose, Clement. 1959. *Caucasians Only*. Berkeley: University of California Press.

Wagner, Richard. 1966. Pressure Groups and Political Entrepreneurs. In *Papers on Non-Market Decision Making*. Charlottesville: University of Virginia.

Walker, Jack L., Jr. 1963a. The Functions of Disunity: Negro Leadership in a Southern City. *Journal of Negro Education* 32:227–36.

Walker, Jack L., Jr. 1963b. Negro Voting in Atlanta, 1953–61. *Phylon*: 379–86.

Walker, Jack L., Jr. 1963c. Protest and Negotiation: A Case Study of Negro Leadership in Atlanta, Georgia. *Midwest Journal of Political Science* 7:99–124.

Walker, Jack L., Jr. 1964. *Sit-Ins in Atlanta*. Eagleton Institute Case no. 34. New York: McGraw-Hill.

Walker, Jack L., Jr. 1966. A Critique of the Elitist Theory of Democracy. *American Political Science Review* 60:285–95, 391–92.

Walker, Jack L., Jr. 1969. The Diffusion of Innovations Among the American States. *American Political Science Review* 63:880–99.

Walker, Jack L., Jr. 1972. Brother Can You Paradigm? *PS* 5:419–22.

Walker, Jack L., Jr. 1977. Setting the Agenda in the U.S. Senate: A Theory of Problem Selection. *British Journal of Political Science* 7:423–45.

Walker, Jack L., Jr. 1978. Untitled. Lecture delivered at American University. Washington, DC.

Walker, Jack L., Jr. 1981. "The Diffusion of Knowledge, Policy Communities, and Agenda Setting: The Relationship of Knowledge and Power." In *New Strategic Perspectives on Social Policy*, ed. John Tropman, Milan Dluhy, and Roger Lind. New York: Pergamon Press.

Walker, Jack L., Jr. 1983. The Origins and Maintenance of Interest Groups in America. *American Political Science Review* 77:390–406.

Walker, Jack L., Jr. 1984. Three Modes of Political Mobilization. Presented at the annual meeting of the American Political Science Association, Chicago.

Walker, Jack L., Jr. 1988. "Interest, Political Parties, and Policy Formation in American Democracy." In *Federal Social Policy: The Historical Dimension*, ed. Donald T. Critchlow and Ellis W. Hawley, University Park, PA: Pennsylvania State University Press.

Walker, Jack L., Jr. 1989. Policy Communities as Global Phenomena. *Governance* 2:1–5.

Walker, Jack L., Jr. 1991. Activities and Maintenance Strategies of Interest Groups in the United States, 1980 and 1985. Ann Arbor, MI: University of Michigan, Institute of Public Policy Studies (producer), 1985. Ann Arbor, MI: Interuniversity Consortium for Political and Social Research (distributor), 1991. Computer file.

Ware, Alan. 1985. *The Breakdown of Democratic Party Organization, 1940–1980*. New York: Oxford University Press.

Waterman, Richard W. 1989. *Presidential Influence and the Administrative State*. Knoxville: University of Tennessee Press.

Webster v. Reproductive Health Services. 1989. 109 S.Ct. 3040.

Wehr, Elizabeth. 1981. Public Liaison Chief Dole Reaches to Outside Groups to Sell Reagan's Programs. *Congressional Quarterly Weekly Report*, June 6, 957.

Weisbrod, Burton A., and Stephen H. Long. 1977. "The Size of the Voluntary Nonprofit Sector: Concepts and Measures." In *The Voluntary Nonprofit Sector*, ed. Burton A. Weisbrod. Lexington, MA: Lexington Books.

Wilson, Graham K. 1981. *Interest Groups in the United States*. Oxford: Clarendon Press.

Wilson, James Q. 1962. *The Amateur Democrat*. Chicago: University of Chicago Press.

Wilson, James Q. 1973. *Political Organizations*. New York: Basic Books.

Wines, Michael. 1981. Should Groups That Set Standards be Subject to Federal Standards? *National Journal.* September 26, 1717–19.

Wines, Michael. 1984. Ma Bell and Her Newly Independent Children Revamp Lobbying Networks. *National Journal,* January 28, 148–52.

Wittenberg, Ernest, and Elisabeth Wittenberg. 1989. *How to Win in Washington.* Cambridge, MA: Basil Blackwell.

Woodward, Bob, and Scott Armstrong. 1981. *The Brethren.* New York: Avon Books.

Wright, John R. 1990. Contributions, Lobbying, and Committee Voting in the U.S. House of Representatives. *American Political Science Review* 84:417–38.

Zald, Mayer N., and Roberta Ash. 1966. Social Movement Organizations: Growth, Decline, and Change. *Social Forces* 44:327–41.

Zald, Mayer N., and John D. McCarthy, eds. 1979. *The Dynamics of Social Movements.* Cambridge, MA: Winthrop.

Zald, Mayer N., and John D. McCarthy. 1980. Social Movement Industries: Competition and Cooperation Among Movement Organizations. *Research in Social Movements, Conflicts, and Change* 3:1–20.

Zald, Mayer N., and John D. McCarthy, eds. 1986. *Social Movements in an Organization Society.* New Brunswick, NJ: Transaction Books.

Zald, Mayer N., and Bert Useem. 1982. Movement and Countermovement: Loosely Coupled Conflict. Presented at the annual meeting of the American Sociological Association, San Francisco.

Zeigler, L. Harmon, and G. Wayne Peak. 1972. *Interest Groups in American Politics.* 2d ed. Englewood Cliffs, NJ: Prentice-Hall.

# Index

Mills, C. Wright, 7
Minorities, 14, 40, 127, 130, 156
  African-American, 13, 36, 40, 52,
    185, 196. *See also* Civil rights
    movement; National Association
    for the Advancement of Colored
    People; Negro Improvement
    Association
  Hispanic-American, 10, 36, 185. *See
    also* Mexican-American Legal De-
    fense and Education Fund
  Native American, 185. *See also* Bu-
    reau of Indian Affairs
Mississippi Freedom Summer, 35. *See
  also* Civil rights movement
Mitchell, Robert Cameron, 85
Mixed sector groups, 57, 60, 62, 66,
    117, 119, 129, 133, 151, 169,
    171, 174, 177–78
Mobilization of interests, 9, 11–13, 16,
    20, 22, 25, 29–30, 35–39, 41–42,
    45, 48–50, 52–55, 75, 101–3,
    105–7, 118, 120, 124, 132–33,
    140, 144, 181, 186–88, 194–97,
    199–200. *See also* Citizen sector
    groups; Collective action dilemma;
    Mixed sector groups; Nonprofit
    sector groups; Olson, Mancur, Jr.;
    Patronage; Private corporations;
    Private sector; Profit sector groups;
    Public sector; Trade unions; Social
    movements
Moe, Terry M., 47–48, 85
Mohr, Lawrence B., 7
Montgomery bus boycott, 35. *See also*
  Civil rights movement
Moral Majority, 34, 37
Mortgage Bankers Association of Amer-
  ica, 60, 187. *See also* Banking
  industry
Mosher, Frederick C., 27
Mueller, John E., 37
Murphy, Walter, 159

Nadel, Mark V., 50
National Abortion Rights Action
  League, 158. *See also* Abortion

National Agricultural Chemicals Asso-
  ciation, 127. *See also* Agriculture
National Alliance for Businessmen, 31.
  *See also* Business interests
National Association for the Advance-
  ment of Colored People, 36, 158–
  60. *See also* Civil rights move-
  ment; Minorities
  in the courts, 158–60
National Association of Automobile
  Manufacturers, 187. *See also* Au-
  tomobile manufacturers
National Association of Broadcasters, 60
National Association of Counties, 60
National Association of Independent
  Colleges and Universities, 60. *See
  also* Education
National Association of Manufacturers,
  6, 83, 95
National Association of Railroad Pas-
  sengers, 2, 95
National Association of Retired Federal
  Employees, 29. *See also* Elderly
National Association of State Alcohol
  and Drug Abuse Directors, 60, 187
National Association of Student Finan-
  cial Aid Administrators, 60. *See
  also* Education
National Association of the Visually
  Handicapped, 61. *See also*
  Handicapped
National Council of Churches, 37. *See
  also* Religion
National Council of Puerto Rican Vol-
  unteers, 57
National Council of Senior Citizens, 29.
  *See also* Elderly
National Labor Relations Board, 31
National League of Cities, 51
National Organization for Women, 31,
  34, 36. *See also* Women's
  movement
National Retired Teachers Association,
  76, 76n.1. *See also* Elderly
National Rifle Association, 31
National Right to Life Committee, 37,
  158. *See also* Abortion